Spiritual Reading

Spiritual Reading
A Study of the Christian Practice
of Reading Scripture

Angela Lou Harvey

Foreword by
R. W. L. Moberly

CASCADE *Books* • Eugene, Oregon

SPIRITUAL READING
A Study of the Christian Practice of Reading Scripture

Copyright © 2015 Angela Lou Harvey. All rights reserved. Except for brief quotations in critical publications or reviews, no part of this book may be reproduced in any manner without prior written permission from the publisher. Write: Permissions. Wipf and Stock Publishers, 199 W. 8th Ave., Suite 3, Eugene, OR 97401.

Cascade Books
An Imprint of Wipf and Stock Publishers
199 W. 8th Ave., Suite 3
Eugene, OR 97401

www.wipfandstock.com

ISBN 13: 978-1-4982-0976-2

Cataloguing-in-Publication Data

Harvey, Angela Lou

    Spiritual reading : a study of the Christian practice of reading Scripture / Angela Lou Harvey.

    xiv + 234 p. ; 23 cm. Includes bibliographical references.

    ISBN 13: 978-1-4982-0976-2

    1. Bible—Criticism, interpretation, etc. 2. Bible—Reading. 3. Davis, Ellen F. 4. Barth, Karl, 1886–1968. 5. Lubac, Henri de, 1896–1991. I. Title.

BS617 H2 2015

Manufactured in the U.S.A.   10/20/2015

For Steve, who helps me read again

I feel that explaining the greatness of the mysteries is beyond our strength. But although we cannot discuss and research everything, we do, however, feel that everything is full of mystery.

−Origen, Homily 3 on Leviticus

Contents

Foreword by R. W. L. Moberly | viii
Acknowledgments | xi
Abbreviations | xiii

CHAPTER 1: Introduction | 1

CHAPTER 2: Spiritual Reading and the Church | 25

CHAPTER 3: Reading Well | 45

CHAPTER 4: Karl Barth and the Reality of God in Scripture | 78

CHAPTER 5: Henri de Lubac and the Spiritual Sense of Scripture | 108

CHAPTER 6: An Artful Reader: Ellen Davis | 140

CHAPTER 7: Ellen Davis's Art in Practice | 170

Conclusion | 209

Bibliography | 223

Foreword

THE READING OF SCRIPTURE for spiritual nurture has been a foundational practice in the Christian Church down the ages. It is a core element in most church services, through reading aloud and preaching on what has been read, and it is also widely practiced by people at home, often as a way of starting, and so framing, the day.

In recent years there has been a striking resurgence of interest in *lectio divina* as a way of reading Scripture spiritually. Although *lectio divina* is a particular practice within the history of the Catholic church, it represents an approach that many Christians have practiced who may have known nothing about *lectio divina* as such; what matters is that they have read carefully and prayerfully with a view to knowing God better. My impression of the literature about *lectio divina*, however, is that it tends to sit light to the questions raised about the origins and nature of the Bible by modern biblical and theological scholarship—not that it is hostile to such questions, but that it tends to bracket them out.

A distinctive strength of Angie Harvey's work is that she explicitly relates the spiritual reading of Scripture to some of the concerns of the scholarly academy. She thereby provides a resource that is especially valuable for those who take a formal course of biblical and theological study, and who want to know how this can enhance their use of Scripture for spiritual nurture.

On the one hand Harvey looks at resources in modern literary studies; and she also considers the approach to Scripture in two of the major theologians of the twentieth century, Karl Barth and Henri de Lubac, who represent the Protestant and Catholic wings of the Christian Church. On the other hand, she looks at the work of a leading contemporary biblical scholar, Ellen Davis, who seeks to bring together biblical scholarship and spiritual significance, and Harvey carefully appraises the value of Davis's writings and the lessons to be learnt from them.

Harvey writes lucidly and accessibly, and provides us with a valuable resource for the better understanding and practice of the spiritual reading of Scripture today. I hope that my own delight in reading this book will be shared by many others.

—Walter Moberly

Abbey House
Palace Green
Durham, UK
2015

Acknowledgments

ANY ACCOUNT OF HOW we got to where we are must begin with God, so Karl Barth insists, and so I have found increasingly true in writing this work. I am so thankful to my Lord and my God for his grace upon grace to me, a grace shown afresh each day I seek to know him and his Word.

This book was born out of my studies at Durham University, a place where that grace came through so many individuals. I arrived at Durham through the kind counsel of Professor Matthias Henze, who has been an inspiration to me since my undergraduate days of struggling with Biblical Hebrew. Many thanks are due to my doctoral supervisor, Professor Walter Moberly, whose own scholarship and reading suggestions have been gems in my studies. His genuine care for his students is obvious, and I appreciate so much the ways he has helped me think through how my studies relate to the even more important work beyond them. Thanks also are due to Professor Francis Watson, my secondary supervisor, for his helpful insights and direction.

So many friends and family have encouraged me along this way—especially in Durham, the Shepherds, the Johnsons, the Jirtles, and the Menzies. Margaret Parkinson's afternoon teas were breaths of fresh air and laughter (and amazing scones—thanks, Margaret!). My family circle of friends in Houston likewise has been so encouraging, particularly the Harmans, the Wilkinsons, and the Swenys. The fellowship and funding of AFTE's John Wesley Fellowship was a great blessing, as well.

My father's preaching and teaching, and my mom's quiet example of reading the Bible have shaped my interest in Scripture and my faith profoundly. Thank you so much, Mom and Dad, for your example of faith, your overwhelming generosity and support, and your immense love. You first introduced me to the wondrous world within the Bible, and have supported us so much as we've traveled back and forth between Texas and England. Your generosity and love really is astounding.

I went to Durham for a degree, but found a husband there on the first day, and Steve has been the most wonderful surprise of my life. He has helped me in more ways than I even know, and it is with him that I encounter with great joy the mysteries of God and this wondrous life that he is giving us (particularly now the wonders of Jedidiah and Talitha!). To Steve, my dearest companion, this work is dedicated, with much thankfulness and love. *Ahavatika.*

Abbreviations

ATR	*The Anglican Theological Review*
CD	Karl Barth, *Church Dogmatics*
ET	Karl Barth, *Evangelical Theology*
EA	*Ex Auditu*
IJST	*International Journal of Systematic Theology*
JBL	*Journal of Biblical Literature*
JTI	*Journal of Theological Interpretation*
Medieval	Henri de Lubac, *Medieval Exegesis*, volume 1
Scripture	Henri de Lubac, *Scripture in the Tradition*

CHAPTER 1

Introduction

SOMEWHERE ALONG A ROMAN road from Jerusalem to Africa, the Ethiopian eunuch sat in his chariot reading Isaiah, pondering who its suffering figure might be. His chariot was stopped, Philip came up, Jesus was proclaimed, and he went away rejoicing.[1] Eleven centuries later, behind Carthusian monastery walls, the monk Guigo II turned over and over again the beatitude "Blessed are the pure in heart," as he prayed to know "what is true purity of heart and how it may be had" so that "with its help" he may know God, "if only a little."[2] Yet still another seven hundred and fifty years later, in an Arkansas small town, Mamma Cissy sat each day with her well-worn Bible, reading it through her small wire-framed spectacles, finding its familiar words ever new. She likely never heard of Guigo but read like him, and her manner of reading left its mark on her daughter's daughter, whose own Bible is being worn out in her own quiet morning readings of its words, words somehow still ever new.[3]

A first-century African official, a medieval French monk, and my great-grandmother, all readers of the Bible. Yet not just readers, but readers of a certain ilk—spiritual readers of Scripture who, like Guigo, seek to know God through their reading. Even as most Christians throughout the ages have encountered the Bible primarily through the communal life of the

---

1. Acts 8:26–40.
2. Guigo II, *Ladder of Monks*, 78. Guigo often pondered biblical texts closely, a practice that led to his writing *The Ladder of Monks*, a guide for other monks on how to seek God in Scripture through intentional ways of reading, meditation, prayer, and contemplation.
3. Flannery O'Connor points out that while the American South is no longer the Bible Belt it once was, the region is still made up of "the descendants of old ladies" who read the Bible on their knees—"You don't shake off their influence in even several generations." O'Connor, *Mystery and Manners*, 202.

church (in its preaching, teaching, liturgy, music, and art that have centered upon Scripture), ever since its writing the Bible has had its passionate readers, as the Bible itself illustrates in Acts' story of the Ethiopian. These readers are those who pick up and read the Bible on their own, trying to make sense of its words and understand what is being said of God through them—even more so, trying to come into a better love of God through them. The point of such reading is more than to know Scripture; it is to know and love God.

Flannery O'Connor once noted, "The writer operates at a peculiar crossroads where time and place and eternity somehow meet. His problem is to find that location."[4] It seems her words apply just as readily to the reader, especially to the spiritual reader of Scripture, one who looks out from her place onto the past and onto eternity. I seek in this study that peculiar crossroads where God, the Bible, and practices of reading somehow all meet today; the problem of this location shapes my work. In this meeting eternal realities mingle with temporal ones, as the work of God and the work of humans come together and merge (at times indistinguishably) in the reading of the Bible. The landscape of the spiritual reading of Scripture is constantly changing according to contingencies of time and place, and my interest here is to study but one segment of it: the spiritual reading of the Christian Bible that takes place in a literate, western culture today. This work is a theological exploration of the realities of God and the postures of biblical readers that enable a good spiritual reading of the Bible in this present day and place; I seek a theological understanding of the work of God and the work of humanity in reading Scripture.[5]

As the wider currents that make up this crossroads are immense, the particular focus of my interest is important to trace out from the beginning, for there are unending ways that one may pursue the nature of God's involvement with the Bible, the nature of Scripture itself and how to interpret it, the nature of spiritual practices, and the nature of the act of reading. Fields of theology, biblical studies, spirituality, and the study of reading are vast, and my work crosses through small sections of all of them. But while touching upon all these areas, the object of my study is focused nonetheless: it centers upon the contemporary western reader of Christian Scripture who seeks to know and love God in and through the practice of individual biblical reading. How is God encountered in reading the Bible this way? How do God's work and humanity's merge in biblical reading? My central concerns

---

4. Ibid., 59.

5. I follow John Webster in understanding that all theology is occasional; there are "'occasions' towards which theology directs itself." And so theology is to "interpret its present situation . . . as an episode in the history of the gospel's dealing with humanity, as one further chapter in the history of holiness." Webster, *Word and Church*, 5.

are what it means to be a Christian reader, how one reads with awareness of the Triune God, whether there might be a distinctly Christian way of reading Scripture, a way of reading that stretches beyond good practices for reading any other work of classic literature. And I aim to work out these concerns as much as possible in concrete ways, as what I am interested in is "the ultimately practical and formational task of actually reading the text in front of us."[6]

I begin in the next two chapters by setting out some of the issues of what it means to read the Bible well, and what it means to read literature in general well. Chapter 2 considers the role the church has in the spiritual reading of Scripture, as the church is the originating context of Scripture and its natural home. I examine the manner in which the church is necessary to provide a framework and guidance for reading the Bible well, and I contrast this setting of the church with two other settings in which the Bible is often placed, namely, the setting of modern, historically-oriented biblical scholarship, and the setting of reading the Bible as a classic work of western literature. Chapter 3 delves more deeply into the issue of reading great works of literature by considering the spiritual dimensions of reading and the spiritual impulses behind certain forms of the study of western literature. I also consider there how literature might be approached through a Christian frame of reference (through exploring the work of C. S. Lewis and Alan Jacobs), and what might be said about the reading of religious works in general (via the work of Paul Griffiths).

With this background of the Bible's setting in the church, and the spiritual dimensions of the practice of reading, my next two chapters center upon how God is involved and working in Christian Scripture, and how Christ is its object. Chapter 4 takes up the question of how it is that God encounters the reader of the Bible; there I follow Karl Barth in his *Church Dogmatics* I.2, §21, and his *Evangelical Theology* lectures. Barth, as one ever pressing for the starting point and object of God in all theological work, sets out an orientation towards God that is necessary to ground the spiritual reading of Scripture. He offers practical marks, as well, of what such a reading looks like, and he points out the necessity of the reader's faith in biblical reading. In chapter 5 I consider the specifically Christ-centered nature of Christian biblical reading, and draw upon another leading mid-twentieth century theologian, Henri de Lubac. In his studies on the medieval exegesis of Scripture, de Lubac highlights the place Jesus has held in traditional Christian readings and interpretations of Scripture, and he advocates a renewed understanding of spiritual reading in the modern world.

---

6. Briggs, *Virtuous Reader*, 10.

In chapters 6 and 7 I turn towards a leading proponent of spiritual reading today, the biblical scholar Ellen Davis. As one who writes from the academy but looks constantly towards the church, Davis considers the form that spiritual reading might take today and she pays attention to the ever fresh and surprising reality of God that the Bible conveys. Chapter 6 is an examination of Davis's background and her theological reading principles, while chapter 7 is an examination of her practices of exegesis. Through several examples of her Old Testament exegesis, I trace out how her manner of spiritual reading works on the ground and how it might provide guidance for spiritual readers.

My conclusion moves from these many thinkers to draw these strands of spiritual reading together in the context of the western church today, and I find that in particular, a renewed understanding of faith is needed for the spiritual reading of Scripture. More than a spiritually-oriented reading, a greater faith in the work and presence of the Triune God in Scripture is needed.

Before entering into the flurry of these issues of spiritual reading and its promising proposals, it is necessary in this introduction to make a few comments pertaining to some background matters on the spiritual reading of the Bible, and the assumptions under which I operate. First is my use of the term "spiritual reading" and the theology of spirituality behind such a biblical reading; second is the manner in which the kind of spiritual reading I propose relates to two significant currents of modern scholarship, that of the theological interpretation of Scripture (a topic debated predominantly in the academy) and of *lectio divina* (a recent lively discussion in the church); and third is the history of the individual reading of Scripture and its place in the modern western church and world.

"Spiritual Reading"

"Spiritual reading" is the term I use to describe the kind of spiritually engaged biblical reading I explore in this work, as this term emphasizes the actual act of reading and the way in which it is oriented. It is the *practice* of reading the Bible that I search out here, that spiritual practice at the heart of the Christian life. While there is no such thing as pure and interpretation-less reading, my interest is less focused upon biblical interpretation as such and more upon the way that one actually goes about reading the Bible—how that reading takes place and to what end. I make a distinction between interpretation and reading here to consider reading as primarily (though not always) an interior activity, whereas interpretation is directed more towards communication.[7]

George Steiner notes that it is difficult to say anything useful about reading in that sense: "Criticism is discursive and breeds discourse. 'Reading' yields no primary impulse towards self-communication. The 'reader' who discourses is, in a certain manner, in breach of the privilege. . . . Reading is done rather than spoken about."[8] Yet here I will try to speak about reading, as I am concerned with the reading practices that enable good understanding and good living of Christian Scripture.[9] For my purposes here, "understanding" might be a better term to use than "interpretation," as my focus is upon readers struggling to understand God and the Christian life through reading Scripture, as opposed to readers who are in positions of leadership and strive to provide biblical interpretations for the church.[10] My envisioned biblical readers are those who more often fill pews than ivory towers (though some are in ivory towers, too).

My understanding of spiritual reading is reading the Bible with a striving towards God throughout the entire process of one's reading. Eugene Peterson, in *Eat This Book: A Conversation in the Art of Spiritual Reading*, has shaped my use of the term "spiritual reading," as Peterson explains spiritual reading as a formative manner of reading, one that is aware of the Spirit of God. He maintains, "spiritual writing—*Spirit*-sourced writing—requires spiritual reading, a reading that honors words as holy;" reading the Scriptures formatively is reading them in such a way that "the Holy Spirit uses them to form Christ in us."[11] Spiritual reading is an approach of reading that looks for the activity of the Spirit of God in Scripture, that recognizes something holy is happening in the words and readings of the Bible. It strives to be in keeping with the Spirit, to make holy its reading and its reader.

---

7. Similarly, John Webster explains that he prefers the term "reading" to "interpretation" because reading is "a more practical, low-level" and "modest term," one less "overlain with the complexities of hermeneutical theory." Webster, *Holy Scripture*, 86; and "Reading Scripture Eschatologically (I)," 247.

8. Steiner, "'Critic'/'Reader,'" 20. Steiner notes, however, on 34, that his heuristic roles of "critic" and "reader" are near-fictions. "Neither can be found at all readily in a pure state. . . . In the ordinary run of things, 'criticism' and 'reading' interpenetrate and overlap."

9. As J. Todd Billings points out, "how we think about our reading of the Bible as a book can have profound effects on how we end up interpreting the Bible as Scripture." Billings, *Word of God*, 32.

10. A point made clear to me through conversation with Francis Watson.

11. Peterson, *Eat This Book*, 4, 59, emphasis his.

Although this kind of reading is basic to the Christian tradition, Peterson notes the difficulty of spiritual reading for many western Christians today:

> [I]n the business of living the Christian life, ranking high among its most neglected aspects is one having to do with the reading of the Christian Scriptures. Not that Christians don't own and read their Bibles. And not that Christians don't believe that their Bibles are the word of God. What is neglected is reading the Scriptures formatively, reading in order to live.[12]

At the start of her own introduction to spiritual reading, Ellen Davis similarly states that "spiritually engaged reading . . . [is] largely unfamiliar to Christians."[13] It is not that Christians have stopped reading the Bible, Davis explains, but that their spiritual engagement with it has declined; many Christians do not know "how to read it for the sake of our souls."[14] Chapters 3 and 6 will briefly explore cultural obstacles in reading Scripture today, but here may it be noted that prevalent patterns of reading in general are often used negatively to define spiritual reading. Spiritual reading is in contrast to manners of reading for information alone, reading in a detached way apart from "the sake of our souls." Peterson notes that "not everyone who gets interested in the Bible and even gets excited about the Bible wants to get involved with God;"[15] his approach intends to counter a perceived common lack of interest in becoming involved with God through biblical reading. Peterson and Davis both use the terms "spiritual reading" or "spiritually engaged reading" to reclaim a self-involving manner of reading Scripture that they feel is lost to many in the present-day western church; their emphasis on spiritual reading is an emphasis on a *way* of reading that is concerned with the formative aspects of reading, of reading with awareness of God and his work through Scripture, work done on each of its readers as they read.

John Webster is another who has recently advocated such an approach to biblical reading; he describes spiritual reading in various terms of "faithful reading," "reading in the economy of grace," and "eschatological" reading.[16] His most helpful description of spiritual reading is perhaps "reading in which we keep company with the holy God."[17] Here lies the essence of

---

12. Ibid., 5.
13. Davis, *Getting Involved With God*, 1.
14. Ibid., 122.
15. Peterson, *Eat This Book*, 30.
16. Webster, *Word and Church*, 43; *Holy Scripture*, 68; "Reading Scripture Eschatologically (I)," 248.
17. Webster, "Reading Scripture Eschatologically (I)," 246.

spiritual reading—keeping company with the holy God of the Christian faith. Following Karl Barth, Webster emphasizes the centrality of God to biblical reading; as Webster argues, "the Christian activity of reading the Bible is most properly (that is, Christianly) understood as a spiritual affair . . . a Christian description of the Christian reading of the Bible will be the kind of description which talks of God."[18] The starting point for talking about reading, Webster maintains, is not the field of hermeneutics or of reading theory, but rather, dogmatics—particularly, who God is and how God has made himself known.[19]

Thus undergirding the broad understanding of spiritual reading that Peterson, Davis, and Webster, among others, set out, and that I follow them in, are many core beliefs about the nature of Scripture and God's involvement with it. As Webster argues, a Christian theology of reading Scripture is best worked out of "the language and belief structure of the Christian faith."[20] I aim here not to argue for, or even to outline, all of that belief structure, but simply to highlight a few Christian beliefs as particularly important for guiding spiritual reading.

The first core belief is an orthodox understanding of God and the Bible—that is, that the Bible is inspired by God and that God is speaking through it still. Precise definitions of inspiration are not needed here, but simply a basic belief that God has worked and is working through Scripture, and that the Bible is central to the understanding of the Christian faith and the living of the Christian life. (More will be said in chapter 4 on Barth's understanding of the nature of God's involvement with the Bible, and inspiration will be returned to in the conclusion.) With this starting point of the Bible as the work of God, also central is the place that Jesus holds in Scripture and its reading. Jesus is more than one of the many subjects of the Christian Bible, but is its proper center, and is its true end, as he is the fullest revelation of God. (More will be said on this in chapter 5, with de Lubac's understanding of medieval exegesis.) And also at the center of spiritual reading is the Spirit of God, the one who both inspired the writing of Scripture and who enables, sustains, and furthers all growth and sanctification. The Trinity is thus behind the spiritual reading of Scripture, as the

---

18. Webster, *Word and Church*, 47.

19. And so, Webster holds that more important than "general theories of religion, textuality, reading or reception" are "the church's dogmatic depictions of encounter with the Bible, depictions which invoke the language of God, Christ, Spirit, faith, church." What is especially needed is to give attention to Jesus, "of whose risen and self-communicative presence in the Holy Spirit the Bible and its reading are a function." Ibid., 48.

20. Ibid., 76.

work of God, the centrality of Christ, and the help of the Spirit are primary to any attempts to read the Christian Bible spiritually.

Beyond this basic confession of the Trinity's activity in the Bible, what is needed is discernment on which other beliefs of the Christian faith are the most fruitful for making sense of this spiritual practice of reading Scripture. Here, I maintain, theological understandings of spirituality and sanctification come in. Spirituality is "the *lived* quality" of the Christian life,[21] how the faith is worked out in the daily lives of Christian believers, and this working out involves both the work of God and the work of believers. In this cooperation, the primacy of God is important ever to bear in mind, as spirituality is not about spiritual self-heroics of individuals, but rather, individuals being increasingly drawn to God. Evelyn Underhill's description of the spiritual life is fitting:

> Any spiritual view which focuses attention on ourselves, and puts the human creature with its small ideas and adventures in the centre foreground, is dangerous till we recognize its absurdity. . . . For a spiritual life is simply a life in which all that we do comes from the centre, where we are anchored in God: a life soaked through and through by a sense of His reality and claim, and self-given to the great movement of His will.[22]

And so, even though a tendency exists for western Christians to become "obsessed with their wonderfully saved souls, setting about busily cultivating their own spiritualities,"[23] all genuine spiritual life and growth is in response to God. What this means when it comes to reading the Bible spiritually is that even "sincere and devout" purposes for biblical reading are displaced, as these can be "self-sovereign" and not in response to God.[24] Spiritual reading is more than having a spiritual agenda; it is a reading

---

21. Peterson, *Christ Plays*, xi, emphasis his.

22. Underhill, *Spiritual Life*, 12, 32.

23. Peterson, *Christ Plays*, 243. Abbot Christopher Jamison similarly notes a "tendency to be self-absorbed . . . characterises so much current western spirituality." Jamison, *Finding Sanctuary*, 170.

24. Peterson, *Eat This Book*, 59. Peterson contrasts spiritual reading with three other dominant approaches: reading the Bible for the intellectual challenge, reading for the acquisition of morals, and "devotionally cozy Bible reading." Although these are aspects of biblical reading, they are not at its true center. "It is entirely possible to come to the Bible in total sincerity, responding to the intellectual challenge it gives, or for the moral guidance it offers, or for the spiritual uplift it provides, and not in any way have to deal with a personally revealing God who has personal designs on you." Ibid., 30. Billings calls such angles "well-intended reading practices that nonetheless point to a lesser story than the gospel of Jesus Christ." Billings, *Word of God*, 197.

which (in Underhill's words) is "soaked through and through by a sense of His reality and claim."

As the spiritual reader of the Bible sets out to read, her essential task, then, is one of participation with God, taking part in the work God is doing. Spiritual reading is working with God, as is the spiritual life as a whole. Orthodox and Wesleyan branches of the church have perhaps best articulated this kind of cooperation between an individual believer and God, as they hold that sanctification is a process of a believer working out his salvation as God is working in him. In Orthodoxy, cooperation with God, or *synergia*, is essential; salvation is a process of *theosis* in which the believer grows in God by cooperating with what God is doing in him. Wesleyan theology likewise believes that Christian perfection hinges upon the believer responding to the grace of God ever at work.[25] The reading of Scripture is one of the most tangible ways that this cooperation between God and the believer may take place, as in the human effort of reading the Bible and seeking to understand it, both the individual's work and the work of God are operative.[26] In the same way that both human and divine processes came together to form the Bible, so too both God's work and the reader's own forms its spiritual reading. Guigo articulates this balance well, "we can do nothing without Him. It is He who achieves our works for us, and yet not entirely without us."[27]

Spiritual reading requires effort, then, but it always holds that effort beneath the sovereignty of God. Illusions may persist that a spiritual reading of the Bible hinges only upon the hard work of the reader. An inclination towards a spiritual reading of Scripture would soon be lost amidst the tide of other desires were it not for the grace of God at work. Spiritual reading is thus not only, as Sandra Schneiders argues, "pre-eminently a reader-centered approach to scripture,"[28] but it is an approach centered upon God's work in the reader. What is necessary is to cultivate the efforts to read well, but to remember that the grace of the Spirit of God is what makes good all

---

25. As Peter C. Bouteneff expresses, Wesleyan perfection is "perfection in love, something that is initiated by the Holy Spirit in us and needs cultivation by us, something dynamic, proceeding from glory to glory in this world and, in a more radical way, from glory to glory in the next." Bouteneff, "All Creation," 197.

26. This is in contrast to Webster's view that "sanctification is not in any straightforward sense a process of cooperation or coordination between God and the creature, a drawing out or building upon some inherent holiness of the creature's own. Sanctification is *making* holy." Webster, *Holy Scripture*, 27, emphasis his. Against Webster, I find cooperative understandings of sanctification are useful at this point to bring together the work of God and the work of the biblical reader.

27. Guigo II, *Ladder of Monks*, 81.

28. Schneiders, "Gospels and the Reader," 103.

strivings and desires. Only the coming of God gives life to reading; there is no intensity of desire strong enough nor any reading approach spiritual enough to guarantee God's presence.[29]

The Theological Interpretation of Scripture and *Lectio Divina*

Many of these thoughts on the nature of spiritual reading find a home in both fields of theological interpretation and of *lectio divina*. A growing field within theology/biblical studies is the theological interpretation of Scripture—Kevin Vanhoozer describes it as "a new kind of interpretation of Scripture that combines an interest in the academic study of the Bible with a passionate commitment to making this scholarship of use to the church."[30] Some of the main characteristics of theological interpretation[31] are taking seriously the text's historical context, bringing together biblical studies and theology, and being governed by an interest in God, both his word and works. Vanhoozer insists that "God must not be an 'afterthought' in biblical interpretation.... A properly theological criticism will therefore seek to do justice to the priority of the living and active triune God."[32]

An array of articles and monographs has been devoted to exploring what "theological interpretation" might mean.[33] In the inaugural issue of the *Journal of Theological Interpretation* (2007), its editor Joel B. Green states,

---

29. David Kelsey articulates this well: "No 'hermenuetic' and no doctrine of the authority of Scripture could hope to discover the key to [Scripture's] perfect employment. Surely, Christianly speaking, it would be improper even to hope for that. For the full discrimen by which theological proposals are finally to be assessed includes the active presence of God. No 'theological position' would presume to tell us how to use Scripture so as to 'guarantee' that God will be present to illumine and correct us. Theological proposals are concerned with what God is now using Scripture to do, and no degree of sophistication in theological methodology can hope to anticipate that!" Kelsey, *Uses of Scripture*, 215.

30. Vanhoozer, *Theological Interpretation*, 13. Earlier works, however, have held these same concerns—see, e.g., Abraham, *Divine Inspiration of Holy Scripture*.

31. Or "theological exegesis" or "theological hermeneutics"—there seems little difference between these terms, other than that "theological interpretation" is more widely used.

32. Vanhoozer, *Theological Interpretation*, 20.

33. See, e.g, Treier, "What Is Theological Interpretation?"; Sarisky, "What is Theological Interpretation?"; Moberly, "What Is Theological Interpretation of Scripture?"; Billings, *Word of God*; Fowl, *Theological Interpretation of Scripture*; Treier, *Introducing Theological Interpretation*; Adam, et al., *Reading Scripture With the Church*; Fowl, *Engaging Scripture*; Fowl, ed., *Theological Interpretation of Scripture*. In addition, other works significant for this movement are Watson's *Text, Church, and World* and *Text and*

> A theological hermeneutics of Christian Scripture concerns the role of Scripture in the faith and the formation of persons and ecclesial communities. . . . Biblical scholarship in the modern period has not oriented itself toward approaches or development of means that would enable us to tune our ears to the voice of God. How do we read the texts as Christian Scripture so as to hear God's address?[34]

Although a desire to hear God's address is at the heart of much theological interpretation, other concerns alongside that desire which are often noted (and can become overriding) are the failings of modern biblical scholarship, and the challenges of negotiating the gap between the academy and the church. Much theological interpretation is caught up with resolving how academic pursuits connect with the life of the church, whether it is possible "to hear God's address" through modern, university-based forms of biblical studies. Those drawn to theological interpretation are often ones who have struggled to articulate their own theological concerns within the perimeters of the academic study of the Bible.[35] Vanhoozer perhaps overstates the situation that prompted the movement of theological interpretation, however, as he likens this "growth industry of late" to the Oklahoma Land Rush of 1893 "when settlers rushed into virgin territory to stake a claim," hoping to find relief from their dire situations: "The recovery of theological interpretation of Scripture is about emerging from the desert to settle in and inhabit the promised land."[36] His imagery is surprisingly careless, as the "virgin territory" of 1893 Oklahoma had, in fact, already been well inhabited—by native peoples whom those settlers of the Land Rush conveniently ignored. Any analogy fails when it is pushed too hard, of course, but Vanhoozer may have unintentionally hit upon a truth in his chosen analogy for theological interpretation—the area of biblical understanding that academic theological interpreters are rushing into is truly an area that has long been inhabited by other readers of the Bible, ones more native to its land. Even when

---

Truth, and the nine theses and collection of essays in *Art of Reading Scripture*.

34. Green, "(Re-)Turn to Theology," 2.

35. Treier suggests theological interpretation's "most natural home . . . with its mix of 'evangelical' and 'catholic' elements tamed by Barthian and postmodern whips, will be among 'higher church' evangelicals and the relatively conservative mainline Protestants associated with the term 'postliberal.' No doubt other evangelicals and Catholics can appropriate some of the movement's language and offer their own contributions; for instance, a Pentecostal scholar could resonate with openness to spiritual exegesis. But that scholar is likely to associate appeals to the 'spiritual' with a non-sacramental framework or a less sacramental one than the classic heritage." Treier, "What Is Theological Interpretation?" 156.

36. Vanhoozer, *Theological Interpretation*, 13–14.

segments of the modern academy have lost interest in hearing God's address in Scripture (though not to say all the academy, as it has ever had its Rudolf Bultmanns and Gerhard von Rads—ones whose scholarly rigor is governed by interest in God[37]), "the promised land" of the Bible has been dwelt in still. As those within the academy turn to listen, they are rejoicing, rather than reviving, a tradition.[38]

Within theological interpretation, a striving to listen to God is not always at the forefront, however. In a review of recently-published theological commentaries on Scripture, Steven J. Koskie finds them curiously lacking the feature of "reading as if Scripture is addressed to the church that is reading right now."[39] What is missing in these theological commentaries, Koskie argues, is the immediacy of address that Barth saw in Calvin and sought for himself. Theological interpretation/commentary can translate for some into paying attention to certain theological issues (e.g., the nature of salvation or community ethics[40]), not necessary to the pressing address of God in a

---

37. Schneiders points out, "In reality the most intellectually rigorous and spiritually fruitful work on the biblical texts throughout history has been done by those who were not only speaking competently and even authoritatively to their academic peers but were also passionately concerned with spirituality: Origen, Augustine, Thomas Aquinas, Bonaventure, Bernard, Luther, Calvin, Bultmann, Barth, Lagrange, Raymond Brown, and many others." Schneiders, "Biblical Spirituality," 141.

38. Briggs notes, "It is a regrettable part of the rhetoric of academia that some who advocate theological interpretation today exaggerate the absence of theological dimensions in earlier biblical studies." Briggs, "Christian Theological Interpretation Built on the Foundation of the Apostles and the Prophets," 311n4. Likewise, Treier argues, "[E]vangelicals have primarily excelled at practicing elements of theological interpretation rather than theorizing about it—maintaining, for instance, forms of canonical reading such as typology or 'Scripture interpreting Scripture' popularly even during their eclipse within mainstream Protestant theology. The renaissance of evangelical biblical scholarship during recent decades undoubtedly galvanizes interest in theological interpretation as a possible provider of the theoretical language within which to articulate or defend how some already pursue biblical theology." Treier, "What Is Theological Interpretation?" 151. Similarly, Billings argues, "The theological interpretation of Scripture is, in many ways, simply the church's attempt to read Scripture again after the hubris and polarities of the Enlightenment have begun to fade." Billings, *Word of God*, 224. Billings's book was the cover story for the October 2011 issue of the evangelical magazine *Christianity Today*: "How to Read the Bible: New Strategies for Interpreting Scripture Turn Out To Be Not So New—And Deepen our Faith."

39. Koskie, "Seeking Comment," 244.

40. Examining Hermann Schelkle's commentary on Romans, R. R. Reno notes that "theological abstractions such as 'redemption,' 'sonship,' and the 'the new, transfigured corporeality' dominate. This approach is typical of much of what we think of when someone commends 'theological exegesis.' Modern theological interpretation relies on words and concepts ('redemption') that stand at least two removes from the text. That is to say, Schelkle is glossing the text with broad generalizations about 'the Christian view of salvation,' a view that seems to float in an ether of ideas." "Biblical Theology," 389.

passage of Scripture. In his article "What is Theological Interpretation?" R. W. L. Moberly questions how wedded one must be to the term "theological" for the task of theological interpretation, asking if other terms might as readily (or better) apply, such as "Christian reading" or "spiritual understanding." The modifier "theological" has become a "high-value term"[41] which can, ironically, detract attention away from God. (And many whose work might be considered in the camp of theological interpretation, such as Ellen Davis, tend not to employ that term.) Moberly is moreover troubled by the lack of exegesis in some recent proposals for theological interpretation,[42] a problem that also bothers R. R. Reno:

> [O]ne of the impediments to clear thinking about theological exegesis on the part of theologians is a drift towards abstraction. To exhort one and all to read the Bible "theologically," or to read it "for the church," offers little insight into what is necessary. Furthermore, digressions into Ricoeurian, narrative and postmodern hermeneutical theory seem to produce more ideas than exegesis.[43]

Thus, as Stephen B. Chapman states, "The problem . . . is not that theological interpretation has been ignored but rather that the *right kind* of theological interpretation has not been done."[44] More attention to God and to biblical texts themselves are recurring concerns for theological interpretation.

While my interests cross into much that is passionately debated in circles of theological interpretation, nonetheless I retain the term "spiritual reading" for my purposes here, so as to make clear my primary aims. Rather than the dislocations between the university and the church, and between the fields of biblical studies and theology, my concern is with the separation between the biblical reader and God, and again, with reading more than with interpretation. How is closeness to God found in the practice of reading Scripture? That question is well-addressed in another area of scholarship that has undergone much recent growth (mostly from church quarters), the area of *lectio divina*, the church's "divine reading" or "reading that is from God."

---

41. Moberly, "What Is Theological Interpretation of Scripture?" 169.

42. "There tends to be more discussion about the nature of theological interpretation and theological hermeneutics than there is demonstration in persuasive and memorable readings of the biblical text." Ibid.

43. Reno, "Biblical Theology and Theological Exegesis," 386.

44. Chapman, "Imaginative Readings," 410, emphasis his.

It is hard to capture the meaning of the expression *lectio divina*. Mariano Magrassi explains that "reading" and "studying" are both inadequate translations of *lectio*, as this kind of *lectio* is closer to meditation, but a meditation that is a loving attention and deep listening while bent eagerly over pages.[45] Magrassi quotes Louis Bouyer to find a more precise definition, explaining that *lectio divina* is "a reading in faith, in a spirit of prayer, believing in the real presence of God who speaks to us in the sacred text."[46] Reading in the way of *lectio divina* is above all else, reading in a posture of prayer, attuned to the presence of God in the text and ready to listen and respond. Early on in church tradition this posture was taken—Cyprian's letter to his friend Donatus, c. 256, was often quoted in the Middle Ages, as Cyprian exhorts Donatus, "Be constant as well in prayer as in reading; now speak with God, now let God speak with you."[47] The close relationship between biblical reading and prayer is central to *lectio divina*; its reading is a deep listening and prayer.

While *lectio divina* is not a precise hermeneutic or rigid practice, beginning in the twelfth century, monastic communities came to give structure to *lectio divina* to guide monks' reading of biblical texts. As mentioned above, the twelfth-century monk Guigo II gives one of the most illuminating looks into medieval practices of *lectio divina*. In his short treatise *The Ladder of Monks*, Guigo outlines the stages of *lectio divina*, reflecting both ancient ideas (such as the ladder of contemplation and the multiple layers of meaning in a biblical text), and fresh outpourings of medieval spirituality.[48] Guigo explains these four rungs of *lectio* being reading, meditation, prayer, and contemplation: in reading one encounters a biblical text and seeks its meaning; in meditation one comes to perceive that meaning; in prayer one asks for the reality of that meaning to be his own; and in contemplation one gazes upon God.

An ancient way of reading the Bible, *lectio divina* never died out as a spiritual practice, surviving through the Enlightenment, the Protestant Reformation, and the growth of modern biblical studies (although much of its survival was in a monastic context still). In the past few decades, however, a

---

45. Magrassi, *Praying the Bible*, 17.

46. Bouyer, *Parola*, 17, translated and quoted in Magrassi, *Praying the Bible*, 18.

47. Cyprian, *Letter* 1.xv, as quoted in Dumont, *Praying the Word of God*, 1.

48. It may be, however, that Guigo's *Ladder* set out a monastic manner of reading just as meditative practices were heading into decline at the end of the twelfth century. See Jamison, *Finding Sanctuary*, 65. In this regard Gugio's guide is similar to Hugh of St. Victor's *Didascalicon*, also written roughly in the mid-twelfth century, and thus also at the end of an era of reading, as Illich argues in his work *In the Vineyard of the Text*, 64, 96.

particular revival of interest in *lectio divina* has taken place in many diverse areas of the church, across denominational lines.[49] In Protestant circles interest in *lectio divina* has grown as part of a larger movement of many mainline denominations and evangelicals in the west reclaiming traditional practices of spiritual formation.[50] On the Catholic side, Archbishop Magrassi traces the Catholic revival of interest in Scripture to the larger renewal work of Vatican Council II and the 1985 Synod of Bishops. Pope Benedict XVI indeed reflects this ongoing work, as on the 40th anniversary of *Dei Verbum*, he urged a renewal of the practice of *lectio divina*:

> I would like in particular to recall and recommend the ancient tradition of *lectio divina*: the diligent reading of Sacred Scripture accompanied by prayer. . . . If it is effectively promoted, this practice will bring to the Church—I am convinced of it—a new spiritual springtime. As a strong point of biblical ministry, *lectio divina* should therefore be increasingly encouraged, also through the use of new methods, carefully thought out and in step with the times.[51]

Lectio divina is thus a promising way the church might find again the freshness of spring in its ancient Scriptures. Yet just as the term "theological interpretation" did not fit what I am aiming at in this work, so too the term *lectio divina* is close to, but not quite the right fit for this study. *Lectio divina* indeed captures the attentiveness to God that marks the posture of spiritual reading, but the term stretches past the actual act of reading to include

---

49. Studzinski offers a helpful survey of the surge of literature on *lectio divina* from the 1970s to the 1990s in *Reading to Live*, 194–95. Most that has been written on *lectio divina* has come from Catholic and Protestant fronts, as traditional Orthodox understandings of Scripture approach its reading in ways more centered upon the ecclesial life of the church. John Breck recently has attempted to bring *lectio divina* into relation with Orthodox theology. He explains, "Any 'personal' reading of Scripture . . . takes place within the Church, as a function of the life of the Church. Like prayer, it draws us into a living communion with the universal Body of Christian believers. Our quest will lead to a *lectio divina* faithful to Orthodox tradition, therefore, only to the extent that it confirms and deepens our commitment to the ecclesial Body." Breck, *Scripture in Tradition*, 67.

50. Both Eugene Peterson (a Presbyterian) and Richard Foster (a Quaker), prominent figures in this movement, have written on the importance of *lectio divina* in spiritual formation. Peterson sets the traditional four-fold movement of *lectio, meditatio, oratio,* and *contemplatio* at the heart of his spiritual reading (though contemplation is explained as the living of biblical texts). He envisages the four parts as non-linear, however, but rather thrown together in "a kind of playful folk dance." Peterson, *Eat This Book*, 91. Foster takes a similar approach in *Life With God*.

51. Benedict XVI, "Address of His Holiness Benedict XVI."

practices of meditation, prayer, contemplation, and Christian living.[52] Such is the real end of biblical reading, and these things are close to my interests here. However, my aim is more modest in thinking more directly and concretely about the practice of reading itself, about how the reader's eyes move over the biblical text and come to be lifted towards God. I search out primarily, then, the meaning of the first step of medieval *lectio divina*—that of *lectio* itself—and to a certain extent, also the meaning of the second step of meditation—yet the kind of meditation I have in mind is, as Sandra Schneiders explains, a modern type of meditation that might entail the use of commentaries or other biblical aids—a meditation aided by scholarship to understand the meaning of texts.[53] My interest is in the type of scriptural reading and thinking that heads toward God.

The Individual Reading of Scripture in the Christian Faith

As the church has sought God in Scripture, the Christian faith from its beginning has had a textual predilection for doing that seeking. Early Christians had almost "an addiction to literacy;"[54] the church inherited a high regard for written Scriptures from Judaism and soon broadened their Scriptures to include Mark with Moses, the epistles with the prophets, Acts with Exodus. Writing was central to the start of the Christian movement, and early Christians even broke with cultural norms in how they went about that. Texts played a role in early Christianity in an anomalous way, as ancient Christians had a strong preference for the codex, which was at odds with the wider culture's use of scrolls—in the second-century, over 70 percent of Christian manuscripts are codices, whereas of all second-century manuscripts, 74 percent are rolls.[55] This codex preference is still perplex-

---

52. Foster explains the practice of *lectio divina* by relating a story of Henri Nouwen once showing him a painting of a woman with an open Bible in her lap, her gaze lifted upward. This, Foster describes, is the essence of *lectio divina*—looking past the text to God. Foster, *Life With God*, 63.

53. Schneiders further points out that *lectio divina* is, in essence, more widely practiced than realized: "I have found that many people who have never heard of lectio divina practice this kind of prayer on a daily basis . . . In other words, even though the term 'biblical spirituality' may be unfamiliar to many people, the reality of biblical spirituality as a practice is not." Schneiders, "Biblical Spirituality," 140.

54. Graham, *Beyond the Written Word*, 123. He continues by pointing out, "even in the face of attacks by outsiders and heretics who themselves cited scripture as a proof text, the young church never resorted to attempts to limit study and circulation of scripture among the laity."

55. Hurtado, *Earliest Christian Artifacts*, 49. He concludes on 53, "[T]he slow but

ing scholars. Larry Hurtado argues that practical reasons often suggested for the Christian use for the codex do not stand up (the codex was neither easier to make or less expensive than a roll, nor was it easier to flip through to access a portion of a text, and nor was transportability a pressing issue). He finds that there is, however, a marked difference in the codex's layout: in contrast to the unbroken form of classical Greek texts, many Christian codices have a layout that aids in reading, with wider margins, punctuation marks, devices to mark off sense-unit sections. Hurtado understands these moves as efforts to help facilitate the public/liturgical usage of texts (and though he does not mention it, these moves may have helped the individual reader, as well). Although such "readerly aids" would come to be common in book production, in their time, "the earliest Christian manuscripts represented the leading edge of such developments in book practice."[56]

Ancient Christian manuscripts attest to an early Christian concern with how its texts are actually read, then, as part of its everyday practices of faith. It seems self-evident that reading sacred writings is a core part of religious practice, but the act of reading itself is not necessary for the Christian faith, or any other faith. William Graham cogently argues that western ideas of sacred texts too often view texts primarily as written objects, and overlook how much scriptures are recited, memorized, chanted, sung, and otherwise engaged orally and aurally; he points out "the historical novelty of our modern relationship to words and books."[57] Paul Griffiths likewise maintains that religious texts may be engaged by modes other than visual reading: "Religious readers, paradoxically, need not know how to read."[58] The importance a religion gives to its sacred writings does not necessarily mean an importance given to the practice of reading its texts, then.[59] Henry

---

steady advance of the codex in general usage across the first three centuries CE contrasts sharply with the early and rather wholesale embrace of this book form in Christian usage." Frances M. Young suggests that the Christian copying of Jewish Scriptures along with their own texts into codices seems to be "not the gradual elevation of recent Christian books to the sacred status of Jewish scriptures, but rather the relativising of those ancient scriptures. They have become secondary to the Gospel of Christ. . . . Jews have never transferred their sacred text from the scroll format." Young, *Biblical Exegesis*, 15, 289.

56. Hurtado, *Earliest Christian Artifacts*, 179. Alan Jacobs wants to take a step further than Hurtado, and he suggests theological reasons are behind early Christian preference for the codex, namely, that "the codex is the technology of typology—just as it is the technology of Biblical integrity." Jacobs, "Christianity and the Future of the Book," 26.

57. Graham, *Beyond the Written Word*, 30.

58. Griffiths, *Religious Reading*, 40.

59. As an example, Graham points out that in Hinduism the Veda was long transmitted only orally to certain castes, as its words were thought too holy to be put into

Gamble thus finds, "It may seem paradoxical to say both that Christianity placed a high value on texts and that most Christians were unable to read, but in the ancient world this was no contradiction."[60]

As the early Christian church used written means of spreading and confirming its beliefs, it was choosing the medium of writing and reading to be central among other possible modes of communicating.[61] This medium of writing in turn had effects upon theological understandings of the Bible; as Jonathan Z. Smith argues, "canonization, in the case of the Bible, is inseparable from modes of production, being as much an affair of technology as theology. The perceived singularity of *the* Bible would have been impossible without the adoption of the codex form; the perceived uniformity of the Bible, impossible without the invention of the printing press."[62]

Although the practice of individually reading the Bible is in many ways a modern practice ("the historical novelty" that Graham notes), from early on the church's members have been encouraged to read Scripture on their own. As early as the fourth century John Chrysostom took up Acts' story of the Ethiopian eunuch as a means to urge his congregation to read Scripture. He asks his hearers to consider "what a great effort" the eunuch made "not to neglect reading even while on a journey," and he admonishes them, "Let this be heeded by those people who do not even deign to do it at home but rather think reading the Scriptures is a waste of time."[63] Jerome's advice to Eustochium, c. 384, likewise insists on individual reading: "Read often, learn all that you can. Let sleep overcome you, the roll still in your hands; when your head falls, let it be on the sacred page."[64]

Yet even with the fathers' common admonition to hold the written Scriptures in high regard and to read them frequently, Chrysostom nonetheless understands that reading itself is not the aim:

> It were indeed meet for us not at all to require the aid of the written Word, but to exhibit a life so pure, that the grace of the Spirit should be instead of books to our souls, and that as these are inscribed with ink, even so should our hearts be with the Spirit.

---

writing or to common use. Graham, *Beyond the Written Word*, 72–73.

60. Gamble, *Books and Readers*, 8.

61. Gamble notes, "No Greco-Roman religious group produced, used, or valued texts on a scale comparable to Judaism and Christianity." Ibid., 18.

62. Smith, "Religion and Bible," 26. Philip Esler offers a different take on the historical significance of Christian texts than I chart above; he argues that a recovery of the oral dimension of New Testament texts is key to their proper understanding. See Esler, *New Testament Theology*, 169.

63. Chrysostom, *Homilies on Genesis*, 35.3.

64. Jerome, Letter 22.17,37.

> But, since we have utterly put away from us this grace, come, let us at any rate embrace the second best course.⁶⁵

Chrysostom holds that the ultimate aim of encountering Scripture is to embody it oneself; it is actually a "second best course" that it must be written to enable that. Early on in the Christian tradition, then, there was both a high regard for written Scripture, and awareness that Scripture was in the service of the greater purpose of knowing God. David Lyle Jeffrey cites Augustine's point that one with a steadfast hold upon faith, hope, and love "has no need of the scriptures except to instruct others," and Jeffrey argues that as a Christ-like life is the goal of reading Scripture, there is "a sense in which the unlettered believer already living this life—one might think of peasant converts in modern China as readily as in the largely oral culture of Europe or Africa during the first Christian centuries—would not himself need the actual Book."⁶⁶

The Christian faith, then, has an almost paradoxical use of its sacred writings—"an unusual complexity and even ambiguity in its treatment of the divine word."⁶⁷ While it inherited its understanding of written Scriptures straight from Judaism, these Scriptures were cast in the light of Jesus Christ as one who gives new meaning and new purpose to all of Scripture. On the one hand, the early Christian movement was eager to write and to circulate and to read publicly its sacred texts, but on the other hand, its Scripture was always subsidiary to the greater goal of knowing Christ and becoming more like him. Not just the writing but the proclamation and the living of the Word were key. Such a dynamic of Scripture carried over even into the Reformation; as Graham argues, the Protestant Reformation sought to recover the preaching and teaching of the word of God, the early kerygmatic orientation of the Church, even though that Word was being set in writing more than ever before.⁶⁸

Setting aside time to read the Bible individually has long been a part of Christian devotional practice in the western world. Edward Wettenhall, for example, gave instructions for devotional reading in *Enter Thy Closet*, written 1666. He explains, "By *Reading* here I understand reading the sole word of God: and this as it should constantly (for the main at least, if not every) have a place in my daily devotions in privated [sic]."⁶⁹ Wettenhall's advice

---

65. Chrysostom, *Homily 1 on Matthew*.
66. Augustine, *On Christian Teaching*, 1.39.43; Jeffrey, *People of the Book*, xvi, xv.
67. Graham, *Beyond the Written Word*, 122.
68. Ibid., 120.
69. Wettenhall, *Enter Thy Closet*, 39, emphasis his. Wettenhall recognizes that not everyone can read or has the time to read, and so the title of his first chapter is, "That

comes after a prolonged struggle for the Bible to be made accessible in English for individual readers, as before the English Reformation it was a crime to publish the Bible in English, or even own a copy of such publication. Wettenhall's instructions reflect just how far the translation and publication of Scripture had come. Although there have been common elements in private devotional practice from the early church to the present, many of the ways in which biblical reading has been done have changed in each new age, as practices of biblical reading are shaped not only through convictions of faith but also through religious and political culture, as well as conventions of type and technology. It is important to recognize the particular time and place in which the spiritual reading of the Bible is considered, then, for spiritual readers today read both like and unlike their fathers and mothers. The particular context in which I pursue the possibility of spiritual reading is the early twenty-first century, western church, enmeshed in a broadly literate and post-Christian culture. Western culture is one whose great literature has historically been influenced by the Bible (a situation not found in every culture), and it is a culture in which books and reading have a common and casual place in everyday lives (again, not a situation found in every culture). Reading is intrinsic to a society increasingly oriented around visual media such as the internet, a primary source of information and consumer goods.

Yet fears have been sounded that modern western culture is becoming postliterate, and for this reason the act of reading has received much attention. "Reading has become one of the hottest subjects in the humanities," Harvard University's library director announced in 2010 with the unveiling of their new online open collection, "Reading: Harvard Views of Readers, Readership, and Reading History."[70] This project compiles vast materials on the nature of reading, all accessible online for free. Its online dimension reflects the scholarly interest in the practice of reading that has been generated by the increasing use of computers for reading. In a computer age, the book is coming into question for its use and permanence, and the textuality of the modern west is akin to how Marshall McLuhan described modern

---

if I am a person of leisure I ought daily twice in day to retire into my closet for devotion sake." Gregory O. Johnson notes that closet prayer was of great importance in early modern Anglo-American Protestant spirituality; "[t]he growth of individualism and privatization in spirituality are significant themes in British—and especially in American—religion." Johnson, "From Morning Watch to Quiet Time," 18, 22. Johnson's work is an engaging history of "the quiet time" and the wider cultural factors that have shaped it.

70. Darnton, "Reading."

life as a whole—it is "dissolving and resolving" at once.[71] The book is in flux and ironically, books are being written to ponder the future of the book.[72]

Within the church and the academy the Bible is now read both through traditional books and through a myriad of forms of modern electronic forms, such as Kindles, iPads, smart phones, personal computers, and online Bibles.[73] Alan Jacobs insists that although "shiny new technologies tend to draw the bulk of our attention," a neat contrast cannot be made between a classic codex and all modern technologies, and a more important difference is that between a codex Bible and a biblical text projected onto a screen. Jacobs finds that e-readers such as Kindles "preserve many of the essential features of the codex"—a Kindle is still "a flat surface on which ink appears."[74] However, the screens used in a growing number of western churches for projecting biblical readings (among other parts of the worship service) are a marked break from biblical codices, and these screens have "a greater influence on Christian encounters with the Bible:"

---

71. McLuhan, *Gutenberg Galaxy*, 1.

72. This has been going on for two decades now; see, e.g., Nunberg, *Future of the Book*. In his introduction Nunberg notes, "One could be forgiven for assuming that anyone who talks about the future of the book nowadays will be chiefly interested in saying whether it has one." Yet Nunberg is "willing to venture . . . by the end of the decade [the 1990s] all our current talk of the 'end of the book' will sound as dated and quaint as most of the other forecasts of this type . . . photography will kill painting, movies will kill the theater . . . and so on." Ibid., 9, 13. Anecdotally, the oddness of this moment in time particularly struck me in 2010 when I was trying to locate Blackwell's *Companion to the History of the Book*. Although the Durham University library catalogue (which I searched online from my home) told me there was not a physical copy of this book in the university's collections, there was a link to "Blackwell Reference Online" with this book's electronic version. How peculiar it was then to read this book on the history of the book by pixels on my laptop screen, unknown miles away from any physical copy of this book I was reading.

73. Some church leaders are seizing on new technologies (at times, recklessly) in attempts to make Scripture appealing. A recent movement in the UK that encourages biblical reading, "Biblefresh," intentionally chose not to present visually the Bible as a codex book. Krish Kandiah explains, "You will see on all of the Biblefresh material that we haven't put a picture of a book and that's because we want to say to people that there are so many great digital ways to engage with God's word today—whether that's through WordLive, smartphones, YouVersion or whatever means you can engage with God's word . . . Paul talked about doing whatever it takes, that he would become a Jew to reach the Jews and a Greek to reach the Greek so that by any means possible he might win some for Christ, and I think that's got to be our opportunistic attitude to these new technologies." "Krish Kandiah and the Weightwatchers Approach."

74. Jacobs acknowledges, "It is true that the e-ink comes from below the surface rather than being impressed on it, but it really is a kind of ink, and must be read under the same lighting conditions that we read paper codices." Jacobs, "Christianity and the Future of the Book," 35, 31.

> [T]he enormous white screen that hangs somewhere near the pulpit of many thousands of churches ... [is] the *primary* way many millions of Christians today encounter Scripture. ... When you consider how thoroughly such a presentation decontextualizes whatever part of the Bible it is interested in—how completely it severs its chosen verse or two from its textual surroundings—how radically it occludes any sense of sequence within the whole of the Bible ... it becomes, I think, difficult to worry about the pernicious effects of iPads and Kindles.[75]

Jacobs might consider more fully that most Christians throughout the ages have encountered the Bible primarily aurally in a church—they did not have their own copies of the Bible to follow along, and so the biblical readings they heard were, in a different way, removed from their "textual surroundings." (Although perhaps the codex Bible from which a reading was done still visually conveyed a wider context of that reading.) Yet Jacobs rightly points out the close relationship between Christian Scripture and the codex—"the interweaving of technology and theology is extremely complex."[76] As the Bible is experienced more and more through technological sound bites, its cohesiveness and its role in the Christian life are harder to grasp. While it is too early to see where our new technologies of reading are leading us (and I will not be delving into analysis of them), they are important to recognize as a factor affecting the direction of spiritual reading.

Moreover, the Bible is also caught up with the immense consumerism of the west, as the glut of Bibles on the shelves of Christian bookstores and online can attest.[77] One result of the explosion of Bible publishing in the past century has most recently been the making of niche Bibles, Bibles marketed for specific demographic groups and interests—a questionable phenomenon in the church.[78] Yet as Graham notes, "we can observe in the past cen-

---

75. Ibid., 33–34, emphasis original.

76. Ibid., 23.

77. In a 2006 essay for *The New Yorker* Daniel Radosh reports, "The situation [of Bible publishing] worries some people. Phyllis Tickle ... told me, 'There's a certain scandal to what's happened to Bible publishing over the last fifteen years.' ... The problem, as she sees it, is that 'instead of demanding that the believer, the reader, the seeker step out from the culture and become more Christian, more enclosed within ecclesial definition, we're saying, "You stay in the culture and we'll come to you." And, therefore, how are we going to separate out the culturally transient and trashy from the eternal?' ... In Tickle's view, reimagining the Bible according to the latest trends is not merely a question of surmounting a language barrier. It involves violating 'something close to moral or spiritual barriers.'" Radosh, "Good Book Business."

78. In a *Christianity Today* review of one such Bible, the environmentally conscious *The Green Bible* (released 2008), Telford Work calls it an "ideological fashion accessory,"

tury or more that, just as availability of the biblical text has greatly increased through growth of literacy and the ubiquitous presence of printed Bibles, the strong biblical saturation of Western culture has sharply decreased."[79] Somehow the Gutenberg revolution has stalled as concerns its first printed text; the Bible is printed on more pages, but on fewer lives.

With emerging technologies of reading and increasing consumerism, there is as well a great proliferation of modern biblical scholarship. While biblical scholarship has existed for some two thousand years, it has grown exponentially in the past century and lodged itself within the modern university context. Yet still there is still a declining biblical literacy in the church and in the broader culture. Robert Jenson remarks, "The scholarship devoted to explaining it, to interpreting it, to applying it, to devising hermeneutical metatheories about it, increases exponentially and becomes ever more desperate; while in the church the Bible nevertheless becomes ever less accessible."[80] The same might be said of the publishing industry devoted to producing new copies of the Bible, both in traditional forms and in new media—biblical publishing and biblical scholarship are increasing ever-rapidly, but a basic biblical literacy in western church and culture is sinking, if not already sunk.

So in this time, in these places, what might it mean to read Scripture well? The situation might seem dire (indeed, Griffiths and others worry about it, as will be considered below), but I hold out there is yet good hope for the spiritual reading of the Bible. The challenge is to understand Christian spiritual reading of Scripture as a spiritual practice that is embedded in cultural practices of reading and yet transcending them; the problem is to perceive

---

yet admits, "I seem to be pointing out the speck in my brother's eye. After all, the Bible is already a fashion accessory. It is available in every shape, size, and price range to suit a dizzying variety of target markets: Bibles for men, for women, for newlyweds, for parents, for children, for teens, for various ethnicities—and of course, Bibles for us academics. In my circle, basic black is the rule, red letters gauche, and utility is its own elegance. First-year students marvel at my bilingual Hebrew and Greek editions, and majors admire my voluminous Bible software. And I can't say I mind it when they do. Why should I begrudge Prius-driving disciples the same satisfaction?" And yet, Work points out that the proliferation of such Bibles is troubling, as niche Bibles are vehicles that "disperse out fellowships into scattered interest groups who represent the various causes and subcultures that rise, clash, and fall in a democracy . . . These are no longer the Word of God for the whole people of God, a whole congregation, or even a whole person. Are they even Bibles?" Work, "Meager Harvest," 30–31.

79. Graham, *Beyond the Written Word*, 167.
80. Jenson, "Strange New World," 25.

how the activities of God and of believers come together over Scripture. It is a bold thing that God has done in placing his Word in ever-turning pages of human words—it seems a risk to use forms of writing and reading, as practices of writing and reading change in every age and culture. Especially evident today is just how much the practice of reading is ever changing, and the Bible is swept up in those changes. But in this risk the spiritual reading of Scripture begins.

CHAPTER 2

Spiritual Reading and the Church

My writing desk sits in front of the window of our second-floor study, with an open view of the row upon row of terraced houses of our neighborhood below. As I scribble out thoughts about Scripture, my eyes are constantly drawn to the people passing by, who ever make me ponder the wider relevance of my work. (It is one of the benefits of working with a public sphere in view instead of library stacks alone.) What these pedestrians make me wonder is how pedestrian my work might seem to them—how much my study on the spiritual reading of Scripture might be dull and uninspiring to those not already reading the Bible and drawn in by its claims.

I set out this image not to speak about academia versus "real life," or the secularization of the west (though those are pressing questions), but to give a context and an illustration for something fundamental to the spiritual reading of Scripture, which is the extent to which spiritual reading depends upon readers having certain expectations of the Bible in place. Without a basic understanding of what the Bible is and why it is worth reading, spiritual reading cannot get off the ground, for a framework is needed to read the Bible well. That framework is one constructed by the church, and my argument in this chapter is that the spiritual reading of the Christian Bible can only take place in and through the church.[1] I will work out this claim

---

1. By "church" I mean the global body of Christian churches who are orthodox according to classic affirmations of faith such as the Apostles Creed and Nicene Creed, and who hold the Bible (in its various Orthodox/Catholic/Protestant forms) as authoritative in matters of belief and practice. Here I will speak of the Christian Bible and the church broadly, apart from any one particular orthodox branch of the church or canonical version of the Bible, as I think that differences both in churches and in their canons do not affect overarching approaches to reading the Bible spiritually.

first through the angle of the sociology of knowledge, and will then consider two alternate approaches to reading the Bible, that of reading the Bible with historical, critical interests, and that of reading the Bible as a classic work of literature. I turn towards historically-oriented and literary-oriented approaches because they have much to offer to the practice of spiritual reading; both historical-critical studies and close literary readings greatly enrich and deepen the spiritual reading of Scripture.[2] Yet taken apart from the life of the church, historical-critical and literary approaches are ultimately unsustainable and even in places misguided, however, and in their limitations the need for the church is made all the more apparent for the spiritual reading of the Bible.

Sociology of Knowledge

The sociology of knowledge is interested in the social nature of knowledge—how knowledge comes through others, how our knowing is related to the knowing of others. Peter L. Berger and Thomas Luckmann gave a landmark study of this in *The Social Construction of Reality: A Treatise in the Sociology of Knowledge*; there they set out that "plausibility structures" are the social forms and relationships that convey knowledge and enable one to take seriously a new way of life through seeing the example of others. Knowledge is generally not gained apart from social relationships, and such relationships are particularly needed to sustain the deep kind of knowledge that shapes one's seeing of the world. With regard to the Christian Bible, sociology of knowledge ties the Bible and the church together, for the church has formed both the Bible (its canonical collections) and expectations for it (through liturgy, preaching, art, devotional practices, etc.). The Bible is not a self-created text—it does not hover out in the world apart from its history—but it is a compilation made by Jews and Christians. Simply in the way that "the Bible" can describe the Jewish Tanak, the Catholic Bible, the Coptic Bible, the Protestant Bible, or any other variation in the Jewish and Christian faiths, it is evident how much the very term "Bible" hinges upon a particular frame of reference and faith community.

In seeking to read the Christian Bible spiritually, then, without the church a reader would have neither a Bible nor a fitting Christian way to

---

2. As Schneiders argues, modern spiritual reading "cannot bypass historical-critical exegesis and literary analysis . . . [N]o one who is serious about biblical spirituality should be excused from the study requisite for a well-grounded understanding of biblical texts in their own historical-cultural contexts and according to their literary genres and theological categories." Schneiders, "Biblical Spirituality," 136, 142.

read it. The historical and the ongoing witness of the church acts as a plausibility structure and shapes the way that readers may come to the Bible today, for the Bible, even when read apart from the church, is never apart from the church's ongoing history and influence. R. W. L. Moberly argues that the church is vital to the possibility of the Christian Bible being taken seriously as Scripture:

> The biblical portrayal of human nature and destiny will present itself to consciousness as reality only to the extent that its appropriate plausibility structure, the church in its many forms, is kept in existence.... [T]he Bible's own understanding [is] that the way of living and thinking of a particular people, called to be the people of God (Israel in the OT, the church in the NT), is indispensable for giving content to and making accessible the enduring and universal significance of the biblical witness.[3]

In other words, without members of the church (perhaps even only a core remnant) keeping on in their reading and their living of their Scriptures, those both inside and outside of the church will not be drawn into reading the Bible in a spiritually-nourishing manner. For a potential biblical reader to see that the Bible offers life, that life must be shown in the lives of others.

The church thus passes down not only a book but expectations for it and manners of reading it that bring out its vitality; what this means for the spiritual reading of Scripture is that it can only be done when biblical readers receive from the church both the Bible and modes of reading well (modes that, while similar to and indebted to wider cultural practices, are accepted by and endorsed by the church). And so, were I to try to speak about the riches of reading the Bible to those pedestrians outside my window, for instance, it might seem an odd claim to them, as most would have limited knowledge of and experience with Scripture. The Bible might be to them an authoritative but remote religious book, or a dull volume, or a political instrument, or a dusty relic of the past. To call for a spiritual reading of Scripture is to call for a particular way of seeing and picking up the Bible, a way taught by the church. Yet moreover, my shouts down to people below might not be effective in that those listening would have no knowledge of my own life and no basis to judge my claims for Scripture giving life to it; and in addition, the unchurched among them possibly would not have very many examples of others who have read the Bible and found its words speaking truly of the living God. What is needed to take on board calls for a spiritual reading of Scripture is acquaintance with Christian believers and personal involvement in the church.

---

3. Moberly, "Theological Interpretation," 20.

Room must be left here for the Spirit of God working through the Bible, however, for all this is not to say that someone unacquainted with Christians, the church, and the Bible might not light upon the Bible suddenly and be convinced of its truth and life (such testimonies have been made, and the Spirit is ever working). Yet what must be recognized in this is that reading the Bible will not inevitably lead the reader towards faith and reading it rightly, for biblical readers' hearts are always at different places in relation to God. Peterson points out, "The Christian community as a whole has never assumed that it is sufficient to place a Bible in a person's hands with a command to read it. That would be as foolish as handing a set of car keys to an adolescent, giving her a Honda and saying, 'Drive it.' And just as dangerous."[4] Biblical readers left to their own devices maneuver in varying ways through Scripture, some figuring out how to shift gears, others stalling at every light.

A few recent, well-publicized biblical readers illustrate this situation: one is that of an American reader, Ted Cooper, who was a "happy agnostic" when he picked up the Bible at age forty-three and determined to read through it in three months. Having come back to church after a long absence, Cooper was curious to read the Bible's claims, and he planned to read through the entire Bible as quickly as possible, so as not to lose interest. He relates that he was somewhat caustic and amused at first by the bizarre stories of the Old Testament, but then somewhere around Isaiah or Jeremiah, he began to believe what he was reading and found his life being changed. He became active in his church and later went on to found the organization "The Bible in 90 Days," a program that offers a curriculum for reading the entirety of the Bible in three months through church-based reading groups (as of 2015, the program has been used in forty-nine states and twenty countries).[5] Cooper's experience points to the role of the church: although his first reading of the Bible was done individually, his reading was prompted by coming to attend church again. Moreover, his reading led him towards greater involvement in a church, and ultimately towards helping others encounter the Bible through their local church communities.

Although Cooper found God in his biblical reading, other self-guided biblical readers have found themselves being distanced from God through reading Scripture. David Plotz, a Reformed Jew and magazine editor, relates such an experience when he began blogging the Hebrew Bible in 2006. His online posts on his biblical reading drew massive interest from Jews,

---

4. Peterson, "Foreword: *Caveat Lector,*" 8.

5. See the website of "The Bible in 90 Days": www.scriptureawakening.com/b90, and Noonoo, "Reading the Bible."

secularists, and evangelical Christians alike, leading to the 2009 publication of his *Good Book: The Bizarre, Hilarious, Disturbing, Marvelous, and Inspiring Things I Learned When I Read Every Single Word of the Bible*. Unlike Cooper, who became a Christian believer right about Jeremiah, Plotz found himself bogged down there.[6] Overall, he emerged from his reading with greater interest in and enjoyment of the Bible, but also with greater ambiguity concerning God. He states, "I guess I'm one of those agnostics who is becoming closer to atheism now because I am so upset by the picture of the God there. I am so disturbed by the God I found there. . . . As Jews, we don't have the comfort of the New Testament to fall back on."[7] When asked why he did not include the New Testament in his project, Plotz explains its omission is fitting for a Jewish reader:

> This is by far the most common question I get, and I sympathize with it. I was giving the Bible a very irreverent, very personal reading. As a Jew, I felt I could do that with my Bible, the Hebrew Bible (the Old Testament, more or less). I did not feel I could do it with the New Testament, because I couldn't treat the life of Jesus fairly. I think that Christian readers would have a right to expect a New Testament reading from someone who belonged to the group, not from some outsider chucking spitballs.[8]

Plotz's statement is striking for how he suggests that membership in a faith community determines at least the broad contours of one's biblical reading, even though his own Jewish tradition did not overly guide his "irreverent" reading. Plotz maintains that being Jewish by birth entitles him to a certain kind of biblical reading/spitball chucking, which, out of respect, he would not extend to the Christian canon.

Just before Plotz's blogging, A. J. Jacobs, another American secular Jew and magazine editor, did something similar but much more radical and farther-reaching, when he attempted to spend a year living "the ultimate biblical life."[9] This, Jacobs saw, consisted in following the Bible "as literally as possible," which he understood meant that he must try to obey all the Bible's commandments, without picking and choosing. Jacobs was prompted by a spiritual curiosity and an interest in biblical literalism, and he chronicles his

---

6. Plotz explains, "If you're reading on your own, I think you should read it straight through, starting from In the Beginning. It will bog down in the middle (I'm talking to you, Jeremiah! And you, too, Micah!) but it makes more sense than reading in any other order." Plotz, "Biblically Speaking."

7. Plotz, "Blogging the Bible," 64.

8. Plotz, "Biblically Speaking."

9. Jacobs, *Year of Living Biblically*, 3.

experience in his memoir *The Year of Living Biblically: One Man's Humble Quest to Follow the Bible as Literally as Possible* (a New York Times bestseller). Jacobs's biblical reading is much more daring and experimental than either Cooper's or Plotz's, as he tries to understand the Bible through allowing its varied commandments to direct his everyday behavior. His focus upon the Bible's commandments is, obviously, a limiting focus, as the Bible contains more than just rules for behavior, and Jacobs writes relatively little on the Bible's non-prescriptive parts.

Jacobs includes the New Testament in his experiment and spends eight months reading through the Old Testament, and four months in the New Testament, though his book relates mostly his stories of juxtaposing Old Testament laws with his life in Manhattan, such as growing an unruly beard, not wearing clothes of mixed fibers, and stoning Sabbath breakers by throwing pebbles at them in Central Park. Although he gathers an advisory board of rabbis, priests, and ministers, and each day tries to meet with one "spiritual sage," on the whole, Jacobs sets out to interpret the Bible on his own. He notes,

> I feel like I have to try to puzzle out for myself what the Bible means, even if it means I take some wrong turns. All this makes me realize: In a sense, my project is steeped in Judaism, since I'm spending a lot of time on the Hebrew Scriptures. But in some ways, it's actually more influenced by the Protestant idea that you can interpret the Bible yourself, without mediation. *Sola scriptura*.[10]

Jacobs's understanding of *sola scriptura* needs refining, as doubtless his biblical reading practices are not what the Reformers had in mind. In Israel, however, Jacobs has a moment that "drives home a disturbing point:"

> My quest is a paradoxical one. I'm trying to fly solo on a route that was specifically designated for a crowd. As one of my spiritual advisers . . . told me . . . "Only the crazy Europeans came up with the idea of individualism. So what you're doing is a modern phenomenon." . . . Maybe I have to dial back my fetishizing of individualism.[11]

Jacobs emerges from his year with greater love for the Bible—he explains, "I didn't expect to, as the Psalmist says, take refuge in the Bible and rejoice in it"[12]—and he finds himself praying more comfortably, but yet, at the

---

10. Ibid., 69–70.
11. Ibid., 213–14.
12. Ibid., 7.

end of the year, his experiment seems just that, a zany intellectual's religious dabbling ended ceremoniously with the shaving of his massive beard. Jacobs conveys great respect and interest in the Bible, and a nuanced understanding of biblically-centered religious communities, but in his memoir he gives no hint of carrying forward his biblical reading or of joining the life of a synagogue or church. He wants his children to know something about God, but that something is undefined. Jacobs sees clearly that the Bible calls for communities of faith in its reading and in its living, but at the end of his quest, he seems uninterested in joining in. Oddly enough, despite having read the Bible intently and trying to live by it, Jacobs does not engage the question of whether or not it is true and pressing, whether or not the God of whom it speaks is still speaking to him.

It is striking how Cooper's individual experience of reading the Bible threw him back into the Christian church, and how Plotz and Jacobs also read the Bible as individuals and came to recognize the necessity of faith communities for biblical reading, but at the end of the day, they themselves are not drawn into one. The Bible can easily be read and blogged and its obscure rules implemented, even in Manhattan, but for its central claims to be wrestled with, for its truths to be considered, for its life to be known, a community of biblical readers is needed. Otherwise the Bible, while it may be interesting and engaging to readers, and perhaps even push them to write best-sellers, has no staying power to shape one's life and understanding of God. Ongoing spiritual reading of the Bible needs the particular frame of reference provided by the church (or the synagogue, for Jewish readers like Plotz and Jacobs) for it to be sustained. A reader who picks up a Gideon's Bible from a hotel drawer is not meant to live in the hotel forever—a home awaits her in the church.

Biblical Scholarship

What complicates such a vision of reading Scripture in the church is the myriad of ways that the Bible is read with great interest and fervor elsewhere—particularly, modern biblical studies offer many other "homes" for biblical reading. One can pick almost any address—text-critical, feminist, postcolonial, and theological homesteads, among many others, are all set up. The history of western biblical scholarship, from the Protestant Reformation to the present secular age, has been a tale of the study of the Bible being increasingly distanced from the church; what has been sought is the meaning of biblical texts, in various stages of their lives and histories, yet all too often apart from the Bible's ongoing life and history in the church.

The scholarly approach of historical criticism is perhaps the best-known example of this tendency in biblical studies, as historical criticism looks to the original roots of biblical texts for their meanings.[13] While this approach began as a way of understanding biblical texts more fully so that they might be better appropriated, as biblical scholarship has lodged itself in the university context it has increasingly distanced itself from practical dimensions of biblical living. As Michael C. Legaspi argues, for biblical scholars of the nineteenth century,

> [H]istorical understanding was never an end in itself . . . professional biblical scholars . . . could not allow the Bible to remain consigned to an alien discursive world. Historical research was expected to throw up new bridges of understanding even as it destroyed old ones. Without slipping into exemplar history, historical research had to become, in Reill's term, "pragmatic." It had to be useful to life.[14]

However, this early instinct of modern biblical studies slowly became forgotten in the university, in part because of the scholarly mantles of objectivity and rationality. Legaspi notes, "the canons of modern rationality" became "modern criticism's leading light. Marooned by confessional interpreters, the Bible entered the university through the back door, where it would find new life."[15] At the heart of much modern scholarship has been the assumption that good scholarly work requires objectivity, and so the faith commitments scholars might hold are viewed as out of place in academic work, as these are thought to color the kind of objective readings of biblical texts sought in modern study. Moberly points out that as modern biblical scholarship has set out to read the Bible apart from any classical creeds or theological formulations,

> This has led to a curious situation. To be a Christian means, at least in part, the acceptance and appropriation of certain theological doctrines and patterns of living. Yet the task of reading the Bible "critically" has regularly been defined precisely in

---

13. This approach has appealed to "liberal" and "conservative" biblical scholars alike—e.g., evangelical biblical scholars Gordon Fee and Douglas Stuart posit, "*the only proper control for hermeneutics is to be found in the original intent of the biblical text . . . A text cannot mean what it never meant.* Or to put that in a positive way, the true meaning of the biblical text for us is what God originally intended it to mean when it was first spoken. This is the starting point." Fee and Stuart, *How to Read the Bible*, 25–26, emphasis theirs.

14. Legaspi, *Death of Scripture*, 8–9.

15. Ibid., 33.

terms of the exclusion of these doctrines and patterns of living from the interpretative process.[16]

As I am brushing out quick and broad strokes of modern biblical studies here, I must be careful with my descriptions and terminology, particularly the term "historical criticism," for as Francis Watson argues, "historical criticism" is often used polemically and ideologically and it does not characterize modern biblical studies as a whole. Watson states, "Historical criticism is a misnomer. Modern biblical interpretation is historically informed, but it is not exclusively historical in orientation. Even if it were, there are many different ways in which a historical orientation might be worked out in practice." He finds that the biblical scholar deals with history in rich ways—"The exegete is a historian only on a part-time basis"—and that historical study serves to make the past more alive to the present, for in good historical contextualization, "the text becomes vividly and poignantly alive." Watson insists, then, that "historical criticism" be dropped from casual usage, for "as a characterization of the field as a whole . . . 'historical criticism' is utterly misleading."[17]

I see great merit in what Watson is arguing, yet I also hold back from full-fledged assent, for although the term "historical criticism" has undoubtedly been dragged through the mud, and it does not characterize the field of modern biblical studies as a whole, the term still holds meaning to many modern biblical scholars themselves who understand their work as being carried out within a particular sphere of academia, and would be happy to be called historical critics. Although the field of biblical studies is wide, many of its scholars' interests are narrow, for modern biblical scholarship is marked by intense specialization and secularization—specialization in that biblical scholars work in increasingly narrower areas of study, and secularization in that the place that modern biblical scholarship has carved out for itself in the western academy is one based upon the *historical* significance of the Bible, its past and residual influence in western culture. A specialized historical-critical approach thus guarantees that the Bible may be picked up within secular university halls. Although many (if not most) biblical scholars have faith commitments and involvement in the church, and may indeed see their work as serving the church, those commitments are bracketed out within the modern university, as there concerns of history and culture give justification for these scholars having a place.[18]

16. Moberly, *Bible, Theology, and Faith*, 5.
17. Watson, "Does Historical Criticism Exist?"
18. Levenson notes, "Many Christians involved in the historical criticism of the Hebrew Bible today, however, seem to have ceased to want their work to be considered

A historical-critical approach has had great influence in the realm of biblical studies, then, even as its practitioners have often been less than self-reflexive on how they employ it. What proves problematic, however, is that western culture is rapidly becoming more secular and unfamiliar with the Bible, and so it is unclear why biblical scholars should keep on having office space in secular academic institutions. As Jon Levenson points out, justifying biblical studies on western cultural grounds is a flimsy argument; why should a university fund classes for "Ugaritic or Coptic (which no one speaks) over Hungarian or Tagalog (which millions speak)"?[19] Levenson offers a searing look into the assumptions undergirding modern biblical studies in *The Hebrew Bible, the Old Testament, and Historical Criticism*, in which he argues that biblical studies needs a framework of meaning outside of itself. The problem with justifying the objective study of the Bible as a part of western culture is that it does not address the question of why privilege this part of culture over other parts; "the very value-neutrality of this [historical critical] method of study puts its practitioners at a loss to defend the *value* of the enterprise itself."[20] An historical approach in biblical studies has created the illusion of biblical texts being detached from their ongoing uses and histories, although the canon itself ever reminds biblical scholars that their texts relate to post-biblical religious communities. When historical-critical questions are pursued apart from any broader concerns, "the enormous historical and philological labors are not justified by reference to any larger structure of meaning."[21] Such structures of meaning exist predominantly within the Jewish and Christian faiths, in which the supposed original contextual meanings of the Bible are only part of the Bible's wider contexts and meanings.[22] (This issue of wider contexts and meanings will be picked up in chapter 5.)

---

distinctively Christian. . . . They are Christians everywhere except in the classroom and at the writing table, where they are simply historians striving for an unbiased view of the past. . . . [Religious] commitment brings scholars to the subject, but the subject of the character of the method with which they pursue it has less in common with the religious traditions than with the Enlightenment critique of them. The incongruity of the motivation and the methods is seldom acknowledged." Levenson, *Hebrew Bible*, 29–30.

19. Ibid., 125.

20. Ibid., 109.

21. Ibid., 99.

22. Levenson notes that the "hidden danger in this neglect of ongoing tradition (hidden usually from the critical scholars themselves, too)" is the implication "that one can become a perfectly adequate biblical scholar without locating the Bible within any larger religious framework or seeing oneself as a generational link in any ongoing tradition." Levenson, "Teach the Texts in Contexts."

Levenson is not against methods of modern historical biblical scholarship by any means, but rather, against the restriction of that scholarship to its own ends, as those ends, he argues, are not only often vacuous but at times hostile to faith. What is needed is for biblical scholars to articulate their own motivations and purposes, beyond mere curiosity in biblical texts. A biblical scholar's intense interest in the history of biblical texts can, in effect, relegate those texts to the past.[23] Although, as Watson has argued, historical study of a text can serve to bring a text nearer and make it alive in the present, more often than not modern biblical scholars have not carried their work forward, leaving that move for theologians to make. Levenson maintains that biblical scholars themselves must make that leap, or at least look over the edge, for their work to have significance:

> Historical criticism . . . can help to heal—though not to reverse—the rupture caused by historical consciousness, or it can aggravate the rupture and help in dismantling the tradition. To the extent that historical critics restrict themselves to descriptive history and avoid the thorny questions of contemporary appropriation, they contribute, even if inadvertently, to the dismantling of tradition rather than to the healing of the rupture. For historical criticism so restricted subtly fosters an image of the Bible as having once meant a great deal but now meaning little or nothing.[24]

Thus the problem with "historical criticism" is not only the possible polemics of the use of the term, but even more so, the way that historical approaches have allowed larger questions of meaning and religious context to be bracketed out in biblical studies. Earlier generations of biblical scholars had many more in their ranks who moved freely between biblical studies, theology, and the church, and they also had a residual Christian culture to give their work a context of meaning, but the pigeonholed areas of study of modern academia, combined with a secular culture, cast greater doubts than ever before upon the reasons for and effects of studying the Bible in a secular university context.

Legaspi, in a similar vein to Levenson (and writing more recently), notes that even as new answers have been offered to what modern biblical scholarship is doing, these answers are still insufficient, as they lie outside of the contours of practices of biblical faith:

---

23. Levenson, *Hebrew Bible*, 98.
24. Ibid., 97.

It has become clear, though, that academic criticism in its contemporary form cannot offer a coherent, intellectually compelling account of what this information is actually *for*. What critics like [John] Collins have done as a result is to shift the rationale for modern criticism away from the intellectual and back toward the social and moral. There is value in the social and moral by-products of academic criticism, in things like tolerance, reasonableness, and self-awareness. The problem is that these rather thin, pale virtues seem only thinner and paler when compared to the classic virtues associated with the scriptural Bible: instead of bland tolerance, *love* that sacrifices self; instead of an agreeable reasonability, *hope* that opens the mind to the goodness and greatness that it had not yet fully imagined; and instead of critical self-awareness, *faith* that inspires and animates the human heart. Academic criticism tempers belief, while scriptural reading edifies and directs it.[25]

What might all this mean for a spiritual reading of the Bible, then? It may seem like an argument is being spun for a kind of spiritual reading over and against an academic approach, but that is far from my intention. I aim not to put academic biblical studies in one corner and spiritual reading in another, and let each go about their own thing. Rather, this look into the field of modern biblical studies is in order to trace out the great extent to which the reading of the Bible calls for a wider context and frame of reference, a reason for the pursuit. Academic biblical scholarship of the Christian Bible loses its vitality without the life of the church; its enormous labors are not justified. It could continue on as an area of historical study, but it would need only a small corner of the ancient near east department, not its own schools and academies. As Levenson has argued, there is great need to constantly integrate biblical studies into a wider structure of meaning for it to have a place in academia today.[26] And just as biblical scholarship is not sustainable apart from a context of meaning, so too spiritual reading needs a context of faith for its reading to do justice to the kind of work that is the Bible. Anything can be studied out of sheer curiosity—one might read the Bible intently out of mere interest—but the nature of the Bible is such that it will constantly point the reader towards larger questions—questions of faith, of life, of the church, of community and love and God.

---

25. Legaspi, *Death of Scripture*, 169.

26. Similarly, Moberly states, "[I]n the present cultural context, the question of why one should continue to attach special expectations to the study of the Bible needs to be specified rather than taken for granted." Moberly, *Bible, Theology, and Faith*, 15.

What spiritual reading of the Bible might learn from modern biblical scholarship is not only its intellectual disciplines, then, but also that it must be clear about its motivations and purposes. Spiritual reading is a vacuous term without the life of the church; it needs the context of a particular kind of belief and spiritual growth for it to have a place in the Christian life. Moreover, in placing spiritual reading firmly within the tradition of the church, the resources of both ecclesial biblical interpretations and modern academic scholarship may be drawn upon, as spiritual reading seeks to hear the wisdom of others.[27] The pursuit of a Christian life is at the heart of a spiritual reading of Scripture, and that pursuit finds its way through the learning and experiences of others who likewise have searched out what it means to know God and understand the depths of Scripture.

Reading Classics

While modern biblical scholarship reflects the need for the Bible to be studied within a wider context of meaning, the nature of reading classics likewise raises issues on why the church must be that structure of meaning. When seeking to read Scripture spiritually this particularly poses a problem, as the nature of both reading and spirituality are fluid enough to lose the mooring of the church. A reader may easily seek spirituality through the Bible without participation in the church; emphasis on the church may seem overbearing for a practice so personal and individual as reading the Bible for one's own spiritual life and growth. Yet although the Bible can be read as a great or inspiring or uplifting or intriguing piece of literature (and indeed is often read so), this kind of reading-the-Bible-as-a-classic stands in contrast to the kind of spiritual reading meant to characterize Christian handlings of Scripture. Reading the Bible for enlargement of one's intellectual and spiritual interests is not the same thing as reading the Bible for growth in the Christian life; the difference hinges upon one's grappling with claims the church makes for the Bible.

Krister Stendahl argues in "The Bible as a Classic and the Bible as Holy Scripture" that we conceive of the Bible as a classic work in western literature precisely because of its normative status for Jewish and Christian communities of faith: "It is as Holy Scripture that the Bible is a classic in

---

27. Abraham notes, "To be sure, critical scholarship does now and then get out of hand, and it can become a kind of cult that would easily divert one from the central message of the Bible. However, the answer to this is not to reject critical scholarship in a fit of alarm but to draw judiciously on every available insight that will bring to us the great riches that the Bible contains." Abraham, *Divine Inspiration*, 30.

our culture. Therefore there is something artificial in the idea of 'the Bible as literature.'"[28] Reading the Bible "as literature" makes the Bible into something it is not; essentially, it is "an attempt at cutting loose the moorings of Holy Writ. It is an attempt at allowing the text to speak as literature freed from the very claims which made the Bible a classic in the first place."[29] Here is an echo of T. S. Eliot's insistence that "the Bible has had a literary influence *not* because it has been considered as literature, but because it has been considered as the report of the Word of God."[30]

When the Bible is read simply as a classic work of literature, as a great piece of culture, what is read is not the Bible but a modern literary construction of it. This is not to overlook the literary and cultural influence of the Bible, but rather, to point out how limiting the Bible's influence to matters of literature and culture does not get at its central content and meaning.[31] As a canonical collection formed by communities of faith, the Bible's literariness is wrapped up in its scriptureness.[32] To read the Bible in keeping with its origins is to recognize how its diverse types of writings were brought together to form a particular type of writing, that of Holy Writ, a writing that reaches intricately into the lives of those who read it in faith communities and in faith.

A note of clarification must be struck here: what I am arguing for is not reading the Bible as something that is not a literary work, but for reading the Bible as something *more* than literature—for seeing the Bible as more than another deep story or profound writing, for recognizing that its literariness is the point where a reader begins, but not ends, their journey of reading.

28. Stendahl, "Bible as a Classic," 212.

29. Ibid., 213.

30. Eliot, *Times Literary Supplement*, Dec. 2, 1944, 583, emphasis Eliot's; quoted in Jeffrey, *Houses of the Interpreter*, 191. Similarly, Sir Arthur Quiller-Couch explains to his students, "There is in fact, Gentlemen, no such thing as 'mere literature. . . . So you should beware of any teacher who would treat the Bible or any part of it as 'fine writing,' mere literature." Quiller-Couch, *On the Art of Reading*, 128-29.

31. The cultural influence of the Bible in the English-speaking world is so well recognized that even the well-renown atheist Richard Dawkins can lend his support to the King James Bible Trust as it celebrated the 400th anniversary of the KJV. He evaluates the merit of the KJV on cultural grounds and states, "It is important that religion should not be allowed to hijack this cultural resource." Dawkins, "Richard Dawkins Lends His Support."

32. Watson states, "The Bible embraces writings in a variety of literary genres, but these genres are transformed by the fact of canonization. The canon converts poetry and prose, narrative, law, prophecy and epistles alike into 'holy scripture'. Genre is determined not only by a text's intrinsic characteristics but also by its communal usage. . . . [T]hese texts function in a peculiar way in the life of . . . interrelated communities." Watson, *Text, Church and World*, 4, 277.

C. S. Lewis articulates well how the Bible's literary nature is essential yet not its end:

> Those who talk of reading the Bible "as literature" sometimes mean, I think, reading it without attending to the main thing it is about; like reading Burke with no interest in politics, or reading the *Aeneid* with no interest in Rome. That seems to me to be nonsense. But there is a saner sense in which the Bible, since it is after all literature, cannot properly be read except as literature; and the different parts of it as the different sorts of literature they are.[33]

In a sense, then, after recognizing that the Bible is more than literature, reading the Bible as literature is part of what it means to read it well. All its history and prose and poetry and prophecy and genealogy and apocalypse and letters call for certain kinds of reading, and through all these genres the Bible weaves a great story, one a reader may receive in a similar way to other stories. Reading the Bible as a story can open up its greater truths; as Madeleine L'Engle relates of her childhood reading, "I'm particularly grateful that I was allowed to read my Bible as I read my other books, to read it as *story*, that story which is a revelation of truth. . . . I had an aunt who was worried that I lived in an unreal world. But what is real? In the Bible we are constantly being given glimpses of a reality quite different from that taught in school, even in Sunday School."[34]

L'Engle's early reading of the Bible as a story opened up the door to a reality far different from what she had been taught, just as Lewis's careful reading of the Bible as literature revealed even more clearly how its subject is about something much more far-reaching than other works of literature. A jettison of basic literary skills is not part of picking up the Bible spiritually, then, but what is needed in reading Scripture is to put such skills towards the end of "attending to the main thing it is about," towards seeing "glimpses of a reality" of the kingdom of God. And it is the church (even its often deficient Sunday Schools) that affirms that this reality of Scripture is truly reality; it is the cloud of Christian witnesses who testify that the Bible speaks truth and life more than is presently known. It is through the church that both Lewis and L'Engle received the Bible and were presented with the possibility that

---

33. Lewis, *Reflections on the Psalms*, 10.

34. L'Engle, *Walking on Water*, 60. It is striking that L'Engle's experience of reading the Bible as a story happens when she is reading the Bible as a child—it may be that seeing the Bible as a story is particularly important to early spiritual growth. Quiller-Couch suggests that the best way of teaching a young reader to read the Bible is to "let him ramp through the Scriptures even as he might through *The Arabian Nights*: to let him take the books as they come." Quiller-Couch, *On the Art of Reading*, 139.

the Bible is true—even if their imaginations were what took them further into Scripture, the Bible came to them through the church, and their understandings of it were held up against those of the church.

What moves the reader from reading the Bible as a classic to reading it as the report of the Word of God is, in principle, the church; without the community of believers making these claims for Scripture a reader would only be able to judge the Bible in comparison to all other books. Although such an individual evaluation of Scripture may bear fruit, a wider community is needed for understanding the Bible's far-reaching claims. As Moberly argues, in seeking "to take seriously the Bible's truth claims, or articulate their implications," the context of the Christian (or Jewish) faith is necessary "to provide the resources, both conceptually and existentially, for enabling this to take place in a disciplined and meaningful way."[35] The church, in short, gives a biblical reader a rule of faith (that which was lacking in the reading experiments of Plotz and Jacobs). Although "membership of a religious community is no guarantee that an existentially searching reading of the text will take place (for many read the text flatly), and lack of religious affiliation need not preclude existential engagement," being part of the church benefits the biblical reader in that she experiences a community with a positive expectation for the Bible, gains an overarching frame of reference for Scripture, and can be encouraged to move past possible fixations on problematic texts to "the tenor of the Bible as a whole."[36]

Even as various parts of Scripture are set into relation to each other (with some parts always privileged over others), when the Bible is read as Christian Scripture, there is no longer the option of simply picking and choosing the bits that appeal the most, and leaving the rest aside, as might be done with other great works of literature. The whole of the Bible has to be reckoned with in some way—all of it requires a degree of listening and discernment and response. Although it has problematic and difficult passages (in chapter 7, three such passages will be considered), the claims the church makes for the Bible pushes the Bible's readers to grapple with it as a whole, to find ways to read all its parts, and to read in light of the wider rule of faith. Sincere and devout Christian biblical readers quite often come to the Bible already knowing what they want to get out of it, but the church has classically seen the Bible as calling for a reading that is much more intense and receptive, one that recognizes the Bible as making demands of the reader relationally, requiring repentance, conversion, and faith.[37]

---

35. Moberly, "'Interpret the Bible," 108.
36. Moberly, "Biblical Criticism and Religious Belief," 95.
37. See Peterson, *Eat This Book*, 30.

With the Christian understanding of Scripture being that the reality of God is present in the Bible, and that personal response is needed in its reading, the church's role is to direct biblical readers towards these aspects. (Readers could possibly come to such convictions on their own through reading Scripture, but most readers will need the church to understand the Bible's centrality to Christian belief and practice.) Essentially, what is needed is the church's ongoing affirmation of its canon. As Watson points outs, the canon itself reflects the corporate reading experience of the church, for it was not an individual reader, but a reading community that became convinced that certain writings were the Word of God and canonical Scripture. And so, there is "a subjective basis to the formation and preservation of the canon, as well as an objective one. If certain writings are to function as canonical Scripture, their origin in the divine speaking must be humanly acknowledged, through the testimony of the Holy Spirit."[38] Just as the reading community of the church was needed to form the canon, and human acknowledgement was part of the work of forming the canon of Scripture ("the subjective basis"), so too the ongoing human witness of the church is part of the spiritual reading of the Bible.

In this regard, reading the Bible is similar to the experience of reading literary classics, in that a wider culture directs one towards its reading and gives expectations for it. As Stendahl states, a piece of literature becomes a classic through "common recognition by a wide constituency of a society;" the social dimension of how a work is received is key. "No inner quality suffices unless widely so recognized."[39] Classics are thus works one is directed towards by others; as Moberly explains, "one reads classics not because one discovers them for oneself but because one is directed to them by the wider culture (in family, school, bookshop, library, cinema, theatre, etc.) on the grounds that they are great literature."[40] Although the catalogue of Western literary classics is increasingly contested, it nonetheless retains some basic continuity and one can recognize in it how classics are works that prove enduring and are handed down through readers' positive experiences. Werner Jeanroad finds that "the classic is a category of reception.... The normative character of a classic stems ... [from] the experience of readers with the text."[41] This experience of readers with the text is so central that without ongoing experiences, a classical work may cease to be such (and

---

38. Watson, "Hermeneutics and the Doctrine of Scripture," 133.
39. Stendahl, "Bible," 211.
40. Moberly, "Biblical Criticism and Religious Belief," 95.
41. Jeanrond, *Text and Interpretation*, 140.

many classics do).[42] A cumulative tradition of readers' experiences with a work of literature is handed down to the next generation of that work's readers. And so similarly, with the Bible, the experiences and expectations of the community of believers in the church provide a starting point for its spiritual reading in each new age.

When it comes to reading the Christian Bible, then, the overriding category of reception one encounters is that of the experience of readers in the church ever trying to hear God speaking through the biblical texts. A potential reader of the Bible has a vast cloud of witnesses handing down the Bible to her; although she can choose to read the Bible as simply a classic, a great sidestepping of the Bible's home community and its majority of readers will have to occur. What will be read then is not the Bible that has come from the church, but a reconstituted Bible of a culture or an individual. (Thomas Jefferson's Bible—a collection of biblical texts literally cut and pasted together—is not the same Bible as the Bible of the church.) An attempt to read the Bible as a classic will sever the reader from the communities that have made it such, for the Bible's concern of God constantly points readers back towards communities of faith.[43]

There are, of course, and always will be, literary aficionados reading the Bible as a great work of western literature. Such a reading, like the reading of other classics, can give the reader inspiration and uplift, but the problem is that inspiration/uplift is not the main thing the Bible is about. What that is, as the church has traditionally understood it, is that the Scriptures are able to make its readers wise for salvation through faith in Christ Jesus. Although in all kinds of biblical readings (even in bad readings) seeds of the gospel may be sown, and literature can be a path towards faith for the literary aficionado, the spiritual benefits that may come indirectly (that is, by God's grace) through a literary-oriented reading do not justify it as a good starting point for a spiritual reading of Scripture. Only in coming to grapple with the Bible's central concern of God being revealed in Jesus will the Bible be read fully and read well. A reader seeking to read the Bible well needs more than anything else a willingness to wrestle with this central content, to have a posture of listening and praying over and pondering the Bible's texts, ever seeking out how they speak of God. In other words, the

---

42. Thus Terry Eagleton points out, provocatively, that it is "quite possible that, given a deep enough transformation of our history, we may in the future produce a society which is unable to get anything out of Shakespeare." Eagleton, *Literary Theory*, 10.

43. "But if the point of reading the Bible as a classic is precisely to sever its links with the specific contexts of Jewish and Christian faiths, the exercise would become self-contradictory (or at least in need of major rethinking)." Moberly, *Bible, Theology, and Faith*, 16.

reader needs growing Christian belief. What is sought in such reading is a consideration of this question of God "so that engagement with the God of whom it speaks, and the transformations of human life which it envisages, remain enduring possibilities; that is to say, 'God is here.'"[44]

A Home for Readers

The disparate ways that the Bible can be read could simply be seen as various options for picking up this collection of texts, but the faith communities behind the Bible, and the claims that the Bible makes for God, ever throw this consumer-mindset into doubt. What is problematic is not that different ways exist for reading the Bible, but that those different ways are seen as self-sufficient, with no need for the church. Although a reader can read the Bible out of sheer curiosity, or scholarly interest, or a bent for literary pleasure, all these approaches ultimately are limited in understanding the Bible for what it is, as they do not bring the reader to reckon with the central content of the Bible that is God and his claims upon humanity. The Bible places questions before the careful biblical reader, pushing her to see that it matters how she reads this book and what she makes of it. Without wrestling with these radical claims of the Bible the reader does not truly engage the Bible; she misses the plot.

The church, then, is a necessary part of the spiritual reading of Scripture, for it is through the church that the story of Scripture is best unraveled, as the church not only explains that story, but is itself in the story. Jenson explains,

> Whatever hermeneutical gaps may need to be dealt with in the course of the church's biblical exegesis, there is one that must not be posited or attempted to be dealt with: there is *no* historical distance between the community in which the Bible appeared and the church which now seeks to understand the Bible, because these are the very same community.... [T]he text we call the Bible was put together in the first place by the same community that now needs to interpret it.[45]

As the community of the Bible, the church testifies to the truth of God as found in it; even though the church does not always get biblical readings or biblical interpretations right, it witnesses to continual engagement with the Bible and taking it seriously as a living Word of God today. A biblical reader

---

44. Ibid., 43.
45. Jenson, "Religious Power of Scripture," 98.

finds in the church a community in which he may wrestle with, understand, and live the words of the Bible; in the church he finds a community of like-minded readers, he finds a home.

CHAPTER 3

Reading Well

IN 1856, THE ANGLICAN theologian F. D. Maurice gave an address entitled "On the Friendship of Books," in which he noted a troubling state of affairs about reading in his Victorian society. Maurice called his time "an age of reading" but was concerned for its masses of readers nonetheless:

> What I regret is that many of us spend much of our time in reading books, and in talking of books—that we like nothing worse than the reputation of being indifferent to them, and nothing better than the reputation of knowing a good deal about them; and yet that, after all, we do not know them in the same way as we know our fellow-creatures . . . This is a great misfortune, in my opinion, and one which I am afraid is increasing as what we call "the taste for literature" increases.[1]

Maurice explained that this situation springs in part from the fact that much of the time spent in reading is "given to Reviews, and Magazines, and Newspapers" as he and his contemporaries are "born into an age in which they exercise great power." Maurice understood there to be a distinction in the qualities of reading good literature and in reading other kinds of works, as "whatever good effects works of this kind may have produced, we certainly are not able to make them our friends."[2] Against a shallow reading of such transient works, he presses for a deep and relational manner of reading good literature, of becoming friends.

Maurice's comments would likely find a welcome with literary critic George Steiner, as over a century later he began sounding out similar fears about reading in his own age. For Steiner, the "Reviews, Magazines, and Newspapers" of Maurice had become a formal body of literary criticism

---

1. Maurice, "On the Friendship of Books," 2–3.
2. Ibid., 3.

that was, as Steiner describes, "little short of ludicrous."[3] Steiner argued that a "mandarin madness of secondary discourse" had "infect[ed] thought and sensibility"—he states, "It is not, as Ecclesiastes would have it, that 'of making many books there is no end.' It is that 'of making books on books and books on those books there is no end.'"[4]

Maurice and Steiner attest to a growing modern concern over the challenges of reading well when faced with an avalanche of printed material, not just of books but also "books on books on books."[5] In light of Maurice's and Steiner's comments, I fear a deep irony exists in my writing this chapter, as I am adding but one more review of all the reviews. I am pursuing here the nature of reading literature well, and it seems that actual readings of works of literature would be preferable to more "secondary discourse." Yet as I am seeking to understand the broad process of reading by listening to other readers and responding to them, my writing about what others have said about reading nonetheless might have potential to bear fruit.[6] Steiner, for all his disparagement of modern literary criticism, nonetheless holds that the task of criticism is "to help us read as total human beings, by examples of precision, fear, and delight . . . without it, creation itself may fall upon silence."[7] Writers like Steiner and Maurice agree that reading is intricately related to living; these writers care about the process of reading because they hold that the reading of good literature can deeply shape readers' lives.

So far we have approached the topic of the spiritual reading of Scripture by considering the time and the place, and the communal framework in which this is done. In the previous chapter the possibility of reading the Bible as a great work of literature was briefly considered, and here in this chapter the matter of reading great works of literature will be taken up in

---

3. Steiner, "'Critic'/'Reader,'" 18.

4. Steiner, *Real Presences*, 26, 48.

5. As Umberto Eco remarked in the mid-1990s, "Look at a bookstore. There are too many books. I receive too many books each week. If the computer network succeeds in reducing the quantity of published books, this would be a paramount cultural improvement." Eco, "Afterword" in Nunberg, *Future of the Book*, 301. W. H. Auden argues that when "ease of access" to art is misused, "it can become a curse. We are all of us tempted to read more books, look at more pictures, listen to more music, than we can possibly absorb; and the result of such gluttony is not a cultured mind but a consuming one; what it reads, looks at, listens to, is immediately forgotten, leaving no more traces behind it than yesterday's newspaper." Auden, *Secondary Worlds*, 128.

6. Davis argues that "one of the emphatically unironic purposes of thinking and writing about reading" is to make it possible to live in the place in a book, or "to live out of the resonance from there, a little bit more, a little while longer." Davis, *Real Voices*, xvi.

7. Steiner, "Humane Literacy," 29.

greater depth. My interest is in the manner in which the practice of reading classical works of literature has received attention in British and American culture throughout the twentieth century and into the twenty-first century. Spiritual impulses and interests seem to be lurking (at times in the dark) behind much modern writing on reading, and for this reason the spiritual dimensions of reading literature are important to trace out, for they relate to practices of reading the Bible. In western culture, in which the Bible is part of a broader canon of written literature (a situation not found in every culture), practices of biblical reading are inevitably related to practices of reading other texts, particularly those texts considered great works of literature. While I argue that the spiritual reading of Scripture is, in important ways, unlike how great literature is read, there are still many overlaps between practices of reading literature well and practices of reading Scripture spiritually. An understanding of what makes for a good reading of classic literature will then make clearer what more is needed for a good spiritual reading of the Bible.

I will proceed by sketching out a brief history of the rise of modern literary studies, noting its concerns for the reasons for reading and studying literature, and then will look at a few Christian proposals for reading well, those of C. S. Lewis's *An Experiment in Criticism*, Alan Jacobs's *A Theology of Reading: The Hermeneutics of Love*, and Paul Griffiths's *Religious Reading*. As my wider interest is in how Christians read the Bible, these authors provide a specifically Christian frame of reference for reading literature and sacred texts.

The Rise of Modern Literary Studies

Concerns with reading are, to a certain degree, as old as written literature itself (Plato's *Phaedrus* attests to a worry over how a written text has both "suitable and unsuitable readers").[8] Western literature has often had clear moral dimensions and early on there has been an awareness that a primary purpose of reading is personal formation. As James M. Houston argues, the rationale a first-century reader would have in reading was to become an exemplary human being: "The purpose of books was to produce persons . . . any other abstract motive was ridiculous. Classics were read to make people into classics."[9] Similarly, Pierre Hadot maintains that ancient philosophies were ways of life for their readers; in the ancient world, the reading of

---

8. *Phaedrus* 275E, as cited by Watson, *Text, Church, and World*, 95.
9. Houston, "Towards a Biblical Spirituality," 154.

philosophical texts was a spiritual exercise intricately related to practices of living.[10]

As reading literature is one aspect of western culture, it is caught up in western culture's "hope, grown almost axiomatic from the time of Plato to that of Matthew Arnold, that culture is a humanizing force."[11] Reading great works of literature is a cultural act and sets one face-to-face with central aspects of a culture, and on that cultural engagement is placed great hope for the common good. This hope came out vividly with the establishment of English departments in prestigious British and American universities in the early twentieth-century—in 1916 Cambridge, for instance, Sir Arthur Quiller-Couch, the first professor of English literature at the university, gave a lecture which argued that classical literature is essentially concerned with the spiritual element of humanity, and so the practice of reading literature "teach[es] us to lift our own souls."[12] He insisted that reading is an art, with its best purpose not to accumulate knowledge, but to produce certain kinds of men and women.[13]

Quiller-Couch was carving out a space for the academic study of English literature, and it is noteworthy that his tactic is to emphasize the spiritual nature of texts and their positive force and lasting effect on readers. In such an approach to literature there is a great belief in the inherent power of literary works; as Quiller-Couch explains, a reader's first obligation to a classic literary text is "to treat it *absolutely*: not for any secondary or derivative purpose . . . we should *trust* any given masterpiece for its operation, on ourselves and on others."[14] Although an approach like Quiller-Couch's came to be radically questioned later that century, he nonetheless reflects enduring concerns within the humanities, as the humanities ever struggle to make clear how their work relates to questions of ultimate significance.[15]

---

10. Hadot, *Philosophy as a Way of Life*. Gamble notes that with "its proclivity to books, as well as in its preoccupation with doctrine and ethics, Christianity appeared to pagan observers more like a philosophical movement than a religious cult." Gamble, *Books and Readers*, 142.

11. Steiner, *Language and Silence*, 15.

12. Quiller-Couch, *On the Art of Reading*, 212.

13. Ibid., 70.

14. Ibid., 200, emphasis Quiller-Couch's.

15. Denis Donoghue argues that often today in the humanities "we make trouble for ourselves, mocking our purposes. As humanists—in the special and limited sense in which we are teachers of the humanities—we are unable or unwilling to say what we are doing, or why our activities should receive support in the form of salaries, grants, and fellowships. . . . We are timid in describing the relation between training in the humanities and the exercise of the moral imagination." Donoghue, *Practice of Reading*, 55.

Quiller-Couch was followed at Cambridge by a generation with an even stronger agenda for establishing firmly the study of English literature, such as F. R. Leavis and I. A. Richards, and literary studies quickly came into its own by the 1930s. Terry Eagleton describes its rise as a dramatic reaction to a post-war industrialized society rapidly losing its spiritual mooring in capitalism; he holds that early English studies grasped at what was significant in life:

> In the early 1920s it was desperately unclear why English was worth studying at all; by the early 1930s it had become a question of why it was worth wasting your time on anything else. English was not only a subject worth studying, but *the* supremely civilizing pursuit, the spiritual essence of the social formation . . . English was an arena in which the most fundamental questions of human existence—what it meant to be a person, to engage in significant relationships with others, to live from the vital centre of most essential values—were thrown into relief and made the object of the most intensive scrutiny.[16]

The optimism for the ability of literature to deepen and to impart society's moral values drove much of the rise of English studies—I. A. Richards reflects this sentiment with his belief that "Poetry is capable of saving us; it is a perfectly possible means of overcoming chaos."[17] As Alan Jacobs explains, leading figures in educational and university circles such George Stuart Gordon (one of Oxford's first English professors) turned to literature to fulfill a role in which Christianity had seemingly failed; literature was looked towards "to save our souls and heal the state."[18] Literature became a replacement for religion, and took on its weight. (Yet not all literary enthusiasts of that time thought so, particularly, not those with Christian commitments; note T. S. Eliot's insistence that "poetry is not the inculcation of morals, or the direction of politics; and no more is it religion or an equivalent of religion, except by some monstrous abuse of words."[19]) With the backdrop of this broad optimism in the saving potential of texts, literary schools such as practical criticism, formalism, structuralism, and New Criticism arose in the first half of the twentieth century; they shared a common approach

---

16. Eagleton, *Literary Theory*, 27, emphasis Eagleton's.

17. I. A. Richards, *Science and Poetry* (London, 1926), 82–83, quoted in Eagleton, *Literary Theory*, 39.

18. Jacobs, "Discussion with Alan Jacobs." http://www.thenewatlantis.com/publications/the-pleasures-of-reading-in-an-age-of-distraction

19. Eliot, *Sacred Wood*, xi.

of reading texts closely, paying exquisite attention to words and structures, finding meaning intrinsically within works of literature.

Although many of the new literary critics did not bring the Christian faith explicitly to bear in their approaches, one might detect in them a Protestant note—a view of a literary work as an infinite other and a belief in the ability of a reader to encounter a text all on his own. David Lyle Jeffrey argues that the impulse of New Criticism springs from the Reformation and Luther's hermeneutics of the individual Bible reader; he finds that in New Criticism, a kind of scripture was made up of secular texts: "The secular text, in short, held much the same place of reverence as the Bible in biblical criticism. It was a distinguished 'other'; what critics might say about the text did not finally compromise the integrity of that otherness."[20] The reverence given to secular literature in modern literary theory, in short, got its cues from the reverence that Scripture had received for ages.[21]

Literary studies could hold its moral high ground for only so long, however, as World War II and its aftermath raised new questions of whether literature was truly doing any good. Steiner, a Jew who escaped Europe as a child in 1940, repeatedly asks this question with urgency in his work. Steiner argues that the "unprecedented ruin of humane values and hopes by the political bestiality of our age" must be the starting point of "any serious thought about literature and the place of literature in society:"[22]

> To think of literature, of education, of language, as if nothing very important had happened to challenge our very concept of these activities seems to me unrealistic. . . . We come after. We know now that a man can read Goethe or Rilke in the evening, that he can play Bach and Schubert, and go to his day's work at

---

20. Jeffrey, *People of the Book*, 92-3.

21. Jeffrey points out that although Christian literary theory in late antiquity and the early Middle Ages was explicitly ideological, with Christians unapologetically reading secular texts for religious purposes and quite often using texts in ways counter to their original meanings, a major shift occurred in Christian literary theory in the mid-twentieth century. Christian writers then largely followed the rise of modern literary formalism, finding it "epistemologically, ethically, and even theologically a comfortable framework in which to operate," and they would later even defend formalism against postmodern attacks, "seeing New Criticism's defense of the autonomy and integrity of the text in particular a sort of moral high ground." Jeffrey notes the irony of this stance, as "what must seem odd about many 'Christian' defenses of formalism is their apparent forgetfulness that the inaugural commitment of Christianity to literature was itself hardly of a formalist character. Relationship with the ultimate Author of the sacred Text was always the end in view for the fathers of the church, and the better understanding of sacred Scripture their only justification for a profitable study of secular texts." Ibid., 95.

22. Steiner, *Language and Silence*, 22.

Auschwitz in the morning. To say that he can read them without understanding or that his ear is gross, is cant.[23]

Steiner explains elsewhere, "The simple yet appalling fact is that we have very little solid evidence that literary studies do very much to enrich or stabilize moral perception, that they *humanize*...What is worse—a certain body of evidence points the other way."[24] And so,

> [S]urely there is something rather terrible in our doubt whether the study and delight a man takes in Shakespeare makes him any less capable of organizing a concentration camp . . . before we can go on teaching we must surely ask ourselves: are the humanities humane and, if so, why did they fail before the night?[25]

Steiner hits upon a dire and intrinsic problem in the study of literature—from its beginning it has had a moral dimension, as literature is read with a belief in its ability to form better lives, but that moral dimension has always been of an ambiguous nature, and can even "fail before the night."

After World War II the study of literature fell upon other challenges in the face of a western culture that was affording it less place. Henry Zylstra, in his essays in *Testament of Vision*, perceived a crisis of literature-reading in 1960s America as its capitalism and pragmatism were deepening, and its education had turned towards over-specialization and practical skills. An impatience "to get on to practical success" marked students brought up in such a system.[26] Zylstra argued, "the need for literature as an integrating discipline is almost desperate in our times" as literature "is forever and essentially the foe of specialization. It is committed to seeing life steadily and seeing it whole."[27] Flannery O'Connor likewise noted serious problems in how works of literature were popularly received, and she found that the common approach to literature is a pragmatic one, wanting it to do something: "people don't know what they are expected to do with a novel, believing, as so many do, that art must be utilitarian, that it must do something,

---

23. Ibid., 15.

24. Ibid., 81, emphasis Steiner's.

25. Ibid., 86. Eagleton similarly notes, "When the Allied troops moved into the concentration camps . . . to arrest commandants who had whiled away their leisure hours with a volume of Goethe, it appeared that someone had some explaining to do." Eagleton, *Literary Theory*, 30.

26. Zylstra, *Testament of Vision*, 19. This problem is widespread still on both sides of the pond; as Moberly laments, common today is the "contemporary culture of quality assurance via immediately measureable learning outcomes in education." Moberly, "Biblical Criticism," 94.

27. Zylstra, *Testament of Vision*, 22, 18.

rather than be something."[28] O'Connor holds that art's doings are not at the center of its being. Mystery, rather than activity, is the core of art and of all literature. "[A] generation has been made to feel that the aim of learning is to eliminate mystery," but "[t]he result of a proper study of a novel should be contemplation of the mystery embodied in it."[29] For American authors like Zylstra and O'Connor, this contemplation of mystery and sense of wholeness of vision were felt to be lost in 1960s society, rendering literature feeble.

Although literature's purposes and effects were even more seriously questioned in the second half of the twentieth century with the rise of poststructural and postmodern schools of theory, there has ever lingered throughout literary studies a profound hope in literature's ability to do good; for literature, in itself, to be an agent of good in the life of its readers.[30] Of course, not all have embraced this hope, and contemporary literary criticism abounds with examples of those who look for systems of power, oppression, and deception in literary texts. But during the rise of such schools, those literary critics who did not take a path of suspicion were forced to find another way to explain literature and its failings, and that quest to resolve the moral ambiguity of literature often led to a concern with practices of reading. As Denis Donoghue argues, "disputes of theory are best engaged as disputes about our ways of reading:"

> The idea of arguing with Jacques Derrida, Fredric Jameson, Edward Said, Annette Kolodny, J. Hills Miller, Stephen Greenblatt, and Stanley Fish about their theories of literature has not lost its charm, but it might be more worthwhile to ask adepts of feminism, Marxism, Deconstruction, the New Historicism, and Cultural Studies what they think they're doing when they read literature. I have come to feel that theories matter only when they coerce someone's way of reading a book. Then they matter a lot.[31]

Like Donoghue, Steiner is one who engages with such disputes of theory (along with the wider cultural situations of western literature[32]) by giving close

28. O'Connor, *Mystery and Manners*, 123.

29. Ibid., 125, 129.

30. Author Blake Morrison has recently explained, "A hope of something beyond our place and time. This is what books— the best books— give us: a lifeline, a reason to believe, a way to breathe more freely." Morrison, "Twelve Thoughts About Reading," 17.

31. Donoghue, *Practice of Reading*, 36. As Stephen Logan argues, "The significance of the contrast between the traditional and contemporary forms of literary theory is ultimately moral and metaphysical." Logan, "Literary Theorist," 30.

32. "Mass culture, the economics of personal space and time, the erosion of privacy, the systematic suppression of silence in technological consumer cultures, the eviction

attention to practices of reading, by asking what is happening when works of literature are read. At the heart of Steiner's resistance to poststructuralism and deconstructive theories is the manner in which they fail to reckon with the actual experience of reading texts and encountering a presence within them.[33] What is missing in modern literary theory is reflection on "the personal phenomenality of the encounter with music, literature and the arts . . . Current critical theory in its investigations of significant form finds almost nothing to say of the literal facts of our experience of the poem. What 'comes to pass' between the lives of the text or painting and our own?"[34]

Steiner thus has directed much effort towards exploring that "personal phenomenality of the encounter." His stirring work *Real Presences: Is There Anything in What We Say?* encapsulates many of his concerns; there he argues that "any account of the capacity of human speech to communicate meaning and feeling is, in the final analysis, underwritten by the assumption of God's presence."[35] Steiner is reticent on the God he envisages, and this results in some confusion over what exactly he is claiming, but he sets out that the reality of God is beneath all hopes of finding meaning in art.[36] Because there is truly a reality that is transcendent, literature is pregnant with transcendent meaning, as well. And so, the possibility of a "real presence" being mediated through artistic work entails that the mark of an "authentic experience" when encountering art is one of "responding responsibility. We are answerable to the text, to the work of art . . . in a very specific sense, at once moral, spiritual and psychological."[37]

Although Steiner speaks of art in an encompassing sense, he offers particularities on what his approach means for reading. In his earlier article "'Critic'/'Reader'" Steiner heuristically makes a distinction between critics and readers (recognizing that no one is purely one or the other): critics are

---

of memory (of learning by heart) from schooling, entail the eclipse of the acts of reading, of the book itself." Steiner, *No Passion Spent*, x.

33. Steiner abhors "the brutalization of style" and "the often repulsive jargon, to the contrived obscurantism and specious pretensions to technicality which make the bulk of post-structuralism and deconstructive theory and practice, particularly among its academic epigones, unreadable." Steiner, *Real Presences*, 116.

34. Ibid., 177.

35. Ibid., 3.

36. Tim McKenzie points out that Steiner's argument runs the risk "that divorcing a religious aesthetic from its roots in a reflective faith tradition leads inevitably to the triumph of the fetish and the kitsch. Steiner is certainly alert to this danger. . . . Yet it seems doubtful whether his religion of high literary culture can avoid Matthew Arnold's temptation towards packaging intuitions of transcendence as aesthetic products." McKenzie, "'I Shall Win At the Odds,'" 361.

37. Steiner, *Real Presences*, 8.

those who consciously or not, compete with the text and want to usurp it with their own judgments, while readers are those who serve the text and always look for more within it. A critic stands back at a distance to judge a text, while a reader moves closer into it; she "proceeds *as if* the text was the housing of forces and meanings, of meanings of meanings, whose lodging within the executive verbal form was one of 'incarnation.'"[38] And so, proceeding *as if* meaning were present, a "true reader" is one characterized by practices such as learning texts by heart (memory is "the pivot"[39]) and transcribing texts, as transcribing "comports a full engagement with the text, a dynamic reciprocity between reader and book."[40] Steiner insists that basic practices such as these must be regained; he maintains that what is needed "are not 'programmes in the humanities'" but rather "places, i.e., a table with some chairs around it, in which we can learn again how to read, how to read together. . . . We need 'houses of and for reading' in which there is enough silence for the sinews of memory to awake . . . it is not more 'critics' we require but more and better 'readers.'"[41]

In *Real Presences* (along with his other essays), Steiner is responding to a particular moment in the academy and in the wider culture of reading literature,[42] yet since its publication, his concerns have continued to be taken up. Ethics of reading is particularly a growing area of research— Martha Nussbaum is one who, for decades now, has raised questions on the relationship between literature and ethics.[43] Like Steiner, Nussbaum is dissatisfied with strands of modern literary theory that have not evinced a concern for morals and character. She imagines

> a future in which our talk about literature will return, increasingly, to a concern with the practical—to the ethical and social questions that give literature its high importance in our lives. . . . In short, a future in which literary theory (while not forgetting its many other pursuits) will also join with ethical theory in pursuit of the question, "How should one live?"[44]

38. Steiner, "'Critic'/'Reader,'" 22, emphasis Steiner's.

39. Steiner, *No Passion Spent*, 15. Memorizing is an "attempt to abolish or sublate that very distance which the critic stakes out." Steiner, "'Critic'/'Reader,'" 25.

40. Steiner, *No Passion Spent*, 8.

41. Steiner, "'Critic'/'Reader,'" 34, 35.

42. Jeff Keuss remarks that *Real Presences* is "part prayer, part lament, part catharsis;" it "reads more like the libretto of a three part opera giving account of the fall of the Humanities in the 20th century than it does as a piece of literary criticism *per se*." Keuss, "George Steiner," 351.

43. See also, e.g., Booth, *Company We Keep*.

44. Nussbaum, *Love's Knowledge*, 168.

Nussbaum presses for "a literary theory that works in conversation with ethical theory" and maintains that an "explicit and deep study of ethical theory will, first of all, clarify for us just what it is that works of literature offer to our sense of life."[45] Literature matters for practices of living because "we have never lived enough. Our experience is, without fiction, too confined and too parochial. Literature extends it, making us reflect and feel about what might otherwise be too distant for feeling."[46] Reading fiction in particular can cultivate sympathy and feelings, especially that of love. Nussbaum maintains, "Reading novels, as David Copperfield learned, is a practice for falling in love. And it is in part because novels prepare the reader for love that they make the valuable contribution they do to society and to moral development."[47]

Steiner and Nussbaum thus hold out hopes for literature's redeeming work, yet in a more nuanced way than earlier twentieth century critics. They recognize the wider issues that must be addressed for literature to be read well and effectively—issues of the possibility of transcendence in literature, of the need for a personal response to literature, and of the need for an ethical framework in which to approach literature. As Donoghue remarks in his own assessment of modern literary criticism, "The moral of the story is not: Back to the New Criticism." Yet he finds, however, that "The moral is interrogative: Are we quite sure that we have devised methods of reading responsive to our own needs and to the literature we have still to read?"[48] Donoghue admires the New Critics for their close readings and presses for that manner of reading to be regained. As Stephen Logan argued in 2003, "Now that we have had twenty-five years of academics, not always notable for their powers of appreciative reading, telling us of the depredations of practical criticism, we need to learn again how to read."[49]

---

45. Ibid., 190. Zylstra expresses this sentiment in his own Christian framework: literature "enables us by vicarious experience in our life to bring to bear on being Christian, myriads of lives not our own . . . there is more of us that is Christian, that can be Christian, than there was before. There is more of you, after reading Hardy, to be Christian with than there was before you read him, and there is also more conviction that you want to be." Zylstra, *Testament*, 57.

46. Nussbaum, *Love's Knowledge*, 47. She continues on 48, "literature is an extension of life not only horizontally, bringing the reader into contact with events or locations or persons or problems he or she has not otherwise met, but also, so to speak, vertically, giving the reader experience that is deeper, sharper, and more precise than much of what takes place in life."

47. Ibid., 238.

48. Donoghue, *Practice of Reading*, 19.

49. Logan, "Amazed and Confused."

It is a stirring call—to learn again how to read. Within that call are foundational assumptions (sometimes hidden, other times more manifest) about *why* one should read, and this question of why has received many varied answers recently. As noted, Steiner argues for the importance of response, of truly responding in a moral and spiritual way to the realities set out in reading, and Nussbaum turns to the ethical, holding that reading helps one learn how to live and to love. Philip Davis similarly asks whether it is "a foolish thing to have aimed for: that I have wanted books to help me make a real life of my own?"[50] These authors read literature to learn how to live well. As Wilber Sanders notes, "The quality of human life is more important than what is said about it, and the justification of literature must lie, if anywhere, in the way it serves that life, not in its own self-enclosed activity."[51]

Harold Bloom offers a markedly different answer than these figures to the question of why to read, however, shying away from the ethical and the broader questions of living. He argues that the "pleasures of reading are indeed selfish rather than social. You cannot directly improve anyone's life by reading better or more deeply." (Here those Nazi readers might come back to mind.) And so, Bloom explains that he is "skeptical of the traditional social hope that care for others may be stimulated by the growth of individual imagination." In contrast, Bloom focuses upon the individual and emphasizes that one reads "in order to strengthen the self, and to learn its authentic interests."[52] Bloom argues that reading offers a transcendent experience:

> [T]he strongest, most authentic motive for deep reading of the now much-abused traditional canon is the search for difficult pleasure... a higher pleasure remains the reader's quest. There is a reader's Sublime, and it seems the only secular transcendence

---

50. He argues that the "serious reader" is one who is "not sure of... the relation of reading to living outside it" and sometimes has "doubts as to the real-life use of reading fiction" yet nonetheless "acknowledg[es] a deep need for art's help." Davis, *Experience of Reading*, 3, 17.

51. Sanders continues, "It's the mark of a great writer, often, to see this very starkly— finding the cloud-capped towers and gorgeous palaces he can so easily conjure up, trifling and ineffectual; feeling that he may as well break his staff and drown his book, for all the difference it makes to the real world. The fictionality of art oppresses him, until writing can come to seem an activity unworthy of a grown man or woman. 'Life is short,' Tolstoy wrote to an importunate publisher in 1859, 'and to waste it in my adult years writing... stories... makes me feel ashamed.' It's the mainspring of Tolstoy's greatness that he doesn't care about literature. Only by not caring about it was he freed to put into literature the life-content that made it *worth* caring about." Sanders, quoted in Davis, *Real Voices*, xv–xvi.

52. Bloom, *How to Read and Why*, 22.

we can ever attain, except for the even more precarious transcendence we call "falling in love."[53]

While Bloom wants to keep clear from any ethics of reading, he ends up with a spirituality of reading—as with the secular New Critics, literature becomes a secular Sublime. His approach moreover has a note of sadness, as Bloom holds that "[w]e read not only because we cannot know enough people, but because friendship is so vulnerable, so likely to diminish or disappear."[54] While for Nussbaum literature expands her experiences with other people, for Bloom, literature seems to actually replace those experiences, as they fade away. Nussbaum finds reading is able to teach one how to fall in love, while for Bloom reading is a similar pleasure as love but it is far less "precarious." Reading is a means of grasping at something permanent and unchanging and ultimate amidst the uncertainties of life and love and death.

Another recent answer, of a different ilk, to the question of why to read comes from Denis Donoghue, who advocates the pleasures of reading through the use of the imagination. Donoghue places imagination at the center of reading and maintains that "the purpose of reading literature is to exercise or incite one's imagination; specifically, one's ability to imagine being different."[55] In this exercise of imagination, great pleasure is found, and that pleasure helps one to grow in sympathy and fellowship to other human beings. Still, however, what is sought is not a sublime pleasure such as Bloom is after; for Donoghue, reading "is certainly not a substitute for anything else—for one's commitments in religion or politics, for instance. It is what it is."[56] Donoghue holds that reading is truly powerful yet is nonetheless limited in its scope, and must not be expected to hold more than it already does.

Donoghue's note of "it is what it is" appears even more strongly in Alan Jacobs, who recently has likewise emphasized the pleasures of reading without looking to reading to fulfill a spiritual or moral role. Jacobs argues in *The Pleasures of Reading in an Age of Distraction* that the "one dominant, overarching, nearly definitive principle for reading" is "*Read at Whim.*"[57] Reading should, above all else, be for the individual's pleasure:

> Forget for a moment *how* books should be read: *Why* should they be read? The first reason—the first sequentially in the story that follows but also the first in order of importance—is that

---

53. Ibid., 29.
54. Ibid., 19.
55. Donoghue, *Practice of Reading*, 56.
56. Ibid., 73.
57. Jacobs, *Pleasures of Reading*, 15, emphasis Jacobs'.

reading books can be intensely pleasurable. Reading is one of the great human delights.[58]

Jacobs reacts against ideas of moral growth and development being set at the center of rationalizations for reading; he is against the heavy doses of duty found in guides to reading such as Mortimer J. Adler and Charles Van Doren's *How to Read a Book: The Classic Guide to Intelligent Reading*.[59] Adler's and Van Doren's work, a popular bestseller, emphasizes that "we must know how to make books teach us well," and sets the exertion of the reader as the key to good reading.[60] A reader must "go to work on a book," using all in her powers to understand it: "To pass from understanding less to understanding more by your own intellectual effort in reading is something like pulling yourself up by your bootstraps."[61] The image Adler and Van Doren evoke throughout most of their work is that of the lonely reader striving upwind in the gale of literature, with good reading hinging upon how strongly the reader leans in. The effort in seeking out good books and reading them well is part and parcel of the "challenge of finding the resources within ourselves to live a good human life."[62] With enough hard work, the reader can pull herself up by her bootstraps to figure out how to encounter not only a work of literature but also life itself.

Jacobs is strongly against this moralistic strand of reading theory and notes, "Adler and Van Doren are strict taskmasters. A word that appears often in their account is 'obligation.' . . . I wouldn't be surprised if many readers of *How to Read a Book* actually like this tone: it is the strongly worded lecture that helps stiffen the backbone, strengthen the resolve."[63] Jacobs

---

58. Ibid., 10. The idea of pleasure in reading is, of course, a long-recognized one, stretching back to the Greeks. Glending Olson traces out aspects of medieval reading and finds that late medieval culture had both "a tolerance of the purely entertaining [aspect of reading], one based in a conviction that pleasure promotes well-being, and at the same time a feeling that such experience cannot stand by itself, that without constant reassertion of its acknowledged values and limits vacation becomes too much like truancy." Olson, *Literature As Recreation*, 231.

59. The 1972 edition is an updated version of the 1940 original written by Adler alone.

60. Adler and Van Doren, *How to Read a Book*, 15.

61. Ibid., 8.

62. Ibid., 345.

63. Jacobs, *Pleasures of Reading*, 8,9. Jacobs might be overlooking some more positive elements of Adler and Van Doren, such as their recognition that literature works somewhat inexplicably upon a reader, particularly when it comes to imaginative types of literary pieces. The most important piece of advice they offer regarding this kind of literature is, "*Don't try to resist the effect that a work of imaginative literature has on you.*" The rule is to "become at home in this imaginary world, know it as if you were

finds this emphasis on obligation misses the point of reading, which is to convey pleasure.[64] However, Jacobs is still aware of the moral dimensions of reading:

> [W]e have gone long enough without raising the question of whether reading makes you a better person. The short answer to that question is No. It doesn't. And the long answer doesn't differ too dramatically from the short one . . . if you really want to become a better person, there are ways in which reading can help. But the degree to which that happens will depend not just on what you read . . . but also why and how.[65]

Jacobs explains in the "how" of reading that attentiveness is worth cultivating (he argues that deep attention in itself is pleasurable), and that the first lesson in reading is having humility, charity, and slowness.[66] Jacobs recognizes that "[s]erious 'deep attention' reading has always been and will always be a minority pursuit," but for those who pursue it, "books are the natural and inevitable and permanent means of being absorbed in something other than the self."[67] Reading can be a means of learning to be interested in others, but only when done rightly. Practices of reading might help one become a better person, then, but becoming a better person is still not the goal of reading. As Jacobs explains in a lecture he gave on *The Pleasures of Reading*, he finds that the virtues of reading play into an Arnoldian narrative he doesn't believe in, and sets people up for exhaustion and frustration. Jacobs explains, "I'm a Christian so I don't look to literature to save my soul. . . . I can actually read literature for fun, because I'm not placing those expectations on it."[68]

It is the expectations that are placed on reading that largely direct how one reads, even though some particular practices of reading are found across the board of readers who have diverse reasons for caring about reading well. Bloom and Jacobs might read texts with a similar measure of care and attention, even though Bloom is ultimately looking for a sublime

---

an observer on the scene; become a member of its population, willing to befriend its characters, and able to participate in its happenings." Adler and Van Doren, *How to Read a Book*, 205, 211, emphasis theirs.

64. Mark Haddon similarly argues that "we do literature no great service if we try to sell it as a kind of moral calisthenics." Haddon, "Right Words in the Right Order," 90.

65. Jacobs, *Pleasures of Reading*, 52, 53.

66. Ibid., 86, 97. These notes of humility, charity, and patience in reading are likewise sounded by Ellen Davis, as discussed in chapter 6.

67. Ibid., 106, 116.

68. Jacobs, "Discussion with Alan Jacobs."

experience, while Jacobs leaves sublimity to his Christian faith and simply looks for pleasure instead. Whether a text is read for response and moral growth, for self-growth, for an experience of sublimity, or for sheer pleasure, practices of patience and close attention and slowness are likely to be present. (And even deconstructive theory brings a manner of close attention to texts, though for other ends than mentioned above.) To some extent, then, what good reading looks like might be easier to agree upon than what good reading is for. Recent literary criticism has shown a bewildering extent of approaches to literature and reading, yet a growing consensus has been that practices of good reading need to be learned anew. More needs to be said, then, on just what good reading actually looks like, and particularly, what good reading might look like for a Christian reader. For that we will turn to the suggestions of C. S. Lewis, Alan Jacobs, and Paul Griffiths.

C. S. Lewis

"C. S. Lewis" is a name that conjures many associations, yet of all Lewis's writings (ranging across fields of literary criticism, imaginative fiction, poetry, Christian apologetics, and prose), it is his professional work of literary criticism that is perhaps least read. Yet because Lewis is such a creative and compelling author himself, he is a particularly helpful literary critic to help us understand the practice of reading. (As Steiner argues, "The readings, the interpretations and critical judgments of art, literature and music from within art, literature and music are of a penetrative quality rarely equaled by those offered from outside, by those propounded by the non-creator."[69]) Lewis wrote about literature as one who deeply loved it and wrote well himself; writing before the dominance of modern literary theory, he "was fully intimate with the older and far longer metaphysical tradition at a time when it was beginning to come under attack."[70] He is well placed, then, to offer insights into a manner of reading literature that is now looked towards anew.

In 1954, the thriving Cambridge literary studies scene had created a new professorship for Lewis, and his *An Experiment in Criticism* (1961), written at Cambridge towards the end of his life, reflects his developed understanding of the role of literature. Lewis's last book published in his lifetime is a brief yet rich consideration of what defines good literature and good reading; he works backwards from practices of good reading to understand works of good writing, as he unravels essential traits of reading well. Lewis's experimental premise is to set readers or types of reading as the basis

---

69. Steiner, *Real Presences*, 12.
70. Logan, "Literary Theorist," 40.

for criticism, and books as the corollary, so as "to discover how far it might be plausible to define a good book as one which is read in one way, and a bad book as a book which is read in another."[71]

Lewis begins by distinguishing between the literary majority and minority—the majority never read anything twice and turn to reading as a last resort, while the minority always are looking for space in which to read, and what they read is constantly on their minds.[72] The literary minority are those for whom reading is deeply a part of their lives; they have a particular disposition to reading. It is not simply about having intelligence or education, then, as even literary scholars "who might be expected *ex officio* to have a profound and permanent appreciation of literature may in reality have nothing of the sort. They are mere professionals."[73] And so, in a house frequently filled with intellectual cocktail parties, it is possible that "the only real literary experience in such a family may be occurring in a back bedroom where a small boy is reading *Treasure Island* under the bed-clothes by the light of an electric torch."[74]

How a book is picked up (and picked up again) is telling about both the book and the reader, Lewis explains, and plenty of bad ways of reading exist, for both good and bad books. One sort of ill-reading that Lewis sees especially prevalent in his age is the "laborious sort of misreading" that reads great literature out of a desire for self-improvement.[75] (Here Lewis preempts Jacobs in emphasizing pleasure over self-improvement.) Reading in order to become cultured is like playing football only to be fit, Lewis argues, with both motives missing the point, as pleasure is absent and the ultimate intention is set only upon oneself.[76] Lewis acknowledges that good art is often used for all sorts of other things than the art itself presents, but real appreciation of art is about receiving what it, in itself, is offering and doing:

---

71. Lewis, *Experiment in Criticism*, 1.
72. Ibid., 3.
73. Ibid., 6.
74. Ibid., 8.
75. Ibid., 10. More recently, Nigel Ford has similarly argued that it is an erroneous idea that "we should read literature in order to improve ourselves. Literature does not give up its real treasures to the status-seeker. The perceived need to be cultured is the true enemy of real enjoyment and understanding of all works of art." Ford, *Lantern and the Looking-glass*, 78.
76. Zylstra similarly argues that when the study of literature is treated as simply a bit of culture, this "puts English in the same class as pink handkerchiefs and tea." Zylstra, *Testament of Vision*, 23.

> The first demand any work of art makes upon us is surrender. Look. Listen. Receive. Get yourself out of the way ... This distinction can hardly better be expressed than by saying that the many *use* art and the few *receive* it.[77]

This distinction between using and receiving drives the force of Lewis's argument; although the "many" and the "few" are the groups engaging in such kinds of reading, Lewis is less interested in categorizing readers than in qualifying their approaches (any given reader can move from "using" to "receiving"). The user takes the work of literature and does something with it (such as using it as a pastime or tool for wish-building or philosophizing), while the recipient rests in it. Using, he argues, is inferior to receiving because if art is used it "merely facilitates, brightens, relieves or palliates our life, and does not add to it."[78] While reading, the reception of a work is to be understood as an end in itself.[79] And so when "pencils go to work on the margin and phrases of censure or approval begin forming themselves in our minds," "[a]ll this activity impedes reception."[80]

What is needed for good reading, then, is to learn how to get oneself out of the way. Lewis finds that books that allow one to do that and reward the effort may be classified as good, while, on the whole, books that may be called bad are ones that do not give anything more when one surrenders to them. Poorly written literature more often than not produces poor reading, he argues, encouraging speed and sentimentality, and when the reader tries to read with true receptivity, nothing deeper is encountered in the work. Yet the hitch is that "We can find a book bad only by reading it as if it might, after all, be very good ... no work [can] succeed without a preliminary act of good will on the part of the reader."[81] A practice of good reading is essentially a practice of letting go and allowing the literary work to offer what it has—with a good literary work, it will be something that is deeply meaningful and capable of shaping one's life.

Lewis's argument is intriguing in how it contrasts so strongly the using and the receiving of a work, and the activity and the surrender of the reader, with both of these similar sets of contrasts hinging upon the "good will on the part of the reader." A reader's will directs whether a piece of literature is used for some outside purpose or whether it is received in itself; likewise, his will directs whether he is overactive in wrestling meaning out of a book,

---

77. Lewis, *Experiment in Criticism*, 18, 19, emphasis original.
78. Ibid., 88.
79. Ibid., 130.
80. Ibid., 92–3.
81. Ibid., 116.

or whether he surrenders to receive what the book in itself is offering. Yet while these contrasts form neat dichotomies, it seems that there is more of a blurry line between the movements of using/receiving and activity/surrender. Steiner's similar distinction between "critic" and "reader," is, he explained, not a simple distinction, but a heuristic one, yet Lewis does not explicitly offer such qualification. And so the difference needs further pressing: although a good reader should not aim to use a piece of literature for her own devices, she nonetheless "uses" literature in the sense of wanting it to come into her everyday life and give her deeper life and pleasure. Similarly, while Lewis holds that the "necessary condition of all good reading is to 'get ourselves out of the way,'"[82] the reader nonetheless has to take initiative in getting herself to the point in which she can get herself out of the way. Attention, surrender, and receptivity take some effort to achieve, as does the "preliminary act of good will" the reader must make.

A balance is struck between the reader's activity and receptivity, then, with the reader at times putting forth effort to receive a work, and at times letting go and allowing the work to take over. What might be clarified in Lewis is the role of receptivity in reading—are "pencils go[ing] to work on the margins" really such a bad thing? Steiner, as noted, presses for response in one's reading. Although receptivity is needed to take in a literary work on its own terms, and is the best way first to read through a work, subsequent reactions to the work while reading can also be a part of good reading. Jacobs describes criticism and commentary as gifts to the author, as they show a true engagement with the author's literary work.[83] Although I find helpful Lewis's differentiation between activity and receptivity in reading, what is needed is more of a flux between the two. Effort is put forth to receive a work, and as the work is read closely, more activity is needed to keep on receiving it and striving to grasp its meaning, even in every fresh rereading.

Lewis's argument is noteworthy, as well, as for the enormous place that is afforded to the practice of reading in the living of a good life. The literary majority who mostly misunderstand the nature of good reading are implicitly depicted as not only missing out on the joys of reading, but missing out on life itself. As a literary scholar, Lewis understandably has a bias towards the role of reading, but what might be clarified is the ultimate significance of reading; how does it relate to the living of the good life, and other ways of learning how to do that? Lewis himself is aware that reading is but one way of encountering the riches of life, and he points out other pursuits enable

---

82. Ibid., 93.

83. Jacobs, *Theology of Reading*, 87. He goes on to say on that not to engage critically with a work is "an ethical failure of engagement" (121).

this, such as worship and love. Yet reading in particular allows this in the way it enables its readers to enter into the experiences of others:

> My own eyes are not enough for me, I will see through those of others ... [I]n reading great literature I become a thousand men and yet remain myself. ... Here, as in worship, in love, in moral action, and in knowing, I transcend myself; and am never more myself than when I do.[84]

Lewis thus gives good reading a place among other spiritual pursuits of life—for him reading literature is certainly not a replacement for the Christian faith, but it has echoes of the spiritual hopes of Christianity, of acquiring deep empathy and losing oneself to find oneself. This is the hope of Nussbaum and others above, that literature might teach one how to live and become more.

Alan Jacobs

Lewis's manner of reading emphasizes the reader's good will and willingness to surrender to a work to see if it will have an effect. As he is concerned with how to recognize good works of literature, Lewis takes for granted that such works will be noble in their intentions and take the reader to a place that is truly good. The complexity of the spiritual tenor of classic works of literature is not considered—for a Christian reader, a classic can say much truth about life but still be spiritually misdirected in some fundamental ways.[85] Lewis, moreover, writes before the general unsettling of the canon of classic literature, and the shift towards nihilism and hopelessness found in much of what is today considered good modern literature.

Alan Jacobs is thus a helpful recent voice to set alongside Lewis, as like Lewis he deeply loves literature and pursues the type of reading that receives literary works well.[86] Yet writing in the present age, Jacobs is more aware of the challenges of modern literature and the need to discern how to receive it, and he tackles this problem by being more explicit about the Christian approach he brings to bear. Although *An Experiment in Criticism* has strong Christian overtones, Lewis does not approach the issue of read-

---

84. Lewis, *Experiment*, 139–41.

85. As modern author Tim Parks notes, "We have to remember that some of the most brilliant writers were not necessarily wise, not trustworthy." Parks, "Mindful Reading," 66.

86. Jacobs also loves Lewis's work and has written widely on it. See, e.g., his contribution to *The Cambridge Companion to C. S. Lewis* and his *The Narnian: The Life and Imagination of C. S. Lewis*.

ing by stating directly his Christian convictions. Jacobs does that, however, in his *A Theology of Reading: The Hermeneutics of Love*, where he explores the intersection of Christian faith and the practice of reading. Jacobs begins his book by setting out the goal "to read lovingly because of and in the name of Jesus Christ,"[87] and he spends his work pursuing just how far Jesus' command to love God and neighbor might stretch, positing that it reaches even to a Christian's engagement with written works. As Jacobs understands the essential nature of the Christian life to be a love of God and others, from that starting point he offers a compelling proposal of what a Christian form of reading might be.

Writing as a scholar of English literature, Jacobs works out from literary examples a vision of how love might affect reading. His work flows between close textual readings, literary theory, philosophy, and theology, resulting in a challenging account of how love might direct one's life so profoundly that even something as seemingly straightforward as reading might be transformed. Love is more expansive than a feeling or action; it is a way of seeing and being that works unceasingly in the life of the Christian believer; it hovers between her and every text she reads. Jacobs argues that Christians are obliged to apply charity to their work of reading texts: "only if we understand this love of God and neighbor as the first requirement of the reading of any text can we fulfill 'the law of love' in our thinking, our talking, and our manner of working."[88]

As set out in his first chapter, some of the broad contours of Jacobs's charitable reading include a resistance to "using" literature rather than loving it (Jacobs is wary of Augustine's analogy of plundering the Egyptians, as he views books as neighbors, not enemies); a preservation of the difference between the self and the other (one loves the other *as* oneself); and a view that "avoiding error is a good thing, but is probably not central in hermeneutics."[89] More than just getting it right, reading and interpreting texts is about deepening in love. Avoiding error is thus at best "propaedeutic to the task of reading lovingly."[90] Jacobs echoes Lewis yet moves a step

---

87. Jacobs, *Theology of Reading*, 1.

88. Ibid., 12. He cites Kevin Vanhoozer, who likewise understands general hermeneutics to be "inescapably theological:" "Understanding—of the Bible or of any other text—is a matter of ethics, indeed, of spirituality. Indeed, interpretation ultimately depends upon the theological virtues of faith, hope, and love" (155n4). Vanhoozer, "Spirit of Understanding," 161.

89. Jacobs, *Theology of Reading*, 14. He leans on Augustine's analogy of one leaving a road by mistake to cut across a field and ending up at the place where the road leads.

90. Ibid., 17.

further than him, in distinguishing not only between using and receiving literature but between using it and *loving* it.

Jacobs notes how there are different kinds of books that require different kinds of receiving (most significantly, "a text identified as sacred makes claims upon our responsive attention that texts not identified as sacred do not and (perhaps) cannot"[91]), yet love is still the universal response to all texts. Jacobs gives nuance to this love, however, as he notes that a Christian reader has to pay attention to the spiritual direction of a work to know how to receive and love it well. He draws from Augustine to point out the necessity of ordering one's loves, as "all things that deserve our love deserve it in proportion to their excellence."[92] Unlike the openness to all good works of literature that Lewis or Steiner might suggest, Jacobs is more discerning on how a reader engages a literary work. The love a reader sets forth is a willingness to hear a book out, but still to keep it as a neighbor, allowing for some distance. What Jacobs does, however, is raise the stakes of neighborly love—a reader need not invite into her home every piece of literature she reads, but neighborly love is more than just passing cordialities across the fence. Love for a neighbor, and for a book, requires deep attention and concern and self-giving.

Jacobs's description of love for books is thus different from the Christ-like love a Christian is to show others, as that is meant to be given regardless of their particular "excellence." A real qualitative difference is present here, as a reader may decide how much a book deserves love according to its own merits, but true Christian love for actual living neighbors, however, cannot be made according to those neighbors' own goodness or excellence. While Jacobs draws from concepts of Christian neighborly love to describe love for books, neighborly love for books is actually much more conditioned than the genuine article.

Jacobs sets out that at the forefront of the task of reading is the reader's will, for only a will directed towards a love of God and neighbor will create charitable reading. Love, Jacobs says, does not just happen, and so charitable reading requires an active will to become increasingly loving and seek the best in every work. He points out that just *how* the will is reformed for love is a disputed theological matter (that formation can be understood, for instance, as the work of the Holy Spirit or as the work of spiritual disciplines), but he emphasizes that the will must be redirected in order to love aright. Jacobs leaves the finer details of this point to theology proper, which is a shame, since his entire argument hinges upon the redirection of the reader's

---

91. Ibid., 17.
92. Ibid., 22.

will. Jacobs takes as his starting point that the Christian reader will have a will bent towards love, but without a deeper understanding of just how that will is bent into place, the sustaining power behind that love is left out of the discussion. (As Jeffrey argues, "the commitment to love with words one's neighbor as oneself can remain lively only so long as the greater Love which precedes it has not been lost."[93]) The reader of Jacobs gets few cues for how to redirect her will to love, or how to sustain that redirected will to keep it lively in order to grow in love in her acts of reading.

In his prelude Jacobs had set out that the central purpose of his work was to read lovingly in and because of the name of Jesus. Yet the reason for Jesus being at the center of his project is not explicitly explored until the end of his book, when Jacobs comes to explain kenosis as the truest way to read lovingly, as Jesus is the example of self-engaging love. As he connects the kenotic love of Jesus and the act of charitable reading, Jacobs points out how charitable reading only makes sense by faith in Christ:

> [O]nly if reading is a theologically significant activity can many of the counsels I am making in this book be justified. The kenotic reading I have outlined makes little sense for a person who does not believe in the claims the Christian church has historically made for Jesus Christ, and who does not participate in the life of that church. Absent such faith and such pretensions, the humble, indeed sacrificial, nature of kenotic reading is pointless.[94]

Here Jesus' command to love God and neighbor, that which has driven Jacobs's work, is seen in light of the person of Jesus, the One who models and sustains such love. Because Jesus shows kenotic love, "kenotic reading" is made possible. What might be further explicated here, however, is how this relates to the double love commandment (an Old Testament idea!), and to the difference Jacobs made earlier between loving books in different ways—Jesus' kenosis was not limited in scope, but was truly given in its all to all.

Jacobs also comes in at the end of his work to name the church as the truest place in which to achieve charitable reading and living. After hints Jacobs has given throughout his work that only in the church is true charity achieved,[95] here he is most explicit in his claims. The church, he hopes, will prove to be the ultimate community of love built upon Jesus. Although absent are any reflections on the reality of this hope, Jacobs's hopeful vision of the church is compelling still as it points out the necessity of a community in which to learn how to love and how to read in love—a reader cannot

---

93. Jeffrey, *People of the Book*, 378.
94. Jacobs, *Theology of Reading*, 111.
95. See ibid., 50 and 63–64.

learn how to love others without others. What would be helpful, however, is to offer here concrete examples of how the church helps its members to read charitably—is it that worship or bible study or fellowship or practical service are the means by which lives of charity are formed? As the church is not a book club, its means of forming charitable reading are indirect; or rather, charitable reading is an indirect outcome of a greater love a Christian is drawn into. Here also would be the place to speak of the Holy Spirit, as oddly enough, the operation of the Spirit on believers' heart and minds has been left unsaid. The Spirit of God at work in both the church and individual believers is a core part of the Christian faith, and it too has strong bearing on the practice of reading.

Jacobs's charitable reading is a program enmeshed in hope—charitable readers "genuinely wish for the best for that book (or its authors, or its characters)"—and he fittingly ends on a note of hope, describing charitable reading as a hopeful "wager on the graciousness of God and on the *imago dei* present in the writers of books."[96] Jacobs's love and hope is thus bound up in the presence of God—part of loving someone is to see traces of the grace of God in them and to hope that they might truly reflect the image of their Creator. Such hope enables one to keep going forward in their relationships with others by remembering that the grace of God is yet at work.[97]

Jacobs offers a serious challenge to his readers (both Christian and non-Christian) to pursue reading as an act of love. Reading well is about more than just receiving a book sympathetically; it is about engaging in the inexplicable, untidy, unpredictable, uncontrollable, and self-involving act that is love. Jacobs's charitable reading is a self-emptying love, and so a risky one, a kenosis without a guarantee of return. Although Jacobs echoes in many ways other literary voices on reading literature, pointing out like Lewis the difference between using and receiving a literary work, he differs from other figures considered here in how much further he involves the reader with the literary work itself. Jacobs's hermeneutic of love refreshingly balances activity and receptivity in reading, as love requires movements of both—the reader is both to offer and to receive love from a work. Effort put forth in such close reading is even more demanding, and receptivity even more personal, when charity is the goal. A book is received as a personal gift, and in that the effort required of the reader is significant; she must

---

96. Ibid., 31, 148.

97. Lewis described such hope in terms of "the weight of glory" of another: "The load, or weight, or burden of my neighbour's glory should be laid on my back. . . . It is in light of these overwhelming possibilities . . . that we should conduct all our dealings with one another, all friendships, all loves, all play, all politics." Lewis, "Weight of Glory," 45–46.

overlay her close reading with much hope for a book's good. Jacobs's understanding of a book as a neighbor (not as a permanent friend) also gives direction to a Christian reader on how to pick up a book on its own terms, without trying to control it, and also on how put a book down, recognizing its limitations. As F. D. Maurice noted, we must not expect from books, as from friends, any more than they profess to give.[98]

The end of reading for Jacobs is quite obvious: reading is meant both to reflect and to increase a love of God and neighbor. A close reading of literature has been given a particular raison d'être, something that is often undefined in other literary approaches. In this hermeneutic Jacobs offers a creative alternative from goals of sublimity or self-growth in reading, as the goal is rather, actively to love God and others, in whatever ways that may come, and for whatever effects they may have. (Jacobs's proposal in *A Theology of Reading* is thus a different approach than his more recent *The Pleasures of Reading*—although written for different purposes and audiences, in the latter it seems one is given more freedom to choose books that are easy to love. *A Theology of Reading*, in contrast, presents a strategy for loving whatever neighbor-books one ends up with.) In Jacobs's understanding, a book is not meant simply to help the reader ponder or to grow, just as the point of love is not simply to help a person to think more deeply or grow more personally. Rather, growth that comes by love is a by-product of the greater good that is purely love itself; personal growth is a consequence, not a goal, of engaging in love with another. Charitable reading might draw readers, then, into lives of love with God and others. Such love reaches beyond the reader in how it is not geared for the reader's credit, but for the ones that he loves.

A point mentioned earlier is that Jacobs only briefly touches upon the different kinds of charity a reader should give to literary works, as he focuses on a neighborly kind of love for a book, not the kind of love as a friend. Jacobs recognizes that different modes of reading may take place, as readers give reverence not just to sacred but also to non-sacred works (Machiavelli, he points out, was known to put on his best clothes to read his favorite authors).[99] Jacobs notes that different kinds of books call for different kinds of love, but this point is not probed deeper, as Jacobs keeps to his theme of the overarching love one must display towards all books. Yet what to make of these qualitative differences of love in reading? Perhaps this is outside of the bounds of Jacobs's work, but the issue of the different kinds of love and reverence one might give to a book is a pressing question for the Christian

---

98. Maurice, *Friendship of Books*, 26.
99. Jacobs, *Theology of Reading*, 103.

reader, whose reading life may encompass a wide range of literature from secular novels to the writings of the saints to Holy Scripture. How might the love for a book that is a friend and fellow member of the people of God be more self-involving than the love for a book that is an unbelieving neighbor? More particularly, how does Scripture come to the Christian reader differently than all other texts, and what is the most fitting way of love in reading it? *Is* there a different way to read it? As we turn towards these questions for the remainder of this study, Paul Griffiths provides a helpful transition from thinking about the reading of great literature to considering the Christian reading of the Bible.

Paul Griffiths

This foray into literature has caught only a slice of a great hope pinned upon literature to do good and to speak into the lives of its readers, and along with this hope, a great hope for readers to read well and take in literary works. For the Christian reader, as Jacobs argues, that hope is taken up in an even wider framework of being a loving follower of Jesus in all acts of life, even in turning the pages of a book. Against the background of these understandings of what it means to read literature well, and how it might be done as a Christian, I want to look at one more proposal for reading, that of Paul Griffiths in his thought-provoking book *Religious Reading: The Place of Reading in the Practice of Religion*. Griffiths is concerned with reading scripture and he comparatively explores characteristics of reading sacred writings in different religious traditions, and his work demonstrates how concerns for reading scripture are similar in many ways to concerns for reading classic literature. Griffiths thus offers a helpful bridge between reading literature and reading Scripture.

The present state of reading in modern western culture is a problem worried over and probed by Griffiths in *Religious Reading*. As a scholar of religion, Griffiths seeks what it means across all religious traditions to read sacred texts well; he sets out a formal account of religious reading and holds that religious reading is for the purpose of enabling religious practitioners to offer an account of themselves and the world. Griffiths's argument has as its backdrop the tide of modern consumerism, and over and against consumerist ways of reading, he calls for a manner of reading religiously that is slow and attentive and lingering, a way of reading as a lover.

As he is working across religious boundaries, Griffiths begins his work by giving a definition of "being religious:" this he understands as being able to offer an account that is comprehensive, unsurpassable, and central, that is, an account that explains one's life and one's world. While Griffiths acknowledges that any definition of religion and religiousness is open to much critique, Griffiths uses this understanding of religion to highlight the place of reading in the religious life. Reading, he argues, is at the heart of that life; to be religious is to read religiously in order to form one's life religiously over and against competing claims for it.[100] Griffiths's broad definition of being religious is thus important for his wider concerns, as he seeks to explore religious reading rather broadly, as well. He argues that the nature of religious reading may be sought apart from any particular tradition, and is in fact, *better* sought in a general manner without specific reference to any tradition.[101] Griffiths has, then, a puzzling tension at work here: he seeks a general method of religious reading, but nonetheless he acknowledges that religious readers will "typically think that the patterns of reading they practice and advocate are constitutively and necessarily tradition-specific."[102] How the particularity of a religion's beliefs might have bearing on its approach to reading is left unexplored, as Griffiths pursues an overarching mode of reading religiously.

Griffiths begins by going to great lengths to describe the impact of consumerism upon reading practices, creating in this a foil for religious reading. (As noted in the introduction, bad practices of reading are often used to define, in contrast, spiritual reading.) The problem, Griffiths argues, is that most readers are consumerist readers, readers who always try to use a text, getting something out of it, rather than being religious readers, readers who listen attentively to a text, giving attention to it as lovers. He notices this troubling state of affairs out of his own experience, as he confesses that he reads "mostly as a consumer, someone who wants to extract what is useful or exciting or entertaining from what is read, preferably with dispatch, and then move on to something else."[103] (Lewis's concerns for "using" a book come to mind here.) Griffiths is concerned with the place of reading in the overarching life of a religious person, and so he fears how consumerism has struck deeply into western life and into all manners of reading, particularly endangering practices of reading sacred texts in a sacred way. Griffiths's work fits into the stream of recent literature that recognizes how

---

100. Griffiths, *Religious Reading*, x.

101. "[M]y interest in this book is principally in the modes of learning and teaching that most effectively foster the ability to come to give, to maintain, and to nurture a religious account. This is a formal question that can be answered largely without reference to the substance of what is read when one reads religiously, a question that is in most respects better answered without such reference." Ibid., 5.

102. Ibid., 74.

103. Ibid., ix.

greatly consumerism has spiritual implications. William T. Cavanaugh notes, "Consumerism is an important subject for theology because it is a spiritual disposition, a way of looking at the world around us that is deeply formative."[104] As books in general are casually picked up, used, and discarded, religious works too come to be affected by such an instrumentalist approach to reading. What marks consumer culture is not an attachment to things, but rather, a detachment; our shopping cart wheels are ever-rolling as we scurry onto the next aisle.

Although it is a wider cultural condition, Griffiths finds consumerist reading especially to be the case among academic readers in universities, some of the worst offenders of good reading, who, as part of the "institutional forms produced by the expansive forces of global capitalism," have contributed to the near-extinction of religious reading.[105] Griffiths gives a sweeping analysis of the culture that informs practices of reading in the west, as he seeks a way of religious reading over and against typical ways of reading in our print-saturated society. He calls the religious reader to resist a culture of consumerism bearing down upon her: "processes of production and consumption . . . dominate almost every department of life in late capitalist cultures like ours"; and so "[r]esisting such pressures means resisting much that is woven deeply into the fabric of our lives."[106]

In contrast to these pressures, Griffiths sets out some key characteristics of religious reading. As he explores reading across religious traditions and across history, he first redefines and broadens what it means to read. Looking at how religious works are formed, Griffiths probes the different ways literary works are composed, displayed, and stored, and he shows how writing is not necessary at any stage. Although in western culture writing is dominant, "compulsive users of writing that we are," literary works may be created, shown, stored, and shown again without the use of writing

---

104. Cavanaugh, *Being Consumed*, 34. Cavanaugh continues, "Consumerism is not so much about having more as it is about having something else; that's why it is not simply *buying* but *shopping* that is at the heart of consumerism . . . This restlessness . . . sets the spiritual tone for consumerism" (ibid.).

105. Griffiths, *Religious Reading*, 184. Elsewhere he points out, "Consumers treat what they read only as objects for consumption . . . [Consider] the consumerist reading done by professional academics in Europe and America at the end of the twentieth century: the attitude toward works implied in their practice is based on metaphors of production, consumption, use, and control" (42). Similarly, Wesley A. Kort argues, "The culture fetishes the result, the Book, the achievement of reading, rather than addressing the process, because it values . . . the commodity rather than the work." Kort, "Take, Read," 101.

106. Griffiths, *Religious Reading*, 59. Yet this resistance is a hard one against deeply entrenched patterns; as Cavanaugh points out, "Even the critique of commodities has itself become a commodity." Cavanaugh, *Being Consumed*, 70.

and without literacy in a narrow sense.[107] Texts of religious works may be learned orally and aurally just as much as visually; learning for Christians in Roman Africa and for Buddhists in classical India was "mostly a matter of ears, memory, and mouth."[108] Griffiths's definition of religious reading is thus inclusive of all manners of taking to heart sacred works: "Religious readers, paradoxically, need not know how to read."[109]

Central to religious reading is not reading per se, then, but rather, establishing certain relations, attitudes, practices, and understandings of the reader to sacred works. Religious readers recognize a canon of reading and commit to "some body of works as an endlessly nourishing garden of delights."[110] The response of the reader is essential, and two main responses to sacred works are making commentaries and anthologies. Anthologies in particular reflect ideals of religious reading, as in them religious readers create "sweet-smelling bouquet[s] for the present," words to ponder and return to again and again.[111]

Like Steiner, Griffiths argues that memorization is the key characteristic of religious reading; it is the ideal mode of internalizing sacred works, and through memorization the religious reader himself becomes textualized. Although it is arguably a lost practice in the west today, memorization of vast portions of religious works was done widely everywhere up to the sixteenth century, partly because of a positive view towards memorization and partly because of the expense of books.[112] Contrasting typical reactions of readers today to religious works, Griffiths notes, "The response of a consumerist reader to a work is to make a critical edition of it; that of the religious reader is to learn it by heart."[113]

107. Griffiths, *Religious Reading*, 34, 27.

108. Ibid., 181. Similarly, Marshall McLuhan calls for a return to orality in visual reading. He notes that "the hushing up of the reader has been a gradual process," as "we have tended to associate lip movements and mutterings from a reader with semi-literacy." Yet there have been attempts to bring orality back into reading, such as in the prose of Gertrude Stein, and the poetry of e.e. cummings, writings that are "carefully devised strateg[ies] to get the passive reader into participant, oral action." McLuhan, *Gutenberg Galaxy*, 83.

109. Griffiths, *Religious Reading*, 40.

110. Ibid., 64.

111. Ibid., 103. He notes that in Renaissance Europe, "cultivated readers then would have felt their reading to be lacking in some fundamental way if it had not involved the copying of excerpts" (105).

112. Ibid., 48.

113. Ibid., 132. H. J. Chaytor offers a similar contrast: "Nothing is more alien to medievalism than the modern reader, skimming the headlines of a newspaper and glancing down its columns to glean any point of interest, racing through the pages of

With such a focus on personal retention of sacred works, religious education in religious communities is a formative matter—the emphasis in learning religious works is on internalizing them and being formed by them. Griffiths points out how remarkable it is that in Roman Africa, Christians did not see any kind of literacy as essential to becoming a Christian; the catechumenal process was a process primarily of being personally engaged with the deep truths of the Christian faith as expressed in its sacred writings. Those works were reread in order to be re-lived.

Griffiths's work is engaging and challenging—definitely not light reading. Most probing is his criticism of consumerism as he proposes it as a principal factor (if not *the* principal factor) that has led religious reading astray in the western world: we are too caught up in a pattern of production and consumption to read beyond ourselves. Stopping that reckless pattern is a near-impossible feat when consumerist pressures colonize our every moment. Griffiths's lens of consumerism throws into sharp relief the hectic, consumer-driven life around us, and the deeper spiritual life that sacred texts call us towards. (Consumers may be more complex and responsive than Griffiths maintains, however; see Michel de Certeau's contrary analysis.[114])

Yet in many ways, however, Griffiths's lens of consumerism has ended up revealing the same kinds of general reading problems as those uncovered by other authors who do not use a consumerist frame. Just as Lewis and O'Connor looked out on their British and American mid-twentieth century cultures and saw pragmatism and utilitarianism chipping away the popular ability to read well, so too Griffiths sees his culture's consumerism wreaking the same havoc on reading practices. His consumer language creates a neat contrast between religious/consumerist reading, but it essentially echoes the contrast of good/poor reading made elsewhere. Lewis, O'Connor, and Jacobs all characterize poor reading in such terms of using and exploiting, wanting a text to do something. The quickness with which Griffiths sees a consumer reading and discarding a work is the same kind of "using" reading that Lewis identified as problematic. Griffiths's constructive descriptions of

---

some dissertation to discover whether it is worth his more careful consideration, and pausing to gather in the argument of a page in a few swift glances. Nor is anything more alien to modernity than the capacious medieval memory which, untrammeled by the associations of print, could learn a strange language with ease and by the methods of a child, and could retain in memory and reproduce lengthy epics and elaborate lyric poems." Chaytor, *From Script to Print*, 10, quoted in McLuhan, *Gutenberg Galaxy*, 88.

114. Michel de Certeau, earlier than Griffiths, made links between consumerism and reading yet argued against a view of the passivity of consumers. De Certeau posits, "[The reader] insinuates into another person's text the ruses of pleasure and appropriation: he poaches on it, is transported into it, pluralizes himself in it." De Certeau, *Practice of the Everyday Life*, xxi.

religious reading are also similar to how good reading has been described by others—the lingering attention Griffiths posits as essential for religious reading is necessary for reading all great literature, as is the willingness to let a text do its own work upon the reader.

What distinguishes Griffiths's depiction of religious reading from other models of good reading considered above is primarily the aim towards which reading is done—Griffiths understands religious reading to be in service of being able to offer a religious account. Other kinds of reading may have similarities in practice to religious reading, but religious reading takes its reading more seriously; here practices of patience and attentiveness and care are of utmost importance. Within the context of a religious community and within a canon of texts, religious readers look to sacred writings to form their lives and give shape to their world. Such reading matters because it is woven intricately into its readers' lives. The end of religious reading is that it pulls the reader into seeing all of life in a particular way, with the reader emerging from his reading to live in a particular way.

As Griffiths sets this out to be the end goal in practices of religious reading, his criticisms of university reading practices then fit in somewhat awkwardly into his overarching schema. At the end of his work, Griffiths recognizes that with his "jeremiad against the pedagogical and reading practices of the academy" in *Religious Reading*, there is, in fact, "a paradox, at the heart of it"—he is an academic who writes from the academy and towards it, and is happy to have his lamentations against academia published by an academic press.[115] Griffiths allows for this paradox to exist, as he finds that the academy has still the virtue of being able to challenge its own assumptions. A deeper paradox is at work in Griffiths's jeremiad, however, one not as easily explained, which is that Griffiths perhaps creates too strong a dichotomy between religious readers and consumerist/academic ones. Francis X. Clooney, in a review of Griffiths's work, comments:

> Agreement would be easier had Griffiths aimed primarily at distinguishing between good reading and bad reading, practices that may occur both within and outside monasteries and divinity schools. Not all religious readers read well, and neither do all academics read disrespectfully, in haste, without passion, and with casual disregard for the deeper meanings of their texts. Scholars are often deeply engaged in the texts they study, and even secular scholars often read with a kind of religious intensity.[116]

---

115. Griffiths, *Religious Reading*, 188.
116. Clooney, "Review of *Religious Reading*," 299.

In identifying consumerist reading with academic reading, Griffiths ends up both being unfair to academics and confusing his definition of religious reading. Religious reading is done to be able to offer a religious account, he claims; how then might religious reading work in an academic context? Must anthropologists and physicists and theologians alike read everything for the purpose of shaping their souls? It seems what Griffiths is after is for the characteristics of religious reading (such as attentiveness, slowness, receptivity, wonder) to mark academic work, but true religious reading, the kind for the purpose of shaping one's life—the kind of reading that memorizes and chews upon works—is not the goal in all reading in academia. And, as Clooney points out, while academia as a whole may have some serious reading problems, individual academics within are still reading deeply with attention and wonder towards their works.

It is hard to place Griffiths's recommendations in the context of academic reading, then, as the kind of reading he calls for is one that would be helpful and fitting for many types of reading, both secular and sacred. The essential difference that seems to exist between reading well and reading religiously is its end purpose and intensity—religious reading is for the sake of becoming more religious, and so its reading is to be more deeply internalized. Texts are memorized and ruminated upon, their words ever before and within the reader. Griffiths assumes there is an essentially different relationship of a reader to a sacred work than to a non-sacred one, but what is left unexplored is how that difference of relationship is established and upheld.

What is needed to understand that difference is to look more into the particulars of each religion, as the content of a religion's beliefs and texts shapes how its practitioners understand its religious texts to operate in their lives. How the particularity of a religion's beliefs might have bearing on its approach to reading is left unprobed by Griffiths, though in a later article he wrote on the nature of spiritual reading, he states more explicitly that Christians might work out the meaning of reading from their faith—the Christian tradition "might have something to teach us about what intellectual work is and how best to do it, and thus also about how best to form in our students and ourselves the habits proper to such work."[117] It is this look into the religious tradition to see how its reading and studying might best function that I am after, as the Christian tradition gives a wider framework for the practices of its reading, particularly for its reading of Scripture. Griffiths's work, while illuminating, thus can only be carried so far to understand Christian practices of reading, for as recent literary theory has shown, beliefs about the purposes of reading are expressed in the very ways that

---

117. Griffiths, "Reading as a Spiritual Discipline," 36.

texts are picked up. A Buddhist belief in the possibility of enlightenment, for example, gives a different slant to the practice of reading than a Christian belief in the fallenness of humankind, irredeemable without the grace of the triune God at work. A good Christian reading of the Bible thus will be formed not only from an understanding of what it means to read literature well or even sacred texts well, but even more so, from an understanding of the God it seeks in all its reading. It is this Christian understanding of God and his work in biblical reading that I pursue in the following two chapters, via Barth and de Lubac.

Without End

Just as the making of books has no end, so too it seems there is no end to the manners in which those books are read. In each time and place reading acquires new means and new meanings, yet the same basic concern seems ever to crop up, seen here from F. D. Maurice to Paul Griffiths—how to read well? Although the practice of reading great literature is not thought of as a spiritual practice (at least, to most readers), it nonetheless has a spiritual aspect to it; reading leads readers into encountering others and the mysteries of life and of God. And this pathway to encountering such mysteries is a still an unpaved one, despite its well-trodden way. Maurice offers an explanation of how it is that books may point to such wonders:

> I have detained you far too long in endeavoring to show you how every true book exhibits to us some man, from whose mind its thoughts have issued, and with whom it brings us acquainted. May I add this one word in conclusion?—that I believe all books may do that for us, because there is one Book which, besides bringing into clearness and distinctiveness a number of men of different ages from the creation downwards, brings before us one Friend, the chief and centre of all, who is called there *The Son of Man*.[118]

It may be, then, that the making and reading of books has no end because books are being used (in ever mysterious ways) to point us to One without end.

---

118. Maurice, *Friendship of Books*, 31.

CHAPTER 4

Karl Barth and the Reality of God in Scripture

IN THE SUMMER OF 1916, Karl Barth sat under an apple tree with the book of Romans, striving to hear its words anew.[1] More than just the summer breeze came upon him then; something peculiar began to happen as he was reading and exegeting Paul's epistle. Barth later told his friend Eduard Thurneysen, "During the work it was often as though something was blowing on me from afar, from Asia Minor or Corinth, something very ancient, early oriental, indefinably bright, wild, original, that somehow is hidden beneath these sentences and is so ready to let itself be drawn forth by ever new generations."[2]

Barth's experience is one that resonates well with readers of Scripture who too have felt something from it blowing upon them from afar. What Barth relates is an encounter with God through the Bible—in his reading of Romans, Paul's words opened up to the living Word, and Barth found his theology and his very life being changed. The relationship of God to humankind, and how this happens through the revelation of the Word of God, would come to be Barth's overriding concern in his theological career. He had set out to relearn his theology after the cataclysmic events of World War I, and had found himself indelibly confronted by God within and through Scripture; this was a confrontation he could never shake off but could only follow. The biblical witnesses pointed to something beyond themselves that he too strained to see.

---

1. Barth relates in a letter to Eduard Thurneysen (26 June 1916), "I sat down under an apple tree and began, with all the tools at my disposal, to apply myself to the Epistle of Romans." Barth, cited in Burnett, *Karl Barth's Theological Exegesis*, 265.

2. Karl Barth to Eduard Thurneysen, 27 Sept. 1917, cited in Burnett, 186.

Barth's impact upon modern theology is monumental, as he broke up existing theological categories and threw off methods of modern theology to work out theology from the starting point of a confrontation with the living God. While his legacy may be debated, Barth's ideas continue to resonate in theological studies, particularly within the recent movement of theological interpretation of Scripture.[3] Barth remains, however, a complex figure, not just because of the immensity of his writings, but also because of his particular style of theological discourse, and the development of his ideas over the course of his lifetime. In *Evangelical Theology* he likened the work of theology to the journey of circling a high mountain—as one travels one is ever catching new views of its object.[4] Barth, gazing upward and enraptured by his subject of God, can be an exhausting trail guide to follow; his theology covers much ground and often moves in surprising ways.[5] Yet in his writings Barth offers a theological journey that is heading constantly towards its object above, and it is a journey worth trekking along.

As I seek to engage the question of how Christians read the Bible spiritually, at the heart of this question is what it means to be confronted by God in reading Scripture. Barth thus proves a worthy guide for this project, as his emphasis is ever upon God. We looked at broad approaches to reading in the previous chapter, and now we turn to see how the Christian understanding of God and the Christian life might shape practices of biblical reading. Here, rather than attempting to grapple with the entirety of Barth's theological understanding of Scripture (a project well outside of the bounds of this work), my aim is to look at one particular aspect of Barth—his understanding of the relationship that exists between God and Christian readers of the Bible. To that end I will first briefly explain how Barth fits into my wider project, and then will offer close readings of two pieces of Barth's writing which are pertinent to this issue: §21 in *Church Dogmatics* I.2, and his *Evangelical Theology* lectures.[6] While much of Barth's writing is relevant to the question of the engagement with God through Scripture, these selections particularly reflect the way that Barth understands what happens on the part of God and

---

3. As Moberly points out, Barth has been seen as the "*éminence grise*" of the entire movement. Moberly, "Biblical Criticism and Religious Belief," 72. See also Madueme, "Theological Interpretation after Barth."

4. Barth, *Evangelical Theology*, 34.

5. William H. Willimon posits, "considering the purposes of Barth's theology, and its peculiar challenges, I do not think that anyone should venture to interpret Barth . . . without being a participant in the Holy Spirit-dependent task that Barth assumes." Willimon, *Conversations with Barth*, 4.

6. *Church Dogmatics* is henceforth referred to as *CD*, and *Evangelical Theology* as *ET*.

on the part of Christian readers of the Bible; they chart out Barth's path of biblical reading.

Barth and Spiritual Reading

A brief note, first, on the place of Barth in this project—as mentioned, Barth reoriented modern theology in many significant ways, pointing it towards its subject of God. For that reason he fits well into this study, as a concern to reckon with God is at the heart of the spiritual reading of the Bible. Yet it must be admitted, however, that in some regards, Barth is a peculiar fit into this work, as Barth is not the most natural theologian to turn towards for thinking about reading Scripture as a spiritual practice. Unlike other figures I consider, Barth does not speak of reading the Bible in terms of a spiritual discipline, or for spiritual formation or spiritual growth. Barth veers away from pietism, particularly, its participatory and subjective elements.

In part this springs from Barth's background, as Barth reacts against subjective and individualistic emphases in liberal Protestantism and sets out differently personal practices and experiences of faith, as he insists upon the agency of God. As George Hunsinger comments, for Barth "the human recipient's active participation in salvation by faith must not be conceived as in any way effecting the occurrence of salvation for that person." Barth holds that both justification and sanctification are solely through Christ; Hunsinger explains, "The transformation of our existence before God, whether in justification or sanctification, is not an immanent process within us, but is a christological event."[7] With this starting point and his wider concerns, Barth does not give a great deal of his attention to explicating in detail just how believers take part in the event of their sanctification.

In Barth it can thus be hard to understand the practical human side of reading Scripture. Stanley Hauerwas takes up a larger issue with Barth's ethics in this regard, arguing that Barth does not offer a resounding account of spiritual growth. Hauerwas notes, "By describing the Christian life primarily in terms of command and decision, Barth cannot fully account for the kind of growth and deepening that he thinks is essential to the Christian's existence."[8] Joseph L. Mangina, drawing from Hauerwas, wonders whether Barth "does not encourage a rather one-dimensional picture of ethics as obedience to the divine command."[9] Mangina argues, "[A] teleological account of sanctification is just what would seem to be missing in Barth's

---

7. Hunsinger, *How to Read Karl Barth*, 110, 119.
8. Hauerwas, *Character and the Christian Life*, 176.
9. Mangina, *Karl Barth*, 171.

thought . . . talk about capacities or growth in relation to God is excluded from the onset."[10]

Objections have been made to such a construal of Barth's theology and his ethics, however—notably, John Webster argues that Barth does indeed "see the anthropological consequences of God's covenant of grace."[11] As the encounter between God and humans is so central to Barth, Barth's dogmatics is a moral theology, as well; it reckons with the complex human response to God. Webster explains that the account Barth gives of divine and human freedom is

> dialectical rather than unilinear, descriptive rather than theoretical, spiritual rather than objectified. If this makes reading Barth a good deal more complex than critics are often prepared to allow, it also makes him a far more absorbing guide to the issues than others who are descriptively more thin. Here, as so often, Barth is a disturber of intellectual and spiritual peace.[12]

And so, in his dialectical, descriptive, and spiritual movements, Barth allows for the richness of the Christian faith. It takes imagination to follow what Barth is doing, then; as Hunsinger notes, "Nothing is more likely to lead the reader of *Church Dogmatics* astray than a nondialectical imagination."[13] Barth is able, as Mangina states, "to craft a rhetoric that is both resolutely non-pietist—and at the same time profoundly personal and self-involving."[14] In Barth's thoughts on reading Scripture in *CD* and in his later *ET*, this complex richness of Barth is evident, as even with his insistence upon God's activity, Barth leaves room for human response. Barth's strong emphasis on God's freedom and command in the Bible does not mean that he diminishes human participation in its reading—more of God does not equal less of the human reader. What Barth does brilliantly for the Bible's spiritual readers is to insist upon the primacy of God's activity and to place the Bible's reading

---

10. Mangina, *Karl Barth on the Christian Life*, 166. Mangina suggests there is more to Barth's understanding of spiritual growth, however; he finds Barth points towards the belief that "the God who summons human beings to obedience is also the faithful God; therefore the moral agent can make some reference to acquired history and experience." Mangina, *Karl Barth*, 147.

11. Webster, *Barth's Moral Theology*, 5, 8.

12. Ibid., 103.

13. Hunsinger, *How to Read Karl Barth*, ix.

14. Mangina, *Karl Barth on the Christian Life*, 31. While Mangina is still uncertain of Barth's ethics, he notes that others have defended Barth against charges of occasionalism. See, e.g., Biggar, *Hastening That Waits*.

always in light of the overwhelming reality of God. More than any other modern theologian, Barth makes the reality of God clear.[15]

Church Dogmatics I.2, §21, Freedom in the Church

We turn then, to the way that Barth grapples with this complexity of God's presence in Scripture in his *CD*. "How does God's Word come to us men in Holy Scripture and how does it exercise sway in the Church of Jesus Christ?" Barth asks in §21, roughly one thousand pages into his first volume of *CD*.[16] Although coming later into his work, this question has really been engaged from the very start, as for Barth, to do theology is to encounter the witness to the Word of God as given in Scripture.[17] When he asks how the Word of God comes to readers of the Bible, Barth is considering formally a presumption operating from the beginning of his dogmatics—for Barth, Scripture is always the primary mediation of how humanity might know God. It is, as Mangina explains, that the church lives and moves and has its being in the "one unified event, the Spirit-testifying-to-Jesus-through-Scripture-and-proclamation."[18]

Before engaging with §21, a brief word is needed on how this section fits into *CD* as a whole. Barth begins *CD* by setting out that the Word of God exists in a threefold form—the Word revealed, written, and proclaimed. The revelation of God (the revealed Word) is the presence of God to humankind, that which is known in the person of Jesus, who is now mediated through the media of Scripture (the written Word) and of church preaching (the proclaimed Word). Scripture for Barth can only be understood out of the

---

15. And so Barth cautions against taking his theology too seriously: "'The angels laugh at old Karl,' he wrote. 'They laugh at him because he tries to grasp the truth of God in a book of Dogmatics. They laugh at the fact that volume follows volume, and each is thicker than the previous one. As they laugh, they say to one another, 'Look! Here he comes now with his little pushcart full of volumes of the Dogmatics!—and they laugh about the persons who write so much about Karl Barth instead of writing about the things he is trying to write about. Truly, the angels laugh." Cited by Godsey, "Barth as a Teacher," 212. As Barth insists that his readers have a personal reckoning with God, Barth casts into doubt the merits of writing more "secondary discourse," as Steiner would say. (A challenge for this work!)

16. Barth, *CD* I.2, 666 (this is 1,155 pages into *CD* volume I as whole).

17. Francis Watson comments, "to regard biblical interpretation as just one among a number of items on Barth's agenda would be to allow the seamless garment of his theology to be torn to pieces." Watson, "Bible," 57.

18. Mangina, *Karl Barth*, 46. The centrality of Jesus to Scripture is deeply important to Barth, and Henri de Lubac's understanding of the place of Jesus in spiritual reading will be explored in the following chapter.

wider context of who God is and how he makes himself known. (As Rowan Williams concisely states, "[A] doctrine of Scripture requires a doctrine of God."[19]) When Barth looks at the Bible he sees it operating within the expansive work of God; its words echo an eternal Word.[20]

The first volume of *CD* is thus structured around Barth's concept of the threefold form of the Word of God. He comes to the written Word in Chapter III, "Holy Scripture," after a lengthy consideration of the revealed Word in Chapter II, "The Revelation of God." As he discusses Scripture Barth builds upon his earlier thoughts on how the Word of God makes itself known; the Bible is always understood in its framework of the activity of God. Within Chapter III are three section divisions—§19, "The Word of God for the Church," considers the nature of Scripture as a witness, then §20, "The Authority in the Church," takes up the relationship between Scripture and the church. In §21, "Freedom in the Church," Barth offers an explication of how Scripture takes effect as God's Word.[21]

§20, Authority in the Church: Scripture as God's Grace to the Church

A note on §20 is needed, then, to understand Barth's claims in §21. While §19 provides insight into the nature of the Bible as a human witness, §20 has most pertinence to the issues Barth will raise in §21, as he draws a parallel between the authority of Scripture in §20, and the freedom of Scripture in §21. In each case Barth is interested in what that authority and freedom mean both for the Bible and for its readers, and likewise how that authority and freedom relate to one another. Barth explains, "authority must necessarily be interpreted by freedom, and freedom by authority."[22]

---

19. Williams, "Historical Criticism and Sacred Text," 228.

20. As Bruce L. McCormack notes, "To say that God's Word has a threefold form is to make a statement with profound hermeneutical consequences. It means that the Bible *belongs* to the Word of God; that when we try to interpret without reference to its proper object, we falsify the nature of the documents that we would understand at the first step." McCormack, "Significance of Karl Barth's Theological Exegesis," xx, emphasis his.

21. Richard Burnett argues that §18 is important to understand the claims Barth makes about Scripture in §19–§21, as well, as in §18 Barth discusses love, that which is "one of Barth's most important hermeneutical presuppositions." Burnett, *Karl Barth's Theological Exegesis*, 208.

22. *CD* I.2, 666.

The Word's authority in the Bible, Barth outlines, means both an authority the Word has over the church, and an authority the Word gives to the church, an authority derived from the revelation of God:

> Scripture confronts [the church] commandingly as Holy Scripture, and it receives revelation from it in an encounter which is just as concrete and concretely ordered as that which according to Scripture originally took place between the Lord and his witnesses. It obeys Scripture. Not as though it were obeying some long-deceased men and their humanity and theology. But it obeys the One whom it has pleased to give certain long-deceased men, in and with and in spite of their humanity and piety and theology, a commission and authority.[23]

Scripture's authority thus consists in how it continually proves itself as revelation and calls forth the church's obedience. Yet as Barth understands this relationship of authoritative revelation and obedience, it is not one of force or coercion, but one of grace. It is in God's grace that he reveals himself in his Word and places that Word over the church, and so a struggle against the Bible "is really a struggle against the freedom of grace."[24] Rather than an "arbitrary attempt" to possess Scripture, the church is to have a "thankful reception" of it.[25] What God has done in the Bible, he has done in his grace to humanity. A biblical reader is to begin, then, with an awareness that Scripture proclaims and conveys God's grace.

Barth further argues that the implication of Scripture being over the church is that Scripture locates itself within the church and gives authority to the church.[26] He explains that the Word of God comes not to individuals, but to the church as a whole, and in doing so, it creates a particular "community of hearing and receiving. Those who really hear and receive it do so in community. They would not hear and receive it if they tried to withdraw from this community."[27]

Barth's emphasis on the church is an important point to grasp here, as later he will not always be as clear about the particular ways in which the church relates to individuals' personal encounters with the Bible. As the Word has formed the church as the proper community for receiving

---

23. Ibid., 544.
24. Ibid., 559.
25. Ibid., 578.
26. This authority is, of course, utterly contingent on the church "being obedient, concretely obedient, and therefore standing not above or alongside, but under the Word." Ibid., 587.
27. Ibid., 588.

Scripture, Barth insists that biblical readers must put themselves in the church to be able to read well. This foundation is beneath his following thoughts in §21, as the church is his basic presupposition for biblical reading. To read alone and apart from the church, Barth states, is dubious:

> We obviously have to ask whether here the Bible individually read and autonomously understood and expounded is not set up with the same sovereignty as others have exalted reason or feeling or experience or history as the one principle of theology? ... [A]lthough it purports to be a laying hold of the Bible, [it] is perhaps something very different from the obedience of faith.[28]

Barth maintains that readers "cannot possibly begin with mistrust and rejection" of the church and its confession, but rather, their "first duty" is to love and respect the church as the body of witnesses to the Word.[29] Barth does not pursue particular implications of the church for individual biblical reading—he does not, e.g., consider how the church shapes its members' expectations for reading the Bible through its worship and liturgies and practices and creeds—but Barth clearly recognizes the church as the necessary community for receiving the Bible as the Word of God.

While Barth's understanding of the church works well to relate the individual biblical reader to the biblical community, what is missing in his description is a recognition of God's freedom to use Scripture to reach one who is not yet in the church, or who has wandered from it. A reader who picks up the Bible in mere curiosity may, like Barth, come to sense something "indefinably bright, wild, original" blowing upon her from afar; just as the wind blows where it pleases, the Word of God is unpredictable in what it does and to whom it goes. The history of the reading of the Bible is fraught with examples of skeptical readers who are surprised to encounter God within its pages; Augustine was not the last to hear a command to "take up and read," as the Spirit continues to draw even the most unsuspecting readers into the pages of Scripture, to the life of God.

§21, Freedom in the Church: The Work of God and Humanity in Reading Scripture

After establishing the relationship between Scripture and the church in §20, Barth's concern when he comes to §21, "Freedom in the Church," is the matter of God's work in Scripture and individual believers' involvement

---

28. Ibid., 608.
29. Ibid., 590.

in that work as they read. Here is where the part of humanity comes into consideration: Barth holds that "a real co-operative responsibility" is taken on when Scripture is read; the Christian reader is the one "who through the Word and love of God has been made alive, the real man, able to love God in return."[30]

The rubric of "freedom" might seem, at first glance, a strange title for what Barth is after in this section. The way in which Scripture makes its readers alive and able to love God is an issue that might well be considered under the authority of the Bible, or its nature as a witness. Barth wants to be clear to emphasize the essentially free and uncontrollable and unpredictable nature of God's operation in the Bible, however, and so the matter of how the Word of God comes to believers in reading Scripture concerns not authority but instead the freedom of God as he works in the Bible. On the side of the Bible's readers freedom will mean something rather different, as will be shown below, but here Barth is primarily after a concept of the operation of God in Scripture. Barth has already established that Scripture is a witness to God and that it has authority, and so his emphasis in §21 is that the Bible works in its own freedom as God works in it in his freedom.

Barth's conceptualization of the Bible as an entity acting freely is thus really a conceptualization of the work of God. When Barth speaks of Scripture having freedom and acting, he really means the freedom God has to do what he wills through it:

> Scripture is itself spirit and life in the comprehensive and profound sense of these ideas—the Spirit and life of the living God Himself, who draws near to us in its faith and witness, who need not wait until spirit and life are subsequently breathed into the document of His revelation in virtue of the acceptance it finds in the Church or the insight, sympathy, and congeniality which its readers bring to it, but who with His own Spirit and life always anticipates the reactions of all its readers.[31]

A fundamental starting point in reading Scripture, then, is to understand its agency as part of the ongoing work of God, a work the Spirit of God persists in doing through all the many dispositions of its readers. Barth ascribes agency to the Bible only because it is part of God's work. This is an important nuance to grasp, as such emphasis on the God above Scripture keeps the Bible from being idolized as the Word of God in itself.[32] The Word of God, Barth says, is what the Bible is constantly becoming.

---

30. Ibid., 662.
31. Ibid., 673.
32. Watson explains this connection: "In the Word made flesh, God continues to

As Barth emphasizes the freedom of Scripture, he puts into perspective, then, believers' own understandings of what the Bible is and what it is supposed to do. They can know that the Bible is a witness, and that it is authoritative, but, he says, they must also know that it is also free, and is beyond all of the ways that they conceptualize it. Beginning in this light to explain the act of biblical reading, Barth points towards a kind of biblical reading that is open to the dynamic activity of God, and is constantly receiving Scripture out of the activity of the God of whom it speaks. The freedom Barth relates is a creative freedom; it is the freedom of God to call things into being.

Barth begins §21 with a clarification of what he means by "freedom:" as Barth understands Christians' relationships to the Word of God, the authority of the Word not only allows for human response but actually creates it;[33] God is the one who sets out the possibility of human response to him. As freedom is given by God, true freedom is not a life apart from God, but one bound to him; freedom is truly "man's real dependence on the God who has mediately addressed and dealt with us."[34] Scripture has its truest effect, then, when believers recognize its inherent freedom and respond by offering back their own freedom (which was given by God).

What all this means for the practical realities of reading of Scripture, and how this relates to the community of the church, is yet to be spelled out, but here Barth points out a fundamental reality of our activity with the Bible: the freedom one has in approaching it is something that is given. As believers come to read Scripture, Barth suggests a mindset in contrast to the ways in which they usually pick up texts—they are to read with a recognition that the ability and freedom they have in reading has been given by God himself, and only has its meaning in him. "Human freedom, like human authority, means nothing if the Word of God is not primary and basic."[35]

Barth understands the Bible as a living entity whose life is not contingent upon its reception by the church; rather, the church comes alive by it as God works through his Word. Believers do not bring Scripture to life, but come into its life. Barth suggests that the Bible is like a river in which the church is taken up into its moving flow, an image conveying the idea that the

---

speak with us, and the Bible attests and mediates this event rather than being the 'Word of God' of itself and in abstraction . . . It is in and through the human words of the biblical writers that God continues to speak the Word that was once and for all spoken in Jesus." Watson, "Bible," 61.

33. *CD* I.2, 661.
34. Ibid., 667.
35. Ibid., 669.

Bible does not just pulse through the church but truly carries it forward.[36] Barth's analogy thus calls for the church's faith—profound trust is needed to move the church's feet onto the banks of Scripture and plunge into its flow. (Yet Barth overlooks here, however, the ways in which the church must learn how to kayak through that river of Scripture, to maneuver through its varied currents and pulsing waters.) Barth holds the church's faith as the starting point of biblical reading.

With these opening thoughts on Scripture, freedom, and the church, Barth defines more precisely what is meant by the freedom of Scripture itself in §21.1. The freedom of Scripture, Barth explains, consists in how it has a unique nature, an unparalleled power, and a particular sphere of influence. His first point, Scripture's unique nature, receives the briefest explanation of the three, as Barth has already spent much of §19 outlining this nature (he explains that in all its human voices, Scripture comes together as a single subject witnessing to God in a way unlike anything else). It is the actual power of Scripture that absorbs most of Barth's attention in §21.1. This power he sees demonstrated in four ways—the first is that Scripture has used its power to enter into "the terrible dialectic" of all things.[37] It has put itself on par with the rest of creation. Yet secondly, however, Scripture's power is such that it has more power than everything else in the world put together. Thirdly, Scripture has power to make itself heard aright. Although each new language might challenge it, Scripture continues to make itself heard: "Nothing human is alien to Scripture. It can speak with original force in every language."[38] With this ability, fourth of all, Scripture has power in how it can change its form. It is not restricted to what it once was but it is always new and making itself what it wills. As Scripture has this kind of power, believing readers are led to realize that in their reading they must wait for the movement of God—"Only then do we realise that we cannot read and understand Holy Scripture without prayer, that is, without invoking the grace of God."[39]

Barth's appraisal of the power of Scripture leads to the last aspect of the freedom of Scripture he considers, its particular sphere of influence in the church. Here Barth considers again the connection between the church and individuals' own receiving of the Bible; he picks up his notion at the start

36. Ibid., 671-72.
37. Ibid., 675.
38. Ibid., 682.
39. Ibid., 684.

of §21 when he stated that believers are made the church through the communication of the Word in their midst. He maintains that in its freedom Scripture creates the church as a community of those who in all their different historical situations and dispositions and sins, are a people who hear the Word of God in Scripture. Barth wants to reorient the role of the church concerning Scripture—he argues that its primary role is to respond to the Bible and be created by it.

This is possible because of the message of Scripture itself. Barth understands the subject of the Bible is the gospel of Jesus, a gospel that tells humankind they are lost without his grace. And so, the freedom of Scripture consists in how it creates the church as those who have "the hearing of obedience, i.e., the hearing by which . . . they are bound to Jesus."[40] As the Bible is meant to bind its readers to Jesus, it has its fullest effect when they allow it to accomplish that work in them; its freedom consists in how it can make believers closer to Christ. In the hearing and being bound to Jesus the church is sustained, and so for this reason Barth is against any idea of Scripture being a deposit in the church. He fears that would allow the church to form a Christian outlook, ethic, view, etc., when rather Scripture is a continuing witness, constantly pointing the church towards Jesus.

In describing Scripture as creating and ruling the church, the activity Barth attributes to the Bible is really the activity of Jesus in establishing witnesses of him who continue to bear witness and speak to the church. The Bible is thus a sign of the ongoing activity and presence of Christ. Scripture was initiated by God; "far from imperilling the immediacy of the relation between the Lord and His Church, it constitutes the true immediacy of this relationship."[41] Scripture shows the closeness of God and the relationship he has sought with humanity. Barth's hope is that "inspiration will prevail in this relationship" and he notes that the danger of an "over-systematized and rigid" conception of the Bible is that the closeness of this relationship is jeopardized.[42] More so than any concept of Scripture, then, Barth is after an understanding of the relationship of God with humankind. He understands that in Scripture the freedom of God means that God is making a way for humanity to be with him.

After establishing the meaning of the freedom of Scripture, Barth turns in §21.2 to consider what this freedom of Scripture means to its readers, for

40. Ibid., 687.
41. Ibid., 694.
42. Ibid.

even as Scripture creates the church, its members must respond. In "Freedom Under the Word" Barth maintains that believers are made participants in the Word; they are made responsible, that is, able to respond to grace. "Response" is a key concept in Barth's biblical reading—for Barth, reading the Bible is always a matter of responding to God. All the particular stances and acts believers are to take on and do are responsive ones. The only real part believers have is to pray.[43] As Watson explains, in prayer "the possibilities of human action and interaction are negated and dissolved but at the same time affirmed and established."[44]

Barth understands freedom under the word to mean the calling of the members of the church and their posture towards Scripture. Barth's explication of their freedom has five points—the first two are that in the church one cannot be a mere spectator, and that the church's activity is to be that of subordination. Barth follows this with three points on the activity of the interpretation of Scripture—readers must first purely observe Scripture, then they are to reflect, and finally, they are to appropriate Scripture into their lives. These activities, as Mangina notes, are not necessarily sequential but are "moments within a single, complex act of interpretation."[45]

These five points of freedom under the Word are significant for grappling with the spiritual reading of Scripture, for here Barth becomes most practical in his thoughts on Scripture and offers a spiritual reading approach. First of all, he explains that believers' freedom means that they cannot be spectators (to be a spectator is perhaps one of the worst things imaginable to Barth[46]). They cannot stand idly by but they must hear and interpret the Word. Barth views Christian believers as standing between the biblical word and the world, and so he insists that all members of the church are to be biblical interpreters. They have an imperative not just to understand the Word themselves but also to proclaim it to others. This freedom given to members of the church is thus essentially a positive freedom, a freedom not *from* something but a freedom *to* something, to do something, that is—to interpret and proclaim the Word. Just as the freedom of the Bible was described as a creative freedom, so believers' freedom is also one of effort.

---

43. Barth makes a short excursus on prayer in his introduction to this section, describing prayer as "literally the archetypal form of all human acts of freedom." Ibid., 698.

44. Watson, "Barth's Philippians," xxxiv.

45. Mangina, *Karl Barth*, 48. Cf. Peterson's explanation of the fourfold movement of *lectio divina* as being a non-linear folk dance.

46. Hunsginer notes that one of Barth's primary rules is "No neutrality." Hunsinger, *How to Read Karl Barth*, 50.

Secondly, Barth explains that in this positive freedom believers have towards Scripture, subordination to Scripture is to be their constant stance. Exegesis, Barth maintains, is first of all about leaving behind our thoughts and ideas that muddle our understanding of biblical texts; believers are to place all their thinking beneath the Bible. Barth's rhetoric may be overblown here, and he recognizes that we cannot completely loosen ourselves from all our own ideas, but he makes this point strongly to insist that believers must learn to set their thinking beneath Scripture. Barth believes that when this is done, the Bible will set forth its own interpretation.

Once again this idea of freedom might be puzzling to modern readers. Subordination is rarely linked with freedom; readers of the Bible might envision their freedom rather to consist in how they can bring whatever they would like to the biblical texts. But the kind of freedom Barth describes is a freedom of travelling light—believers are freed from all the clutter of their minds and distracting thoughts. This is a freedom that has to be learned, for we are so caught in asserting all manner of things over Scripture that to subordinate our thoughts to it is near impossible. Yet Barth views believers' freedom under the Word as consisting in how they can allow the Bible to rule their thinking.

Barth's emphasis on subordination frees believers from their minds' clutter, but at the same time, his point comes to be further strained, in that by throwing off everything before reading Scripture, Barth does not reckon with what is to be done with all that has been gained through all previous readings.[47] The reality is that most serious biblical readers will become biblical re-readers, reading and hearing the same texts over and over again in faith. Can such readers not bring positive ideas to Scripture, remembering how it has already spoken, not exerting their ideas over the Bible, but re-entering it as ones who have trod there before and return again? Barth's concept of subordination seems to ignore this possibility, as he advocates reading the Bible in such a way that believers come to it each time almost as if they had never seen it before. There is an immediacy in Barth, a need for a freshness in reading, and while this newness of reading reflects the sovereignty of God (who is over the text, its readers, and its reading), and encourages constant reading of Scripture, it is ambiguous how such ever-new biblical reading relates to the lifelong process of spiritual growth. While God's mercy is fresh every day, it also calls its recipients towards further growth each day.

Barth then outlines how this kind of freedom of interpretation and subordination takes place concretely in the act of biblical exegesis. He sets

---

47. A point raised to me in conversation with Francis Watson and Walter Moberly.

out that three phases of biblical interpretation take place: observation, reflection, and assimilation. The first phase in the act of interpretation (and third aspect of freedom under the Word), is observation—believers are to try to hear and see biblical texts as they are in themselves, in their own historical, linguistic, and cultural situations. This point is related to Barth's earlier point on subordination, on leaving our own thoughts behind, but here the emphasis is on looking to see what is there in the biblical texts. The kind of observation, Barth notes, is similar to acts of other hermeneutics in general, but Barth traces a floundering of general hermeneutics, in that general hermeneutics does not follow the path of observation to its very end; it allows other elements into the process to color what it sees. Yet in Scriptural interpretation, in following subordination, observation is to be truly pure observation in that what is seen is allowed to reshape the very act of seeing. Christian readers find in the biblical world not just things that are different from what they usually see, but even more so, they find a new way of seeing the world.

The second phase in biblical exegesis is reflection, an act that is not totally separate from observation, but rather a movement of the biblical words into the thinking of the reader. Although readers are simply to observe a biblical text, Barth recognizes that we cannot have only observation; he notes that we cannot let Scripture "speak to us without at least moving our lips (as the readers of antiquity did visibly and audibly) and ourselves speaking with it."[48] The simplest biblical reader (perhaps even with a particular force) translates what is read into his or her own thinking. Our ways of thinking are then not to be disparaged, nor exalted. No way of thinking is particularly apt for understanding Scripture, Barth insists, but it can be made so through a free submission to God. It is only through encountering the Bible's Word that believers acquire an ability for it. Thus the scheme of thought brought to the Bible must be recognized as such, seen as provisional and penultimate, and left to God's remaking.

Finally, Barth understands freedom in exegesis to consist in how readers are to assimilate Scripture into their lives. "Exposition has not properly taken place so long as it stops short of assimilation,"[49] Barth explains. There is no "theory and practice" divide in genuine biblical exposition: "From the point of view of the biblical text and its object, concern about a so-called practice limping behind a so-called theory is not only superfluous but impossible."[50] Christians must be willing, then, for their lives to be reordered as they read

48. *CD* I.2, 727.
49. Ibid., 736.
50. Ibid., 737.

Scripture. By faith the Bible becomes the determining force of their entire existence—"for the sake of redeeming our life we abide by faith and therefore by this looking away from self and looking to Scripture."[51]

Christians readers' freedom under the Word thus consists in how they are able to relate to Scripture and have their whole lives made by it. Barth does not want to set out a rigid method of reading, for the freedom of God in the Bible overrides any attempts to chart just how it is God is known through its pages.[52] Barth will cling to this freedom of God in all instances of reading Scripture, and so the work of biblical readers is one of response to this freedom. The freedom Barth describes is one of first being able to come to the Bible responsively, taking up the task of interpretation and subordinating oneself to it, and secondly being able to read the Bible responsibly, taking up acts of observation, reflection, and assimilation. Barth posits, then, that freedom is about learning a particular posture and response. Although he could say more about how that proper response is learned and sustained, Barth's point here is to emphasize that freedom before Scripture is about faith, the "whole life as a life lived in God."[53]

Evangelical Theology

More than a quarter-century after he wrote his first volume of *Church Dogmatics*, Barth delivered in Switzerland, and then again in America in 1962, the series of lectures encompassed in *Evangelical Theology: An Introduction*. These lectures vary greatly in form and content from Barth's heavier works—written as addresses upon his retirement, they briefly consider the nature of theology as a whole, and emphasize the proper response of a theologian to the realities of God. While these short lectures touch only briefly upon issues *CD* considers in full volumes (and are far less commented upon than Barth's other works), their "sheer openness, simplicity and modesty"[54] is compelling, and they reflect well the maturing of Barth's thought, particularly the manner

---

51. Ibid., 749.

52. Eberhard Busch describes that Barth "refused to involve himself in a discussion which was purely about the method of exegesis and was not involved in the exegesis of particular texts. He thought that 'hermeneutics cannot be an independent topic of conversation; its problems can only be tackled and answered in countless acts of interpretation.'" Busch relates that in a letter to Gerhald Ebeling, Barth stated "[T]he question of right hermeneutics cannot be decided in a discussion of exegetical *method*, but only in exegesis itself. And I think that I can see that discussion of the question of the method *per se* now threatens to run into nothingness." Busch, *Karl Barth*, 348, 390.

53. *CD* I.2, 708.

54. Lewis, "Review of *Evangelical Theology*," 255.

in which his theology of Scripture grew. As *ET* speaks much about the situation of the biblical reader, it invites and rewards a close look.

ET is structured in four parts, with sections of lectures considering the place of theology, theological existence, the threat to theology, and theological work. Barth emphasizes in *ET* that God discloses himself anew, and so theology is to discover him anew and to be always a procession after God. Theology "can in no way become monolithic, monomanic, monotonous, and infallibly boring" because it is to be "oriented to the unceasing succession of different loci of the divine work and word."[55] Most of all, theology is to be centered upon the free love of God, a dimension of God often overlooked in theology, but one Barth presses for as an essential mark of theology.[56]

Barth explains from the beginning of *ET* that he means "evangelical" not in a confessional sense, but in a biblical sense of the Bible being the basis for theology.[57] Also, while Barth is focused upon the proper study of theology, much of the work of the theologian encompasses the work of any Christian believer, theologically trained or not. Barth explains in *ET* that "every Christian as such is also called to be a theologian."[58] His thoughts truly do apply to every Christian believer serious about properly understanding God, as for Barth, theology is not a discipline only professionals can engage, but is a work most relevant to the life of faith. In addition, Barth's description of evangelical theological work points most prominently to the act of biblical reading, because for Barth the Bible is the basis of all theology. What Barth says about how theology is to be done thus applies to the act of reading Scripture by any believer. As Francis Watson points out, in Barth's overarching theology, his "theological hermeneutic is at the same time an ethic of reading."[59]

Sections I, II, and III: Participation in Biblical Reading with the Spirit, Faith, and Hope

Here I will pick up pieces from the first three sections of *ET* that are most pertinent to biblical reading, before looking at Section IV in greater depth. Barth begins in Section I, "The Place of Theology," with a consideration of the nature of theology as a response to the Word of God. His lectures in this section are on the Word, the witnesses, the community, and the Spirit, and

---

55. *ET*, 34.
56. Ibid., 12.
57. Ibid., 5.
58. Ibid., 40.
59. Watson, "Bible," 65.

he draws throughout each lecture his overriding principle that theology is our being confronted by God. It happens as we hear, understand, and testify to the Word.

Barth's second lecture on the biblical witnesses focuses upon the nature of the biblical authors and suggests a particular posture modern readers are to take towards them. The biblical witnesses, Barth explains, are those who stand in a special relationship to God by virtue of the ways that the Word of God has confronted them. All theologians and believers are to place themselves beneath the authority of these witnesses: "Even the strangest, simplest, or obscurest among the biblical witnesses has an incomparable advantage over even the most pious, scholarly, and sagacious latter-day theologian . . . the biblical witnesses are better informed than the theologians. For this reason theology must agree to let *them* look over its shoulder and correct its notebooks."[60]

Barth offers a compelling invitation to learn from the biblical witnesses, as their confrontation with the living God is what modern readers are likewise seeking, and his rhetoric is strong to make his point. As elsewhere, his rhetoric might be too strong, however; Moberly points out that this kind of language of Barth may encourage "too undifferentiated an approach to the Bible." Moberly's concern is that with such rhetoric the wider concern of Barth (and even more so, other theological readers of the Bible) may be missed, for "unless those wishing to gain a wider hearing for a renewed theological engagement with Scripture are careful with their language and the nature of the claims they make for Scripture, their substantive concerns may well not be heard because their audience may be too busy reacting to and pointing out problems with their rhetoric."[61]

What needs qualifying at this point in Barth, then, is the extent to which any given biblical witness can correct modern theological notebooks. Are biblical witnesses not still limited in what they see? Could it be that even in being confronted by God, a biblical witness does not have that confrontation extend to the entirety of his vision? Even in seeing God, the "obscurest" biblical witness may not have all the answers. Obadiah knows the day of the Lord is near but he offers only one vision of its coming. And even Isaiah, while he saw the glory of the Lord and spoke of a royal descendent of David yet to come, did not yet behold the living Jesus Christ. The entire biblical

---

60. *ET*, 31–32, emphasis Barth's. This is a point in which Barth's principles and practices may not be in full agreement, for, as Willimon argues, Barth had somewhat of a canon within the biblical canon (rarely engaging, e.g., wisdom literature or apocalyptic literature): "Although Barth says he is listening carefully to scripture, Barth listens to a limited range of scripture." Willimon, *Conversations*, 43.

61. Moberly, "What Is Theological Interpretation?," 171–72.

tradition is needed, and a way to pull all the biblical witnesses together, and moreover, a way to discern how to match the perspectives of these witnesses with the present community of faith and the world. In other words, the church and its rule of faith are needed to listen well to the biblical witnesses in the world today, and this is where Barth might say more.

As Barth relates together the Word, the witnesses, and the community, he fittingly ends this section of lectures with the Spirit. It is the Spirit who creates each believer and calls the work of theology into being. All believers are made theologians through it, and the Spirit does not just enable theological work but is also the reality of that which theology seeks.[62] The coming of the Spirit is the end goal of theology, then, the presence of God that is theology's true end. Believing theologians are called simply and earnestly to pray, "*Veni creator Spiritus!* 'Come, O, come, thou Spirit of life!' Even the best theology cannot be anything more or better than this petition made in the form of resolute work."[63]

In Section II, "Theological Existence," Barth's lectures are on wonder, concern, commitment, and faith. Barth takes up the question of "how theology encounters a man . . . how it confronts him, enters into him, and assumes concrete form in him."[64] This question echoes a similar one at the beginning of *CD* §21 when Barth asks how it is that God's Word might come to us. Barth is ever conscious that God is in heaven and we are on earth, and so the problem of just how that bridge between God and us is forged is a matter he wrestles with his entire theological career. Always Barth insists that God must enable faith; only the activity of God can create belief.[65] Yet here in *ET* a new note is sounded, or rather, a stronger repeat of a note struck earlier, as

---

62. As Brevard Childs states, "The Christian doctrine of the Holy Spirit is not a hermeneutical principle, but that divine reality who makes understanding of God possible." Childs, *Biblical Theology*, 87.

63. *ET*, 58. Willimon notes on Barth, "Our fertile imaginations are not the key to biblical interpretation but rather the Holy Spirit. The source of any interesting interpretation is prayer. When it comes to making sense of the Bible, we are always beyond our own resources." Willimon, *Conversations*, 24.

64. *ET*, 63.

65. Willimon states, "In Kierkegaardian fashion, Barth saw Christ as 'the paradox' and the great 'divine incognito,' describing faith as a 'leap into the darkness of the unknown, a flight into empty air.' Perhaps his disappointing experience with preaching in Basel and Safenwil prompted Barth to agree with Kierkegaard that faith cannot be communicated from one human being to another; it can only be revealed by God. There is no access from here to there except that which is divinely given." Willimon, *Conversations*, 18.

now he emphasizes the importance of the personal stance of the theologian. In his first lecture in Section II, Barth understands that a certain posture is necessary to study theology, and his concern is to work out the existential marks of the theologian, what it is that characterizes him. Barth holds that first mark is wonder:

> If anyone should *not* find himself astonished and filled with wonder when he becomes interested in one way or another with theology, he would be well advised to consider once more, from a certain remoteness and without prejudice, what is involved in this undertaking. The same holds true for anyone who should have accomplished the feat of *no longer* being astonished, instead of becoming continually *more* astonished all the time that he concerns himself with this subject. . . . [I]n theological wonder it is a sheer impossibility that he might one day finish his lessons, that the new might appear old and familiar, that the strange might ever become thoroughly domesticated. If a man could domesticate this wonder, he would not yet have taken the step into theology, or he would already have stepped out of it again.[66]

Barth's words are beautiful and compelling, as the mark of wonder is often missing in university seminars and church bible studies alike. It is more the case that this kind of wonder only occasionally brushes past those of us studying Scripture. Yet for Barth, this is an unacceptable state of affairs; he argues that wonder must be a defining mark of Christian engagement with Scripture and theology as a whole. Wonder is meant to precede the smallest dabbling with theology and only to grow the longer and deeper that engagement. Just how this wonder occurs is a bit ambiguous, however; on the one hand, Barth holds that a detached contemplation of the nature of theology should lead to a realization of the importance of the place of wonder, yet on the other hand, that wonder is something that can only seize the theologian; she cannot attain it on her own. This is similar to how Barth understands faith as beginning in the work of God; Barth is working with an unspoken presumption that the activity of God will in fact create that sense of wonder in believers—wonder is bound to take place when they consider what it is they are doing in theological work. Barth views this wonder as what happens out of a true encounter with God, and so he connects that

---

66. *ET*, 63–64, 65, emphasis Barth's. As Mangina points out, the wonder Barth speaks of in *ET* is also pervasive in *CD*; see "God With Us," §57.1.

wonder to the primacy of grace—"To become and be a theologian is not a natural process but an incomparably concrete fact of grace."[67]

Concern is secondly the mark of a theologian, for the wonder is that which claims the theologian personally. Concern, Barth explains, is the manner in which the theologian recognizes that the subject of his work is deeply relevant to him. "Theology cannot be an easygoing (or even interested and perhaps fascinated) contemplation of an object."[68] We are made involved with theology; a theologian is one who is struck to the core by God. Again, the essential activity is that it is God who acts. Barth constantly links the theologian's existential state to the external activity of God. Concern, like wonder, is something that must come upon the theologian from without.

Applying Barth's thoughts to the act of reading Scripture, there is particularly a need for God to create that sense of wonder and concern in believing readers, for often a biblical text can seem lifeless and removed. Wonder in reading the Bible, and concern for its words being deeply relevant to our lives, is not a natural state of our reading. Scripture often seems too foreign and unapproachable for us to pick it up in such a manner. As Richard Hays points out through his reading of the story of the healing of the blind man in Mark 8:22-26, we readers of Scripture need Jesus to touch our eyes (repeatedly) to see what is already before us. "I fear that," Hays says, "most of the time, even if we have been touched by Jesus, when we biblical scholars look at a text, we see trees walking."[69] Barth understands that we cannot alter this state of affairs on our own, and so a change must happen in believing Christians as readers. In *CD* §21 Barth's interest was in the realities of God that make biblical reading possible, that which he described as the freedom of God and our freedom. Here in *ET* his interest has shifted to what must happen inside believers as biblical readers. Barth maintains that out of a dependence upon the Spirit, wonder and concern must come upon the reader.

What is left unsaid is what happens if it does not, however, and this is a weakness in Barth's argument, for he does not grapple with how even the most faithful Christian biblical reader can struggle with lack of interest or with complacency, or with sheer frustration in trying to understand difficult texts. Although wonder and concern are to mark the overall Christian life, and the Spirit makes that so, at times they are bound to be absent—some days simply see less light. Even a theologian whose eyes have been touched by Jesus can wake up to stare bleary-eyed at Scripture still. Perhaps what

---

67. *ET*, 73.
68. Ibid., 75.
69. Hays, "Reading the Bible," 7.

Barth might be clearer to distinguish between, then, is the *feeling* of wonder and concern, and the *reality* of that wonder and concern that surround the Christian reader. The spiritual reality of what occurs in reading Scripture is not always readily apparent to the believing reader.

A continual perseverance is needed in theological study, then, and so Barth explains that wonder and concern lead to the third mark of a theologian, commitment, which is where the part of believers begins. Commitment, Barth describes, is total life obedience to the living God. It is a resting in the sufficiency of God and knowing that believers are "God's beloved and chosen people, called as such to praise him."[70] What makes this wonder, concern, and commitment possible is faith, Barth's final category of theological existence. Although he sets it last, like the Spirit in the first section of lectures, faith really comes first and underlies all the work of true theology.[71] Without faith Barth holds that no one can become and be a Christian or a theologian: "[A] person who is not freed for faith will not be able to hear, see, or speak theologically, but will only display a splendid triviality in every theological discipline."[72] Barth's "splendid triviality" may (again) be rhetorically overstating the case, but he points to the kind of confused purposes when what is pursued in theology is something other than God. At its foundation, theological knowledge does not exist for its own sake—for some vague advancement of some general body of knowledge—but it exists rather for the continuance of the Christian faith. And so while a theological project pursed apart from God may yield interesting results (and there may be legitimate different contexts in which to pursue biblical reading), and while God may not forsake all theological endeavors even when they forsake him, theology's nature is such that it must ever be pulled back towards God. Faith is the end goal of theology, and theology serves faith by giving it ever-fresh orientation, for "Faith is a history, new every morning."[73]

The pressing issues that come against the work of theology and the theologian are taken up in Section III, "The Threat to Theology." Solitude, the first

---

70. *ET*, 95.

71. "Faith is the special event that is constitutive for both Christian and theological existence. Faith is the event by which the wonderment, concern, and commitment that make the theologian a theologian are distinguished from all other occurrences which, in their own way, might be noteworthy and memorable or might be given the same designation." Ibid., 100.

72. Ibid., 102.

73. Ibid., 103.

danger, is the problem of theology's isolation from the world, the church, and the university. Barth finds such isolation is in contrast to the essence of theology, which is a proclamation to the world of the grace of Jesus. Theology has a "missionary charge."[74] Doubt is the second danger Barth mentions—this doubt is that believers are never quite certain of God and must always work through what they believe again. Barth then describes the third temptation of theology, which is to become so engrossed with one's own theological efforts that God removes himself.[75] Our best theological work is useful to God only when God takes it up in his grace. "There is no theology which could live otherwise than by the mercy of God."[76] Hope is thus the answer to these dangers, and the crowning lecture of this section. Barth explains hope as "the present reality" in which theologians do their work: it is the realization that Christ died and was raised for them, and so their work is done in his life and power.[77] An understanding of this hope thus might encourage biblical readers, for it sets their work in light of Christ who is greater than all the difficulties they might face in reading.

In these first three sections of *ET* lectures, it is evident how Barth is setting out the course of theology in a different manner than in *CD*—although his overarching concerns are much the same, in *ET* he has turned his attention increasingly towards the individual Christian believer. All along his theological career Barth has insisted that believers cannot be passive spectators, yet here Barth sets out that the *way* they participate really matters. Perhaps in his increasing experience Barth saw a need to spell out more the particulars of participation: one encountering the Word must be a participant in the kind of manner that reflects that Word. Not just any kind of participation will do.

Barth's concern for the manner of a believer's participation reflects a broader hermeneutical development, as in his later writing he shifts his attention more towards the immediacy of a reader's encounter with the biblical text. As Watson notes, although in Barth's Romans commentary Barth

---

74. Ibid., 115.

75. "It does happen that the real relation of God to theology and the theologians must be described by a variation of the famous passage of Amos 5: I hate, I despise your lectures and seminars, your sermons, addresses, and Bible studies, and I take no delight in your discussions, meetings, and conventions. For when you display your hermeneutic, dogmatic, ethical, and pastoral bits of wisdom before one and other and before me, I have no pleasure in them." Ibid., 135.

76. Ibid., 143.

77. Ibid., 149.

made a distinction between what Paul said to his contemporaries then and what he says now to our own age, Watson argues that "In the Philippians commentary, *the disjunction between then and now has largely been abandoned.* That is the fundamental point at which Barth's hermeneutic has changed and developed."[78] Just as Barth dissolves his strong distinction between what Paul *said* and what he *says*, he also becomes more particular on how one must respond to Scripture.

Barth holds that it is not enough for believers to recognize God as the source of all theology; that recognition is to reorder their lives anew each day. Each time they pick up Scripture they are to be made increasingly more into the kind of readers they are meant to be. Much more than in *CD*, Barth speaks in *ET* of the manner believers must take up to be involved with theology. Their active participation is under the living God, the One who begins and sustains and is the end of all theological work. The Spirit is how theology is started, faith is its existential stance, hope in Christ is how it moves forward.

Section IV: Participation in Biblical Reading with Love

As biblical reading is the foundational work of theology, Barth points in *ET* to a kind of reading that is deeply involved, and moreover, involved on the terms of God. Barth's lectures in his final section, "Theological Work," consider what that involvement looks like. These lectures have most bearing to the matter of reading Scripture, as here Barth engages the specifics that must be done in the work of theology—acts of prayer, study, service, and love.

All theological work first is to be begun and carried forward by prayer. Barth explains in his first lecture in this section that prayer as "the first and basic act of theological work;" theology is to be "that sort of act that has the manner and meaning of prayer in all its dimensions, relationships, and movements."[79] (As he has said in *CD*, "Because it is the decisive activity prayer must take precedence even of exegesis, and in no circumstances must it be suspended."[80]) What Barth envisions in *ET* is that theological work is a room that has windows opening to the church and the world, and most importantly, a skylight above opening to theology's real object. Prayer is about turning one's work to God so that it might be done under him and become fruitful. Listening to God is the essential work of theology, and the work that is offered is to be a response to God. Theology, and the biblical

78. Watson, "Barth's *Philippians*," xxv, emphasis Watson's.
79. *ET*, 160.
80. *CD* I.2, 695.

reading that is at its core, is always to be a fresh and original listening and response to God; it is to be an offering in which everything is placed before the living God.

The prayer that is underneath Barth's thoughts in *CD* is thus brought to the forefront of *ET*—here prayer really matters in such a way that theological work is barren without it. Prayer as an aspect of biblical reading means that the reader prays (in some unspecified way) on each page of her reading, asking for the grace and the illumination of God; she constantly is drawn to look not only downward at the biblical text but also upward at the skylight giving light to it. Such a kind of biblical reading will call for a slower, more attentive approach, travelling through the biblical text at the pace of prayer. This reflects Barth's concern in *CD* §19 that readers "turn with all the more attentiveness, accuracy and love to the text as such."[81] Here in *ET*, however, what is made clearer is that prayer is not just tacked onto biblical reading, but it permeates it. Barth never spells out what such prayers will be, only that such prayers *should* be. In this context, prayer is more of a posture than a liturgical act; it is what settles the reader down into her biblical reading and meets her on every page.

Barth might need to make clear, however, that prayer does not inevitably lead towards good biblical reading—many sincere biblical readers and churches pray adamantly while they read Scripture and yet still arrive at misguided results. It is easy to deceive oneself in prayer and not truly be listening. A wider context of the church is needed in which to place prayer, then, as well as ways to judge biblical interpretations. However, while Barth could say more about the content and ecclesial setting of prayer, Barth has all along assumed the church as the foundation of theology, and for that reason he focuses upon particular activities of the church and ways in which it is often lacking.

Barth indirectly answers the objection that prayer needs direction in his second lecture that emphasizes theological study, that which is the second step of theological work. Barth pays close attention to the way that study is undertaken, for theology's place beneath the living God means that *how* one studies it matters. It is not enough just to study, but one must study in such a way that reflects the nature of theology: "The real value of a doctorate, even when earned with the greatest distinction, is totally dependent on the degree to which its recipient has conducted and maintained himself as a learner. Its worth depends, as well, entirely on the extent to which he further conducts and maintains himself as such."[82] The worth of theological

---

81. Ibid., 494.
82. *ET*, 172.

study depends, then, upon the spiritual growth of the learner. Learning of any sort, but particularly that of theology, is a deeply personal act, one that involves not just the mind but also entire person of the learner and the wider life he or she leads.

The way in which one conducts oneself as a learner is a key point, yet it might be strengthened by linking such learning more concretely to practices of spiritual and intellectual disciplines. Again, Barth needs to say more on the process of spiritual growth. Barth recognizes that there are good and poor theologians, but beyond emphasizing prayer, he does not say much more on how to move from one camp to another. Yet good and poor theologians—and good and poor biblical readers—are not divided by a fence but rather are points along a spectrum. A biblical reader is constantly travelling the road towards good reading. How does any sort of reader become a better reader? Spiritual and intellectual disciplines and virtues are certainly needed. As part of the Christian life, these practices and virtues are not picked up instantly, but are learned as they are lived into through being part of a community. R. R. Reno argues that communal spiritual disciplines must undergird the practice of biblical reading: "Only as we are formed by the common life of the church, her ancient teachings, her ceaseless prayer, and her patterns of self-discipline and mutual service, can we read rightly." He notes that today "spiritual reading gains little traction because the moral and ascetical practices the Father thought essential to the Christian life are now divorced from intellectual training. Who would imagine that fasting might contribute to exegetical insight?"[83]

Barth would likely welcome such spiritual and intellectual self-disciplines, but for his purposes in *ET*, these practices are left relatively unmentioned. After his opening remarks on the nature of the learner, Barth's focus in his second lecture on study turns towards the areas of theology. He maintains that theological study consists of a primary and secondary conversation—the first one consists of the voices of the biblical witnesses, while the second, the voices of patristic, scholastic, reformation, and modern scholars. A student of theology is to take part in both conversations, never neglecting the first, nor being so self-confident to ignore the second. As Barth goes on then to survey the various sub-disciplines of theology, biblical exegesis is put first as the foundational task of theology. While all aspects of theology are to engage Scripture, Barth sets biblical interpretation apart as the keystone act of theological work and the act that directs all following types of work in theology. In understanding Scripture both historical-critical research and theological exegesis are needed: the first

---

83. Reno, "'You Who Once Were Far Off,'" 180.

recognizes that all manner of contextual knowledge is part of interpretation; the second recognizes that Scripture must be interpreted in light of its nature as a kerygmatic text.

Barth then touches upon the secondary conversations in church history, dogmatics, ethics, and practical theology. Explaining the place of dogmatics, he opposes any concept of systematic theology, as such a formulated system is against the nature of theology as a response to God: "What should rule the community is not a concept or principle, but solely the Word of God attested to it in the Scriptures and vivified by the Holy Spirit."[84] When Barth comes to practical theology as the last sub-discipline, he views this work not as the peak or the periphery of theology, but rather, at the heart of theology as being the proclamation of God. Practical theology is the way this proclamation is carried out and it reflects the life of the community, and so it is to be studied for all of one's life.

Barth's concern with the life of the community of Christian believers is taken up in his third lecture on the next act of theological work he describes, the service of the theologian. Theology, Barth understands, cannot be otherwise than service or ministry to the Word, a service that is directed to the community. Theological work cannot be done for its own sake, then—service of God and service of man are "the meaning, horizon, and goal of theological work."[85] The Word cannot simply be contemplated; it must be attended to. The theologian is then to have humility beneath the Word, and never to try to control it or think that she knows how that Word is best served. The theologian must "reckon with the possibility that quite suddenly some minor character in the community (the 'little old lady' in the congregation, so well known to every pastor!) or perhaps some stranger might be better informed in a most important respect about the subject on which everything depends."[86] The Word is always free and believers cannot take for granted that their work is serving it; it is this mindset of service to the Word that constantly draws them back beneath it.

What service might mean for the act of biblical reading is that the value of a biblical interpretation depends upon the extent to which it can give life to the Christian community, calling believers to live the gospel. This cuts two ways—on the one hand, biblical reading gains its orientation not to an historical past but to a living present (though, of course, the historical context of Scripture is still key to this orientation). On the other hand, biblical reading, while spiritually formative to the individual reader, is also

---

84. *ET*, 180.
85. Ibid., 187.
86. Ibid., 189.

about more than the individual; the Word of God addresses an entire people of God. An individual Christian's reading of the Bible is to be likewise outward-focused, striving to serve others through her reading and the spiritual change it affects within her.

As theological work is pursued in prayer, study, and service, the most important element in all this, Barth insists, is love. Love is the concluding lecture in this section, and the conclusion of *ET* as a whole. Like the goals of the Spirit, faith, and hope in the previous three sections, love is both the ending and beginning of his section; it has been at work all throughout. Barth sets out that love is the goal of all theology:

> We must now venture the statement that theological work is a good work when it is permitted to be done in *love*. It is a good work *only* there (but nevertheless there with certainty) where it is resolutely done in love. Therefore, love alone counts. But love *really* counts. . . . Without love, theological work would be miserable polemics and a waste of words. . . . But as a *good* work it may and should be done in love.[87]

As he explains how this love is key, Barth distinguishes between the kinds of love that might operate in theology. An *eros* kind of love is a love by which a human seeks fulfillment—in the pursuit of an object, a human desire is sought to be met. Barth sees this kind of love happening when we seek out knowledge simply because it is interesting. This type of love will always be present in theology, Barth states, but what must be sought over that is *agape* love, a love in which one is free from selfish desire and loves the other for the sake of the other—to love "concentratedly, not haphazardly, ramblingly, or distractingly."[88] Barth maintains that theological work must be this kind of love, for evangelical theology, he explains, has as its prototype the work of God in the love of Jesus. What this amounts to is that "those who are occupied with theology are compelled all along the line to look beyond themselves and their work in order properly to do what they do."[89]

Barth began *ET* by pointing out the absence of love in theology, and perhaps this absence is most keenly felt in the act of biblical reading—not just academics but ordinary lay readers as well are often quick to criticize and interpret Scripture, but not to love it, and to seek the love of God through it. A kind of reading made out of love is seen as a nice sentiment but not an essential duty in serious biblical study; love is not always readily related to theological study. As Alan Jacobs notes, a lack of love is a problem not just

87. Ibid., 196–97, emphasis Barth's.
88. Ibid., 200.
89. Ibid., 204–5.

in theology but in reading as whole, and so love is needed to approach any text.[90] Yet perhaps more than any other book, the Bible requires its readers' love, as love for it is really a love for God, the community of faith, and the world. Such love, moreover, is bound up in the joy and enjoyment of God. Beverly Roberts Gaventa notes that too little enjoyment of God is evident in the church's biblical reading, and she argues that a proper Reformed approach to Scripture begins with the enjoyment and glorification of God.[91] Stephen I. Wright similarly argues, "If our chief end is to know God, and enjoy him forever, it is fitting that the texts through which he reveals himself should be enjoyed as well as studied and obeyed."[92]

Barth points towards this kind of passionate joy and love in theological work, a kind of concern that stretches past simply loving what one reads. It is an *agape* love for the other; it is not mere interest. It is not enough just to love the Bible, then, but believers must love and enjoy God in their very act of reading. What Barth is suggesting is truly a reorientation in *modus operandi*; he presses for the love of God and others being the spirit by which believers read Scripture and do all proper works of theology. Quite frankly, this makes them much harder to do; even knowledge and understanding are easier end goals of theology than love. Yet if what is sought in biblical reading is an encounter with God, believers must pursue love. To read Scripture in love is to encounter most deeply the presence of God in one's reading. He who is love is known most truly in love.

From Freedom to Love

In trekking along with Barth on his theological journey, it often happens that we come back to the place where we first began, but in this (as T. S. Eliot has so memorably stated), we know it for the first time. Barth's theology of Scripture is richly developed throughout *CD* and his other writings, yet *ET* particularly offers a retracing over the ascension of his movement; we see how Barth struck out and where he ended up. When Barth looks at Scripture and how believers encounter God within it, his understanding of the broader activity of the Word of God holds throughout his career, but what changes is the way he views readers as relating to that Word. Most significantly, what *ET* reflects is that Barth sets out the importance of the God-given Spirit, faith, hope, and love shaping Christians in all their theological

90. Jacobs, *Theology of Reading*; see previous discussion of Jacobs in chapter 3.
91. Gaventa, "To Glorify God," 107.
92. Wright, "Experiment in Biblical Criticism," 265.

endeavors. A work of God has to be done inside of them for them to be able to hear and read the Bible as the Word of God—they cannot be spectators because this Word is at work on them. More than just believers' freedom to respond to God in Scripture, their love is needed, for ultimately it is the love of God that meets them in the Bible. In *CD* Barth set out that believers' wills and freedoms must be remade by God to read Scripture, yet in *ET* he goes even deeper to emphasize that believers must be remade so to love God. And so prayer, study, and service allow them to come into that love more each day.

Barth thus comes to recognize the love of God as the determining force of believers' biblical reading and theological study. What needs to be further developed is just how that love takes root in reading Scripture—the faith, hope, and love believers must have are fruits of the Spirit that take time to ripen. Barth's ethics of reading needs further working out on the ground. A process of sanctification in reading is required, as the kind of reading Barth presses for is one that is the product of spiritual growth. We must learn to read well, and ever be learning. The hazy vision brought to the Bible is to be reformed each day.

What Barth might teach Christians most in reading the Bible is that they are always to be involved. There is no theory and practice divide; one cannot objectively set one's personal faith aside to study Scripture. In all our scrutiny of it—in the broadest historical investigation, in the smallest linguistic question, in the most troubling theological issue—our very selves are bound up with that study. All parts of our reading and study are part of our encounter with God in the biblical text (whether we see it or not). As believers seek God in Scripture, then, they are to read with the operation of the Spirit within them, the faith they come into, the hope they are given, and most of all, the love that comes from God. Just as God is entirely present in the biblical text, believing readers must also be entirely present. More than in his freedom, in his love God encounters us in Scripture, and so it is love that brings us to him.

CHAPTER 5

Henri de Lubac and the Spiritual Sense of Scripture

As KARL BARTH WAS putting the finishing touches on his *Evangelical Theology*, across the Swiss-French border the French Catholic theologian Henri de Lubac, SJ, was in the thick of his most monumental theological project, *Exégèse Médiévale*. De Lubac, like Barth, was seeking an understanding of the Bible that reckoned with its true subject and nature; yet whereas Barth went about that effort through dogmatic theology, de Lubac charted a course through somewhat dusty pages of church tradition. His pursuit first bore fruits in his work on Origen, *Historie et Espirit* (1950), followed by *Medieval Exegesis*, an extensive study of medieval spiritual interpretations of Scripture (published in four volumes from 1959 to 1964), in which de Lubac traces out the patterns and reasoning of hundreds of early and medieval biblical readers. He writes in this massive project not just a history of biblical interpretation—even more, he unearths ancient voices to guide again the church's reading of Scripture.

Henri de Lubac is, with Barth, among the most influential Christian theologians of the twentieth century. With figures such as Jean Daniélou and Louis Bouyer, de Lubac was instrumental in the *ressourcement* movement, reclaiming ancient sources for modern theology. De Lubac's influence was later felt in the Second Vatican Council and the drafting of *Dei Verbum*. His theological work covers an astonishing range of areas, from Thomistic theology and atheism, to ecclesiology and the history of biblical exegesis. As his student Hans Urs von Balthasar said, one "feels as though he is at the entrance to a primeval forest" when he comes before the more than ten thousand pages of de Lubac's writing, with their hundreds of thousands of quotations.[1] Yet more than just his prodigious outpouring of writing, de Lubac is noteworthy among modern theologians for how, as a Jesuit deeply committed to the church, he worked theology out of the continuing tradition of the church he was planted within. His was a theology intricately woven out of the past and present striving of the faith.

In this chapter I survey one particular area of the verdant forest of de Lubac's work, his exploration of the spiritual meaning of Scripture. In the previous chapter we followed Barth's resounding account of how God is involved in biblical reading; here we turn to de Lubac for his understanding of what "spiritual reading" means, and how it relates to the person of Jesus. Just as Barth makes the primacy of God clear, de Lubac sets out compellingly the centrality of Jesus for the spiritual reading of Scripture.[2] Moreover, de Lubac has a strong interest in the church, as he insists upon the historic continuity of the life of the church and the ongoing and fresh work of the Spirit of God within it. In his tracing of that work, de Lubac finds that earlier exegetes have much to teach biblical readers today.

Here I follow de Lubac's approach to spiritual reading through his work *Scripture in the Tradition*. Published in 1967, *Scripture* is an abridged collection of several of de Lubac's other pieces—the conclusion of *History and Spirit* (which makes up part one of *Scripture*), the fifth chapter of the first volume of *Medieval Exegesis* (part two of *Scripture*), and selections from volumes two, three, and four of *Medieval Exegesis* (part three of *Scripture*). Although I also consult those works directly (as de Lubac requests in his introduction to *Scripture*), and in exploring part two of *Scripture* I comment more widely on other sections of volume one of *Medieval Exegesis*, primarily I focus upon these pieces in *Scripture* because they make evident what de Lubac thought was most important in his scholarship on spiritual exegesis. Set together, these selections focus his concerns and cogently present his understanding of spiritual reading. In his exploration of medieval exegesis de Lubac offers a vision of spiritual reading that centers upon Jesus—through spiritual exegesis the church not only comes to understand the depths of Scripture and salvation, but moreover, comes to know Jesus as a living presence in their midst.[3]

---

1. Quoted by Robert Louis Wilken in his foreword to de Lubac, *Medieval Exegesis*, Vol. 1, ix.

2. Barth also places Jesus at the center of his biblical reading, but for my purposes here, I look to de Lubac for his understanding of how Jesus relates to the spiritual reading of Scripture, as de Lubac works through church tradition to insist upon Jesus' centrality for spiritual exegesis.

3. Brian C. Hollon explains that "spiritual exegesis mediates the church's ontological participation in Christ." Hollon, *Everything is Sacred*, 4.

Spiritual Understanding

We begin, then, with part one of *Scripture*, "Spiritual Understanding," which presents the early stages of de Lubac's theology of the spiritual exegesis of the Bible, formulated out of his study of Origen. While writing on Origen's interpretative methods in *History and Spirit*, de Lubac began to pursue a fuller study of spiritual biblical interpretations made by other early and medieval authors, and the broad patterns at work across these figures.[4] Part one of *Scripture* explores the role of history, the definition of "spiritual meaning," the spirit and meaning of the New Testament, early and medieval spiritual interpretation and its decline, and spiritual interpretation's prospects for the present day. In this section I will conclude my discussion with de Lubac's history of spiritual interpretation and its decline, and will wait until the end of the next section on *Medieval* to comment briefly upon de Lubac's thoughts on spiritual interpretation's prospects, as his final subsection in part one of *Scripture* summarizes well his hopes for spiritual exegesis.

Jesus and History[5]

History is where it all begins, yet history understood in a particular way. When de Lubac looks at human history, he sees it moving as a spiritual force.[6] Human events are not just cyclical, but are moving towards something. With this view, the history of the church matters: in its past are the energies that have shaped and sustained, and continue to shape and sustain, the lives of the faithful. As de Lubac begins with this explanation of history, he lays down at the onset a clarifying point: we would be mistaken if we "admired past constructs so much that we longed to make them our permanent dwelling" or if we tried to "slavishly" copy them.[7] The goal is not to repeat what has been done. Rather, being free from illusions of going back to the past, we might see just how much early exegesis has nourished

---

4. As he was writing *History and Spirit* in German-occupied France and was moving about from place to place, de Lubac kept a sack full of note cards of citations that he carried with him; those references that he could not fit into *History and Spirit* became the starting point for *Medieval Exegesis*. Accounted by Wilken, "Foreword," x.

5. The subheadings for this section are my own, following the order of part one of *Scripture* but grouping its subsections under my own titles. De Lubac did not use subheadings for the conclusion of *History and Spirit*, and his argument flows freely from one section to the next. "Jesus and History" equates to 1.1 of *Scripture*.

6. As de Lubac states elsewhere, "There is a spiritual force in history; by reason of their finality, the facts themselves have an inner significance; they are already, in time, charged with eternity." De Lubac cited by Wood, *Spiritual Exegesis*, 45.

7. *Scripture*, 2.

the soul of the church, as it is embedded in "the permanent foundation of Christian thought."[8]

At the beginning of his pursuit of spiritual interpretation, de Lubac thus finds it necessary to defend clearly how his exegetical direction is not a u-turn to the past. (He has still been misunderstood on this point, however, and criticized for supposedly setting back the church's appropriation of historical methods.[9]) De Lubac holds that in the past a way was carved out that the present community of faith can walk upon still. Such a view of the necessity of ever pressing onward in the tradition is linked to de Lubac's belief that history is significant in itself: the tide of events ever unfolding has spiritual importance.[10] Spiritual meaning is not an escape from the everyday happenings of life, but rather, it is an understanding found by living more attentively within the everyday and discerning its worth. As Susan K. Wood articulates, "De Lubac's mysticism is a discovery of spiritual meaning in historical realities. It is thus a mysticism of the incarnate rather than an escape to something otherwordly or disembodied."[11] For this reason, a simple return to how exegesis was done in the past cannot bring about a true spiritual interpretation of Scripture, as what must be followed is the Spirit's moving in the present day.

What de Lubac wants the church to recapture from the past, then, is its earlier posture towards history and spiritual meaning which so readily sought within history the spiritual sense of it all. Brian C. Hollon argues that "For de Lubac, spiritual exegesis enabled the Church to move beyond the external facts of biblical history in order to 'plunge into' the history of salvation through the same Spirit that animated it."[12] De Lubac looks to what the church did in its early exegesis to encourage the church to plunge in anew to what the Spirit might presently be doing. This nuance is an important one to catch, as it is the *impulse* behind early spiritual exegesis, not necessarily its methods, that de Lubac holds as having a lasting place in the church.

8. Ibid., 5.

9. See the introduction to the 2000 edition of *Scripture*, xiii. Writing recently, Susan K. Wood is sympathetic to de Lubac's work but is restrictive about the use of de Lubac's spiritual exegesis today; she classifies spiritual interpretation as "a hermeneutical method of theological reflection on the relationship between these mysteries [of the faith] rather than an 'objective' method of biblical study." Wood, *Spiritual Exegesis*, 144.

10. In arguing for a retrieval of patristic sources, Brian E. Daley has noted a need for Christians "to approach history with the conviction that God is present and active within it as its fundamentally real, although fundamentally transcendent, ground and source." Daley, "Is Patristic Exegesis Still Usable?," 87.

11. Wood, *Spiritual Exegesis*, viii.

12. Hollon, *Everything is Sacred*, 101.

In outlining the contours of spiritual exegesis in this section, de Lubac makes several statements that he will further pursue in *Medieval Exegesis*, and his most central claim is that Jesus is the cause for all spiritual interpretation. It is in Jesus that history and spiritual significance are bound up together more intimately than ever before, as the incarnation is a spiritual reality made known precisely through history. De Lubac posits that the reality of history and spirit coming together in Jesus is what prompted the early church to look at all history anew and seek out its spiritual meaning; the event of Jesus opened up the flood of early spiritual interpretation.

Spiritual exegesis of the early church, de Lubac argues, was not a clever game or unnecessary work, but rather, it was a practice that was needed to help first translate the Christian faith from Judaism to Jesus, and to connect the New Testament to the Old Testament. Christian faith was not handed down without any images or traditions, but rather, from the start it was linked to the Old Testament in a deeply intimate way. The way the revelation of God began in the Old Testament shaped the way the ultimate revelation of God came in Christ.[13] Jesus begins this link, as he breathed life into ancient biblical categories and made them "converge upon himself."[14] De Lubac's understanding of history and christology are bound up in each other, as the coming of God into history means that history can never be without spiritual meaning, for its meaning is in Christ.

It is obvious, then, how de Lubac's use of the term "history" differs from much modern usage. History for de Lubac is not dispassionate research about the past. It rather involves spiritual understanding and decision—e.g., this is seen in the structure of the Christian canon, as the Old Testament's books are ordered to point towards the New Testament: Malachi's promise of the prophet Elijah leads straight into Matthew's account of John the Baptist preparing the way. The kind of history sought in spiritual exegesis is thus not that of Israel's religious history, or of the origins of its texts and collections, but rather, salvation history. In this, the interest in "what really happened" is not in historical data and reconstructions, but rather, in how historical happenings are taken up in the wider happenings of God. Although historical events of any kind are constantly undergoing reevaluation (histories are constantly being written of the French Revolution),[15] spiritual

---

13. Our methods of categorizing revelation in such terms of before/after perhaps are out of keeping with ancient biblical writers, de Lubac suggests, for "[i]t may be that the mental operations of the New Testament authors transcend any such duality: simultaneously they express the New Testament by the Old and spiritualize the Old by the New." *Scripture*, 9, ft 12.

14. Ibid., 7.

15. Sandra Schneiders, explicating Gadamer, points out that the meaning of World

exegesis uniquely looks to Jesus as history's definitive turning point, a point still orienting historical understanding today.

De Lubac offers a compelling vision of history filled with meaning, but where he could say more is how the church's history has not always been a linear progression. He indeed recognizes this reality when he comes to account for the history of spiritual interpretation and its decline, and his project on medieval exegesis is aimed at reorienting exegesis in the church today. Yet more clarity is perhaps needed on the criteria de Lubac uses for determining what constitutes setback and growth in the church; more explanation is needed on how the church's movement towards Jesus is discerned in practice.

"Spiritual Meaning"

Having grounded spiritual interpretation as happening within the history of the church and because of the incarnation of Jesus, de Lubac proceeds to outline a loose definition of the term "spiritual meaning." He sets out that spiritual meaning is the meaning of Scripture concerning "the spiritual realities which, no longer past or future, eternally perdure."[16] The spiritual meaning is rooted in history but goes past it, reaching into the eternal significance of things. As this meaning is only that which can be worked out by God, the inspiration of the Bible means that there is more to Scripture than what its authors could perceive.[17] The spiritual meaning of the Bible thus moves past how the biblical authors spoke to the overarching, unfolding salvation plan of God.

Spiritual meaning, de Lubac explains, is essentially the meaning of Scripture that addresses the spirit of its reader: "this spiritualization is simultaneously an interiorization: in saying 'spiritual,' we are also saying 'interior.'"[18] Although all meanings of biblical texts, from the literal to the allegorical, come from the Holy Spirit, the spiritual meaning is that which brings the cosmic realities of salvation to bear upon the reader—it is that which arrests his or her soul. As this meaning springs from the Spirit, not from the human authors or readers of the Bible, there is no set method that is capable of making a reader of Scripture aware of that spiritual mean-

---

War II "in 2006 is different from its meaning in 1945 because its effective history is now part of the meaning of the event itself." Schneiders, "Gospels and the Reader," 106.

16. *Scripture*, 17.

17. Inspiration of Scripture means "that things signified by its words possess a signification willed by God, a signification that relates to salvation." Ibid., 14.

18. Ibid., 17.

ing; there is "no resource of the human mind, no method, no scientific procedure which will ever be enough to make us hear 'the music written on the silent pages of the Holy Books.'"[19] This point is key to de Lubac, as the Spirit's bringing out the spiritual meaning of a biblical text reflects the Spirit's ongoing activity with Christian readers:

> [T]he spiritual meaning, understood as figurative or mystical meaning, is the meaning which, objectively, leads us to the realities of the spiritual life and which, subjectively, can only be the fruit of a spiritual life.... It is certain that the Christian mystery is not something to be curiously contemplated like a pure object of science, but is something which must be interiorized and lived. It finds its own fullness in being fulfilled within souls.[20]

Scripture is thus understood as the Spirit sets it within the souls and lives of its readers. The spiritual meaning can be accessed only through the biblical reader's present openness to the Holy Spirit, and as it leads to a life of faith. This spiritual meaning is not a gnostic quest for knowledge, as knowledge in itself of spiritual matters is not the aim; it is rather the way to a more lively faith being truly lived.

De Lubac admits that his definition of "spiritual meaning" has ambiguity, yet he finds value in that. He is not after a cut and dried definition of the spiritual meaning of Scripture, but rather, a pattern of movement through Scripture that seeks the Spirit. What that movement might look like will vary in different texts, e.g., whether one is wrestling with a prophecy or a parable or a point of the Sermon on the Mount.[21] As we will see, the fourfold method of medieval exegesis was one way to allow for differing movements in seeking out spiritual meaning.

Such movements require faith that the Spirit is working in all of Scripture. Like Barth, de Lubac holds faith to be central—faith in Jesus is needed to see the Old and New Testaments as telling one plan of salvation centered upon him, and faith is needed for the biblical texts to be interiorized in the soul of the reader. As in Barth, this seed of this faith comes up a bit mysteriously; de Lubac does not explain just how that faith is planted. It is hard to see how it gets off the ground, and so spiritual exegesis can appear

---

19. Ibid., 19. Barth similarly argues, "[O]ne cannot lay down conditions which, if observed, guarantee hearing of the Word. There is no method by which revelation can be made revelation that is actually received, no method of scriptural exegesis which is truly pneumatic... no method of living, rousing proclamation that truly comes home to the hearers in an ultimate sense." Barth, *CD I.1*, 183.

20. *Scripture*, 20–21.

21. Ibid., 20.

circular.²² Faith in Christ is simply the starting point for spiritual exegesis, and without that faith neither the heights nor depths of Scripture may be explored. Just how much faith is required is not mentioned—perhaps what is needed for spiritual exegesis to begin is just an initial amount of faith, however mustard-seed-sized.

With such an understanding of spiritual meaning and its connection to the faith of believers, de Lubac casts the process of biblical understanding in different terms than much modern biblical scholarship. The goal is not to acquire an historical understanding of the Bible that will then equip one to go on and form a spiritual understanding of it, but rather, to seek the Spirit of God at every stage of biblical learning. A believer "does not study this salvation history as a historian, whose goal is to see the spectacle of events unfold before him; he meditates on it as a believer—in order to live by it. This is his own history, from which he cannot remove himself. It is a mystery which is also his mystery."²³ To enquire into ancient near east history is to enquire what God was doing within it. Spiritual exegesis is about seeking God in every stage of a biblical text's history and in every task of enquiry.

Here de Lubac preempts concerns of more recent scholars who also have sought to articulate their own personal engagement in studying Scripture. Brevard Childs explains,

> I do not come to the Old Testament to learn about someone else's God, but about the God we confess. . . . I do not approach some ancient concept, some mythological construct akin to Zeus or Moloch, but our God, our Father. The Old Testament bears witness that God revealed himself to Abraham, and we confess that he has broken into our lives.²⁴

De Lubac and Childs share the view that the Bible's history is their own history, the Old Testament's God is their God. Such personal claiming of Scripture and its story is key to spiritual reading; it is the awareness that one is already implicated in the biblical plot. (In Barth's terms, it is the awareness that one cannot be a spectator.) An understanding of being implicated within the Bible gives biblical reading a different slant than other manners of reading, as in reading Scripture one cannot choose whether or not to be personally involved. When one is in the church, the stories of the Bible are one's own stories.

---

22. Wood finds, "The solution to the hermeneutical problem is a priori, namely, revelation in the person of Jesus Christ. . . . The reasoning within spiritual exegesis is circular since it both begins and ends with Christ." Wood, *Spiritual Exegesis*, 142.

23. *Scripture*, 27.

24. Childs, *Old Testament Theology*, 28–29.

What is necessary to step into this personal and radical kind of biblical reading and living, de Lubac finds, is a conversion of the reader. At the "root of the problem of spiritual understanding" is the need for this act of conversion.[25] Just as a conversion is needed to come fully to Christ, a conversion is required for the spiritual reading of the Bible—a conversion that is a continual turning to God, a constant drawing near to him and abandoning old ways in favor of his. It is the process of learning "to recognize the inner nature of God, to appropriate to oneself God's thoughts about the world."[26] Such conversion is not a one-off moment, but is an ongoing process.[27] This insistence on the biblical reader's conversion has cropped up in recent theological scholarship (see chapter six)—John Webster, e.g., has insisted upon the primacy of conversion for reading Scripture; he argues that biblical reading requires a "hermeneutical conversion" for "[f]aithful reading of Holy Scripture in the economy of grace."[28]

De Lubac's conversion of the biblical reader is one caught up in this "economy of grace;" conversion in reading is something the believer never completely finishes but always strives towards. What sparks this conversion is left unsaid, however; it seems the eyes of spiritual reading are opened somewhat mysteriously as an act of grace. Like the faith that is necessary to see all of Scripture as pointing to Christ, the conversion bound up in this faith also defies neat explanations of origins. Conversion is a daily outworking of a deeper faith that comes from God; just as faith grows, conversion too is meant to grow, in a visible yet enigmatic way.

The conversion necessary for spiritual reading is different, then, from a simple change of ways. It is not a dead-set striving of human will, but rather, an openness of the reader to be changed and converted by the work of the Spirit. More than carving out a new way of reading the Bible, the spiritual reader is led into it. The activity of the Spirit is key, as conversion for spiritual reading is distinct then from any other self-imposed discipline.[29] Although

---

25. *Scripture*, 22.

26. Ibid., 23.

27. "[T]he entire process of spiritual understanding is, in principle, identical to the process of conversion . . . the expression 'passing on to spiritual understanding' is equivalent to 'turning to Christ'— a conversion which can never be said to have been fully achieved." Ibid., 21.

28. Webster, *Holy Scripture*, 87–88.

29. Analogously, David Steinmetz holds that a kind of conversion is necessary for all learning, from linguistics to law: "[S]tudents who wish to learn any subject whatever must be prepared to undergo a radical change in their customary habits. . . . The university looks like a cloister because it is one. Without self-denial, without conversion to a new and inconvenient way of living . . . no new knowledge is possible." Steinmetz, "Calvin and the Irrepressible Spirit," 96. While Steinmetz strikingly sets forward moral

it is difficult to see just how this conversion gets off the ground, perhaps that is one of its points, as spiritual interpretation begins only when the Spirit sets to work in ways beyond human searching. Eyes of faith are opened and only after can one trace inklings of how that took place.

What is most important in coming to read Scripture spiritually, then, is a continual following of the work of the Spirit. "We must, above all else, reproduce a spiritual movement," de Lubac argues, even if our methods themselves differ from those of earlier readers.[30] A recapturing is needed of the way ancient and medieval spiritual readers heard the Spirit of God speaking to them through Scripture. Early biblical readers held the postures that spiritual readers today too must learn.

The Spirit of the New Testament

After this exploration of the broad definition of "spiritual meaning," de Lubac considers more closely the role of the New Testament in creating this sense. De Lubac has argued that the spiritual meaning of the Bible comes only through Christ, and he goes on to explain that for the Scriptures to take on their true spiritual meanings "a new element had to be introduced, one which could not be reduced to anything which went before."[31] He recognizes that within the Old Testament itself there was a process of "spiritualization" at work, but he distinguishes this from the spiritual meaning of the Old Testament itself: "a *spiritualized* meaning could be obtained from the biblical facts, but it was impossible to obtain *the spiritual meaning* in the full and proper sense of the term."[32] More than a recontextualization of Old Testament texts, then, a reunderstanding of the entire story is taking place. Jon Levenson explains that "just as each piece of a chessboard changes the meaning and value of every other piece, so does each text in the Bible change our reading of all the others."[33] Spiritual exegesis indeed views texts of the Old Testament as changing in relation to the gospel of Christ, but in some ways the change is even more radical than the moving of chess pieces—a new end has been introduced, one that alters all play.

---

aspects of self-denial and conversion as a core part of intellectual learning, de Lubac is moving beyond even this, as at the root of the conversion of spiritual interpretation is a work of the Spirit that enables conversion to begin and carries it forward.

30. *Scripture*, 24.
31. Ibid., 31.
32. Ibid., 35, emphasis de Lubac's.
33. Levenson, *Hebrew Bible*, 104.

De Lubac holds that the connection between the Old Testament and the New Testament is to be sought by following the activity of God in Christ, as the bond between the two testaments is not in external facts but in the spiritual realities that encompass them both. For example, with the manna and the Eucharist, or the paschal lamb and the death of Jesus, their connection is not in "extrinsic resemblance alone, no matter how striking this might be. There is actually an 'inherent continuity' and 'ontological bond' between the two facts, and this is due to the same divine will which is active in both situations."[34] Apart from how things might appear to be connected, then, the real resonance between the Old and New Testaments is in what God is doing. At the center of that is Jesus Christ, the one who was the "mystery hidden from all prior generations."[35]

Early and Medieval Spiritual Interpretation and Its Decline[36]

De Lubac then offers a history of the process of the unfolding of this mystery, as he recounts the development of spiritual exegesis from its beginnings to the Middle Ages. He argues that there is "a secret logic" presiding over the process of the spiritual interpretation of Scriptures, starting with Paul and the author of Hebrews, and carried forward by early church fathers.[37] These interpreters drew the Old Testament together with the gospel of Christ as they worked out the spiritual meanings of texts from their literal meanings, and began to develop a hierarchy of meanings. It was Origen, de Lubac finds, who was the watershed figure in the early movement of spiritual exegesis; his interpretations sought to give a spiritual sense to all of Scripture. De Lubac admires how Origen "never studied the Holy Books as a pure scholar or disinterested intellectual. He is less intent on explaining Scripture than on illuminating everything by it."[38]

In the Alexandrian school of exegesis that developed around Origen, the emphasis was on a search for spiritual constants in Scripture, while the later approach of the Antiochian school focused on the manifest meanings of texts. De Lubac finds that Alexandria and Antioch were not in as much opposition as they often have been held to be against each other; the difference,

---

34. *Scripture*, 37.
35. Eph 1:9, Col 1:26. *Scripture*, 39–40.
36. 1.4 and 1.5 of *Scripture*.
37. *Scripture*, 43.
38. Ibid., 46.

he argues, is "less rooted in space than in time."[39] Yet the demise that Origen and his exegesis was to meet, de Lubac argues, is because the Antiochian school of exegesis left little room for the spiritual meaning of Scripture to be sought alongside its historical meaning. As the historical meaning was separated from the spiritually edifying one, the literal and spiritual senses came to be torn apart. For early exegetes, the two senses were not seen in such tension and put against each other. De Lubac traces a hazard in the opposite direction in later monastic interpreters of Scripture, in which the spiritual sense comes to be interiorized to such a degree that biblical reading becomes cut off from its social and eschatological context. Spiritual contemplation itself becomes the goal, and the ultimate danger in this, de Lubac argues, is a "narrowing of the dimensions" of the Christian life.[40]

While the Antiochians and monks may have set the spiritual sense of Scripture further apart from its historical meaning, spiritual exegesis nonetheless continued throughout the Middle Ages up to the sixteenth century. De Lubac identifies science and Protestantism as the two challenges that then rose to spiritual interpretation. Although the Fathers had delighted in difficult passages of the Bible, the church came to find the obscurity of Scripture as a reason to emphasize the place for an authoritative Tradition. Moreover, the problem of inerrancy stole attention away from spiritual exegesis, as increasingly, pressure was felt to explain Scripture. The disciple of theology, de Lubac argues, took, on the whole, an anti-mystical bias. He recognizes there were those who attempted to revive spiritual interpretation, but such efforts were clumsy and misunderstood what earlier exegetes were truly after; it is much easier "to side with the ancient than to recapture his spirit."[41]

Yet even though spiritual interpretation came to crumble in its original beauty and force as a way of understanding Scripture, de Lubac does not lament its decline as an era forever lost to the church. Rather, he sees a natural

---

39. Ibid., 48. More recently, Frances Young has argued the same, finding many common assumptions between Antiochian and Alexandrian schools. Young, *Biblical Exegesis*, 183.

40. *Scripture*, 53. John Milbank explains, "in accordance with the paradox of the supernatural, the movement of inspired reading is not entirely spiritual, or forwards and upwards. To suppose this would be to commit the *Joachite* error of spirit escaping from historical form: an error which de Lubac deemed to be especially heinous. Every allegorizing exegesis also points backwards: if baptism 'fulfills' the crossing of the Red Sea it does not supersede the latter, but in part can only be expounded in terms of the latter. For allegory to work and be renewed we are always returned to the literal— just as, for the mystical path to be taken, we are always returned to the social, political, and ecclesial." Milbank, *Suspended Middle*, 58.

41. *Scripture*, 60, 61.

process at work in the history of the faith: "Spiritual exegesis accomplished an essential part of its task a long time ago. . . . It would be impossible to restore it today in all its fullness . . . in the spiritual order it is an illusion to think that anything can be absolutely acquired, once for all."[42] What is most important, de Lubac argues, is to understand spiritual exegesis as a mode of the Spirit's operation in the earlier church, and to seek that same Spirit in reading Scripture today. Where that Spirit might lead is hard to say, as "it is impossible to give a precise definition of the ways in which the Holy Spirit will nourish the Church on that Word in times to come. Always faithful and always consistent, the Spirit is also always unforeseen."[43] Even though the history of spiritual exegesis is told as one of decline, its story may not yet be over, as the same Spirit is working in the same church still.

Medieval Exegesis: Volume 1

Carrying forward from his work on Origen, de Lubac continued his pursuit of the nature of spiritual understanding in his four-volume *Medieval Exegesis*. The fifth chapter of *Medieval* makes up part two of *Scripture*, "The Dual Testaments." As many of de Lubac's interests in *Medieval* are important for my wider concerns of spiritual reading, rather than limiting my comments here to what is found in *Scripture*, I will range across volume 1 as a whole and pick up relevant pieces of its wider discussions.

Synthesis and the Spirit

In his introduction to *Medieval*, de Lubac explains that he seeks to follow the thoughts, spiritualities, and wider "current of thought" of ancient and medieval commentators on Scripture.[44] Ancient and medieval exegesis indelibly shaped the Christian tradition, de Lubac argues, and he understands the nature of progress to be about the integration, not the elimination, of earlier thought. Again, he is not suggesting a full-fledged return to the particular methods of this type of exegesis (we should not "ensconce ourselves" in the past[45]), but rather, he finds that medieval exegesis has cast light on some of the most important aspects of the faith. In particular, a most vital element of the Christian tradition is made clear through it, in that early and medieval

---

42. Ibid., 64–65.
43. Ibid., 67.
44. *Medieval*, xiv.
45. Ibid., xxi.

exegetes had an enormous sense of synthesis—in the Bible they saw all the mysteries of Scripture and the Christian life as bound up together in the mystery of Christ. It is this "extraordinary powerful sense of the synthesis" that gives medieval exegesis its enduring place in the Christian faith.[46]

In *Medieval* de Lubac is working out again his vision of history, as he argues that the way to move forward in the faith is to follow the Spirit's movement in the present age. Synthesis is found through the Spirit. More so than just human exegesis, de Lubac is tracing the activity of God. He holds the sweep of ancient and modern exegesis in one view and concludes, "What has happened is the Holy Spirit has changed its outward trappings in keeping with the times."[47] At the onset of his work of *Medieval*, de Lubac displays an overwhelming trust in the activity of the Spirit of God—earlier exegesis matters not just as an historical fact, but even more so, as a spiritual reality of the Spirit's work within the church. De Lubac thus looks to the early church to see the ways in which they followed the Spirit. His starting premise is not, "How might we now appropriate early exegesis?" but rather, "How might we learn from the early church to follow that Spirit's present working?"

Discipline in Exegesis

Our entry into medieval exegesis begins with a poem, one coined around the early thirteenth century and picked up by countless readers of Scripture:

> *Littera gesta docet, quid credas allegoria,*
>
> *Moralis quid agas, quo tendas anagogia.*[48]

Articulating the fourfold way in which Scripture could be interpreted through history, allegory, morality, and anagogy, these verses by an anonymous exegete put into words how ancients and medievals approached the Bible. Such layers of the different senses of Scripture were a widespread feature in early exegesis and were seen as so classic that they were correlated to the great doctors of the Church—Jerome, it was said, had taught history; Origen and Ambrose, allegory; Chrysostom and Gregory, morality; and Augustine, anagogy.[49] Amongst a multitude of medieval exegetes, de

---

46. Ibid., xx. Frances Young likewise holds, "patristic study is most significant for the discovery of the inseparability of theology, exegesis of scripture and spirituality, an integration by no means apparent in the modern world." Young, *Biblical Exegesis*, 265.

47. *Medieval*, xx.

48. "The letter teaches events, allegory what you should believe / Morality teaches what you should do, anagogy what mark you should be aiming for." Ibid., 1.

49. This list varies up to the twelfth century, however, and in many forms, such at

Lubac finds the fourfold distich existing in many different forms, but in all its various manifestations it expresses the same sentiment—in Scripture there are layers of meaning, relating to both historical and spiritual senses. Although Protestantism would denounce stratified layers of meaning in biblical texts, for much of church history the fourfold sense of Scripture was an accepted norm. De Lubac strives to recapture the significance of this doctrine for the church, as he sees that the fourfold meaning has provided a framework of thought for generations.[50]

With the ever-present danger of the fourfold sense of Scripture being misunderstood as an unstable and subjective approach to biblical exegesis, de Lubac begins *Medieval* in 1.1 with a section on discipline, by which he means the accepted rules of interpreting the Bible, in light of its open-ended fourfold meanings. He finds that from its earliest beginnings there was in the fourfold approach a recognition that the truly pious biblical interpreters are the ones who respect the contexts of a passage of Scripture. One could not jump or wander aimlessly through the Bible; as Jerome states, "spiritual interpretation ought to follow the guiding order of history; seeing that many people who are mired in ignorance wander in frantic error through the pages of Scripture."[51] Spiritual understanding, while open to mysteries, thus has its own structure and order.[52]

David Steinmetz notes that "medieval interpreters, once you grant the presuppositions on which they operate, are as conservative and restrained in their approach to the Bible as any comparable group of modern scholars."[53] Moreover, this discipline involved not only the rules of interpretation, but also the self-discipline, morals, and virtues of the learner: "the person who seeks after knowledge must be very much on his guard not to neglect discipline."[54]

De Lubac makes it clear from the start, then, that rightly directed human participation is needed for spiritual reading, even as that participation

---

that of Bede's, only the Latin fathers are named. Ibid., 4.

50. Ibid., 12.

51. Ibid., 280, ft 16.

52. Moberly notes the problem of calling premodern interpreters 'uncritical;' he argues, "One of the most arrogant self-depictions of modern biblical study was to call itself 'critical' and what preceded 'precritical.' . . . [T]he great premodern interpreters were neither less intelligent nor less 'critical' than moderns; they were simply 'critical' by different criteria." Moberly, "Christ in All the Scriptures?," 94. Young similarly finds, "The difference between ancient and modern exegesis lies in the massive shift in what is found to be problematical. We have had problems about historical coherence; they had problems about doctrinal coherence." Young, *Biblical Exegesis*, 207.

53. Steinmetz, "Superiority of Pre-Critical Exegesis," 32.

54. *Medieval*, 281, ft 34.

is beneath the mysterious workings of God. John Milbank explains, it was "the patristic and high mediaeval paradox of the supernatural which de Lubac sought to recover: that which is wholly done for us by God, namely deification by grace, is yet also our highest act and as such properly our own—even that which is most properly our own."[55] In beginning with a section on discipline to explain spiritual exegesis, de Lubac commences with the paradox that the human is involved in the work of divine grace in Scripture. As Lewis Ayres notes, the Christian transformation is "mysterious because it is we who act and yet our acting here is experienced as the work of the Spirit."[56] Spiritual exegesis starts in this mystery and challenge.

De Lubac's description of discipline is moreover a challenging notion for the fragmented church today, in which biblical exegesis is often carried out in an ad hoc manner across diverse denominations, universities, and seminaries. An order of discipline implies an overarching order that binds the life of the faithful, yet the relevance of such an order to exegesis is lost among most modern mainstream biblical expositors. No longer is there commonly felt to be a need to submit to a larger rule of life in order to carry out biblical exegesis.[57] The discipline one submits to in exegesis is, instead of a rule for life, a methodology, with an historical-critical approach still attracting the strongest following, although its hegemony has broken down this past half-century with the rise of other schools, such as liberation theologies and literary readings. Such approaches have their own rules, yet in earlier exegesis, discipline meant more than exegetical rules, but that the reader set himself or herself within the sanctifying work of the church and its rule of faith. Diversity of interpretation was held underneath a greater unity of faith and mind, to which we now turn.

Unity in the Life of the Mind

De Lubac moves in 1.2 to the relationship of exegesis to theology. He argues that theology and exegesis "cannot but be one and the same thing," as one finds in the writings of early fathers of the church (such as Augustine) that

---

55. Milbank, *Suspended Middle*, ix.

56. Ayres, "Soul and the Reading of Scripture," 176.

57. As Sandra Schnieders states, "[E]ven among believing biblical scholars there are those who acknowledge the relationship between faith and the Bible but do not think that that relationship has any practical bearing on the scholarly work of exegeting a text. . . . [Such scholars] generally content themselves with a fervent avowal of their reverence for the text as the word of God but carry on their scholarly pursuits in a manner indistinguishable from that of the nonbelieving scholar." *Revelatory Text*, 12.

"[k]nowledge of the faith amounted to knowledge of Scripture."[58] More so than texts being explained, the mysteries of God were explored in early exegesis. There was "a unity in the life of the mind."[59] A theme that de Lubac will carry throughout *Medieval Exegesis* is that Scripture and tradition are not two separate entities; the unity of theology and exegesis in medieval interpretation is basic. Here Barth's concerns are detected; de Lubac too was seeking integration of theological and biblical studies, and spirituality, as well.

With a unity in the life of the mind, secular knowledge could prove to be helpful. Like Origen, medieval exegetes found that such knowledge could be used to explore the mysteries of faith, yet de Lubac is careful to define the nature of this "usefulness": "There are many ways of understanding the usefulness or relationship of means to end," he cautions.[60] The mindset of the medieval was such that beauty and truth were admired simply for being beautiful and true, not as being somehow useful to another end. De Lubac thus laments the starkly different nature of modern thinking, in that "our rude and clumsy pragmatism" reflects a "feverish preoccupation with utility!" We are fundamentally removed from the thinking of the medievals, for never did the church have "so many poets in her ranks as she did in their era of her history."[61] Concerns of Flannery O'Connor and C.S. Lewis are heard here—usefulness and pragmatism do not equal goodness. The love of beauty in exegesis more often marks earlier exegetes than moderns. Jason Byassee, in his study of Augustine, argues that for all of Augustine's limitations, "his exegesis itself is lovely, and it is more precisely aimed at the church's goal of reshaping persons in the image of Christ than ours tends to be. Even when he is 'wrong,' there is often a certain beauty to his readings."[62]

In his discussion of the relationship of theology to other academic disciplines in section 1.3, de Lubac relates how the study of Scripture ("librorum exercitatio," "lectionis studium," or "lectionis sacrae studia"[63]) was distinct from the meditative reading of Scripture ("lectio divina"[64]). A com-

58. *Medieval*, 27–28.
59. Ibid., 34–35.
60. Ibid., 36.
61. Ibid., 37.
62. And so, while the fathers had their faults, "their *telos* in exegesis is often right, precisely where ours is frequently wrong. They see exegesis as one of the tasks the church undertakes as part of its pilgrimage to the heavenly city." Byassee, *Praise Seeking Understanding*, 1, 3.
63. *Medieval*, 303, ft 55.
64. Ibid., 303, ft 59. De Lubac notes also on 305, ft 87, that "lectio" originally could mean the text or book itself, but came to mean uniquely the fact of reading, and then the act of explicating a text. Its usage can be vague even within the same author, however.

mentary on Scripture was not the same as a kind of reading by *lectio divina*, yet this study nonetheless was not dissociated from the spiritual life. All things were taken up for spiritual growth, as spiritual edification was the constant aim.[65]

De Lubac traces a shift beginning in the twelfth century when the reading of Scripture begins to be desacralized. Learning Scripture takes on a different bent during the beginnings of scholasticism, as some students "seek to be taught only with a view to making a career and have already begun with drive to achieve honors. They do not draw on the wisdom and simplicity of life to be found in Scripture."[66] The term "disputatio," which once was linked to practices of *lectio divina* and could mean the research/exposition/discussion/explication/ meditation—and even the "collatio" of spiritual conversation among interpreters—came to take on the tone of scholastic question and disputation.[67] In 1.4 de Lubac charts the even more definitive breaks mainstream exegesis would make from the spiritual life, as from c. 1000 the study of Scripture began to be relocated from monasteries to cathedral and chapter schools, which preceded modern universities.[68] In these places de Lubac finds that theology comes no longer to be oriented towards practices of spiritual living, though it is still bound up with exegesis until the mid-thirteenth century when questions of a scientific curiosity begin to proliferate and the dialectical approach wins out. Summas take the place of commentaries.

What de Lubac charts in this broad sweep of the history of spiritual exegesis, then, is a process of biblical studies being increasingly oriented away from spirituality, as the Bible comes to be studied first as a problem in its own right, and then as a part of a growing body of academic studies, and finally as a discipline separate from theology. The end result is a loss of concern to arrive at "a better discernment of the presence of Christ" in scriptural studies.[69] The wonder and humility that marked earlier readers is lost as well.[70]

65. Ibid., 48.
66. Ibid., 49.
67. Ibid., 53.
68. De Lubac is, of course, tracking church history in the west. William Abraham notes that when in the west theology moved into the universities, in the east it remained in the monasteries and was understood "as much as a healing art as an academic discipline." Abraham, *Canon and Criterion*, 69.
69. *Medieval*, 61.
70. Byassee admits that ancient exegesis can seem fanciful (such as when Augustine extrapolates the meaning of 153 fish in John 21:11), but this manner of exegesis nonetheless "offers a remedy against the malady that strikes contemporary biblical exegesis,

Scripture's Depths

After surveying these broader strokes of the history of the fourfold method of spiritual exegesis, de Lubac turns in 2.1 to consider the principle at the heart of this exegesis, the sense that Scripture has untold depths. Early on biblical readers saw the Bible as more than could be plumbed. Ambrose calls the Bible a "vast sea," echoing an idea of Origen, who sees such an image before him in reading Scripture: "it is just like someone embarking on a small vessel in order to sail the sea . . . it is something like this that we too seem to undergo . . . when we dare to embark on so vast a sea of mystery."[71] This idea would not be lost to the Christian tradition, as interpreters from John Henry Newman to Barth would pick up such imagery, likewise seeing the Bible as a land uncharted and unchartable.[72] Scripture's inspiration is assumed, for it is the active involvement of God in the Bible that accounts for its manifold depths and meanings.[73] Although modern literary theory has emphasized the endless fecundity of texts, what is envisaged here is far more than sheer literary power—it is rather the work of the Spirit of God that gives the Bible its depths and endlessness.

Although many meanings of Scripture may be recognized, de Lubac argues in 2.2 that there is a need to go beyond a hazy notion of multiple layers to the traditional structure of a threefold or fourfold sense of interpretation. He traces in 2.3 the various ways that such spiritual senses of the Bible have been explicated by medieval authors: sometimes a threefold sense of history, morality, and allegory existed, and other times the fourfold one. In medieval biblical exegesis these different orders exist simultaneously in time, and sometimes even within the same author. Yet in this complex multiplicity de Lubac discerns two most dominant patterns: one of morality preceding allegory in the order of senses, and the other of morality following

---

namely that it is boring. Not always, nor in all hands (for many contemporary exegetes have their own greatness that Augustine himself lacked). Rather, it is their premise that is so frequently dull. The goal of discovering the intention of an original author or redactors, while bearing an antiquarian interest that will captivate the few, cannot feed the many whom the gospel seeks to attract." Byassee, *Praise Seeking Understanding*, 131.

71. *Medieval*, 325, fts 10, 11: Ambrose, PL 16:738 C, 880 AB; Origen, *In Gen.*, h.9, n.1.

72. De Lubac quotes Newman's striking description: "(Scripture) cannot, as it were, be mapped, or its contents catalogued; but after all our diligence, to the end of our lives and to the end of the Church, it must be an unexplored and unsubdued land, with heights and valleys, forests and streams, on the right and left of our path and close about us, full of concealed wonders and choice treasures." *Medieval*, 80. Compare also Barth's essay "The Strange New World Within the Bible," in which Barth speaks of a wondrous world within the Bible, an unending country. Barth, *Word of God*.

73. *Medieval*, 81.

allegory. As he argues in 2.5, the order in which the different senses are given is not without consequence; he finds the second formula of history-allegory-morality-anagogy is the most frequent and argues it is the one that "yields the true formula" of spiritual exegesis.[74]

De Lubac defends this argument by moving in his third chapter to trace patristic origins for the fourfold sense with allegory preceding morality.[75] The fountainhead of medieval exegesis, de Lubac argues, is the profound yet controversial Origen. Origen, he argues, went beyond the age of his time, as he did not merely replicate the allegorizing approaches of Philo, but oriented all biblical exegesis to the mystery of Christ: "It is this mystery that he always presupposes. It is from this mystery that all his 'mysticism' springs ... Jewish exegesis is really and truly surpassed, since what is at stake now is a new principle which owes nothing to it."[76] Most church fathers after Origen copied his commentaries, even those who were opposed to his thinking; Origen was "one of the foremost educators of the Latin Middle Ages."[77] In chapter 4 de Lubac accounts for Origen's wide reading in the Latin world, with Origen "copied, summarized, amplified, adapted, or plagiarized, sometimes in the most massive way."[78] Origen's exegetical and homiletical principles were found everywhere, which makes it all the more perplexing that he was labeled a heretic. De Lubac thus wonders, "How, therefore, are we to understand that so faithful an interpreter of all the Scriptures had at the same time corrupted them, to the point of becoming a heterodox purveyor of doctrine?"[79] The history of spiritual exegesis is itself full of mysteries.

---

74. Ibid., 115.

75. Augustine is strong a candidate for its beginning, but de Lubac finds Augustine's understanding of a fourfold interpretation has to do with different genres of texts within Scripture, not with different senses within texts themselves. Augustine's concern is to defend the place of the Old Testament and so allegory is its saving device; just as for other early writers like Junilius the African, the fourfold sense means for him the four kinds of texts within the Bible as a whole. *Medieval*, 124-127. The boundary between the four types of biblical texts and four senses of a text was a blurry one, however, and Gregory the Great bridged the two meanings as "one of the principal initiators and one of the greatest patrons of the medieval doctrine of the fourfold sense." Ibid., 134.

76. Ibid., 150. In contrast, Young argues that Origen was much more a child of his time, as Origen built "an alternative paideia based on the alternative biblical literature, pirating all the methods used in the Hellenistic schools for the exegesis of barbarian books." Young, *Biblical Exegesis*, 285.

77. *Medieval*, 159.

78. Ibid., 161, 167. De Lubac traces how Bernard of Clairvaux takes inspiration from Origen and even preaches like him. Gregory and Bede likewise drew from Origen. *Medieval*, 167-68.

79. *Medieval*, 198.

Jesus as Unifying Event

After a lengthy coverage of Origen's influence, de Lubac moves in chapter 5 to explain the unity of the two testaments as the core of spiritual exegesis. He starts 5.1 with a recapitulation: "To summarize the whole thing briefly: the Christian tradition understands that Scripture has two meanings, The most general name for these two meanings is the literal and the spiritual ("pneumatic") meanings, and these two meanings have the same kind of relationship to each other as do the Old and New Testaments to each other."[80] Here de Lubac reaches the crux of his argument in setting out Jesus as the defining element of spiritual interpretation. Everything in Scripture is spiritual, de Lubac argues, and its purpose is to engender spiritual joy and living, but in this process Christ is the essential element. All talk of spiritual edification through reading texts is no different from uses of Scripture in other "religions of the book" until Jesus enters in. In the way the New Testament testifies to the present reality of Jesus, the New Testament is not just new in time, but new in its essence. After the advent of Jesus, the Old Testament can only exist in relation to him, and thus the believer can only read the Old Testament in its relationship to the New Testament.[81] A break happened with the coming of Jesus; the Fathers saw Jesus not as one moment in a line of happenings, but as the eternal instant, the unique *kairos* who reoriented all happenings.[82]

In 5.2 de Lubac explains the coming of Jesus as more definitive than any other development in history: "Even if there were several transitions, there was only one transition, however, the final one, which forever merits the name 'Easter.'"[83] The result of this is that all biblical reality, as part of human history, has Christ for its end. "Scripture leads us to him, and when we reach this end, we no longer have to look for anything beyond it."[84] Moreover, Jesus is both the exegesis of Scripture and its exegete, as his presence is discerned in the Bible only through his presence today. Again, de Lubac has a similar concern as Barth, for it is the present action of God that makes the Bible the living Word.

The harmony of the two testaments is taken up in 5.3, where de Lubac argues that both testaments lay unsearchable wonders before the reader. A belief in the unity of the Scriptures preceded the establishment of a set canon, as exegetes saw the writings of the Bible existing together as one great

---

80. Ibid., 225, emphasis de Lubac's.
81. Ibid., 227–28.
82. Ibid., 233.
83. Ibid., 235.
84. Ibid., 237.

library telling of Christ.[85] In 5.4 de Lubac again identifies the necessity of a conversion to come to such a view of the Bible; spiritual understanding requires an existential faith commitment: "Christian exegesis is an exegesis in faith . . . it is an act of faith in the great historical Act that has never had and never will have its equal: for the Incarnation is unique."[86]

At the end of chapter 5, de Lubac concludes that the gospel must be received in faith for spiritual exegesis to take place. Spiritual understanding is essentially not a matter of intellect or technique, but it "depends on the illumination, which can only be given from on high."[87] A starting point of faith is necessary for the ending point of spiritual exegesis, as its aim is not better historical knowledge, but better spiritual edification. Yet this goal of spiritual edification is not in opposition to modern exegetical methods, de Lubac insists, for there is a need to be both learned and spiritual readers: "we need both the learned in order to help us read Scripture historically, and the spiritual men (who ought to be 'men of the Church') in order to help us arrive at a deeper spiritual understanding of it."[88] Learning is needed for spiritual exegesis, but learning that is rightly directed towards the life of faith.

The Christian Newness

What de Lubac begins in his first volume of *Medieval Exegesis* is filled in with intricate detail in his following three volumes, which offer focused studies on each of the four senses of spiritual interpretation, as well on key figures and historical developments. De Lubac's theological writing is similar in style to Barth's in that he too often circles around his issue, coming at it from different angles to see each of its facets. As he progresses through a history of medieval exegesis, he does so through its themes, drawing each part into the whole and the whole into each part. The pieces selected for the third section of *Scripture*, "The Christian Newness," recapitulate some of de Lubac's central arguments—there he argues that Jesus is what sets apart Christian exegesis; there is a Christian dialectical relationship to the Old Testament; Jesus brings all things in Scripture together; allegory is about heading more into the mystery of Christ; and that the four meanings of the Bible are unified in the organic whole of the spiritual life. Here I only briefly survey these arguments, as they pick up themes already mentioned.

85. Ibid., 247.
86. Ibid., 260.
87. Ibid., 265.
88. Ibid., 267.

As de Lubac explicates the meaning of medieval allegory in "The Fact of Christ,"[89] he again turns to Jesus to explain how Christian allegory is a particularly Christian act. Allegory, de Lubac argues, considers history not only in terms of time, but considers history in terms of its nature, as allegory is about a qualitative change in history, a difference in its essence. What makes Christian allegory different from pagan allegory is its basis and its term, then, as its basis is the coming of Jesus, and its term is the historical reality of history. Allegory in spiritual exegesis is by no means "a flight from history"[90]—because something as tangible and fleshly as the Incarnation is the reason for reading the Old Testament allegorically, it follows that the tangible and fleshly historical level of Scripture is not without meaning.[91] Yet its meaning, like the Incarnation, is one that stretches beyond its historical manifestations. Here de Lubac picks up tones from *History and Spirit*, in which he addressed the issue of Jewish allegory and differentiated between a "spiritualized" and a "spiritual" meaning. What is most distinct about Christian exegesis, he argues, is how the spiritual meaning of a text is defined; for early Christians, it could only be through Jesus' breaking into the world. De Lubac presses for the fact of Christ as making a true qualitative difference in allegory—the incarnation directs exegetical methodology, as it means that history can never be set aside.

De Lubac sets out that there is no myth or abstraction in spiritual exegesis: "we are really going, at least taking a first step, from history to history—although certainly not to history alone, or at least not to the mere exterior of history."[92] A deeper level of meaning is sought not outside of history, but within it. How this happens is that "a reality is inserted into our history at a given moment"—Jesus comes into history and everything culminates in him.[93] What is necessary, then, is that the biblical reader recognize the momentousness of this reality of Jesus; "anyone who failed to recognize for himself the Fact of Christ, in all its individuality, would encounter a bit of difficulty in fully understanding the impact of that great Fact on the consciousness of those who first perceived it and interpreted the Bible consistently with it." A "startling of the very being" of the exegete has occurred with the coming of Jesus.[94] Origen, e.g., had his soul startled by Christ and

---

89. In *Medieval Exegesis*, v.2, 8.3.

90. *Scripture*, 162.

91. "In de Lubac's theology, grace is concretely embodied in the world because revelation has, in Christ, taken a historical form." Wood, *Spiritual Exegesis*, 24.

92. *Scripture*, 163.

93. Ibid., 164.

94. Ibid., 168.

so looked for him in all of Scripture; de Lubac finds that this "ever-living activity of the same reality" sustains spiritual interpretation today.[95] As Hollon notes, allegory "enables the church to see Christ everywhere in the present and future."[96]

A Christian allegorical reading of Scripture holds tightly to Jesus, and so the Old Testament is a dialectic, de Lubac argues in "The Christian Dialectic."[97] Christian thought alternates back and forth between seeing the Old Testament in contradiction to the New Testament, and seeing the two as one. After the incarnation, de Lubac argues, the Old Testament cannot be read in the same manner in which it used to be read.[98] The time now is resurrection time. What Christians must hold together at once, then, is that the patterns of religion in the Old Testament are abrogated and yet that God is still speaking through Old Testament texts.

De Lubac pursues this claim in "The Abridged Word,"[99] in which he argues that the unity of Scripture is solely in Christ. Jesus brings the essence of biblical words together, as through them the Word is first pronounced, then finally heard as one.[100] Jesus is the abridgement of all the words of Scripture, yet unlike any other abridgement, which condenses and is less than that which it abridges, Jesus is greater than all that he abridges in Scripture. And so, "Contrary to the laws of human language, which becomes clearer when it is explained, it is when the *Word* appears in abridged form that what had been obscure becomes manifest."[101] Christianity, de Lubac argues, is not a religion of a book, but a religion of this living Word.[102]

Early generations of Christians looked always for Jesus in reading Scripture, and de Lubac sets out in "The New Testament"[103] that this basic instinct of early exegesis should be the norm for Christian biblical reading today. While the New Testament is not to be allegorized beyond itself in the way that the Old Testament is, there is allegory of a different sort operating in the New Testament. Whereas the Old Testament leads to Christ, the New Testament leads the reader further into the mystery of Christ. The

---

95. Ibid., 171.

96. Hollon, *Everything is Sacred*, 171.

97. In *Medieval Exegesis*, vol.3, 2.3.

98. "[A]s soon as the miracle of transformation was accomplished in Christ, the pretense of preserving the prior state of reality by preserving the prior reading of the Book becomes a doomed undertaking." *Scripture*, 176.

99. In *Medieval Exegesis*, vol.3, 2.5.

100. *Scripture*, 183–84.

101. Ibid., 190, emphasis de Lubac's.

102. Ibid., 194.

103. In *Medieval Exegesis*, vol.4, 7.5.

literal meaning of the New Testament, de Lubac argues, is itself the spiritual meaning, yet the "intention of the Spirit is that one stop no more at the letter of the New Testament than at the letter of the Old."[104] Early exegetes looked beyond the surface of New Testament passages, such as with the Nativity or the miracle at Cana, in which every detail contains "the mysteries and joys of our salvation."[105] Such exegetes understood that more than any other part of Scripture, "nothing can possibly be as 'filled with mysteries' as the words and actions of the Saviour."[106] The coming of Christ was such an event that "never ceases, from the very first instant, to bear fruit within itself for centuries to come and for eternity."[107]

The concluding section of *Scripture*, "The Unity of the Quadruple Meaning,"[108] weaves each meaning of the Bible into each other and presents the spiritual life as an organic whole.[109] Although we speak of the four senses as separate entities, de Lubac understands this is really a reflection of "language's inevitable parade"—a parade that did not fool the ancients.[110] All meanings of Scripture are bound up in each other; "The passage from one meaning to the other is, more precisely, the passage of the one meaning into the other, the becoming of the one by the other."[111] As Wood explains, the principles of spiritual exegesis are "neither successive nor progressive 'methods' of reading a biblical text that can be separated one from the other, but rather demonstrate a compenetration of meanings within the historical events which ground the biblical text."[112]

Just as one meaning turns seamlessly into each other, these meanings come to be more seamlessly woven into the soul of the reader. All spiritual interpretation is made possible by the spirituality of the reader, and the more the Bible is interiorized, the greater is the possibility for growth in understanding it. "The Word of God never stops creating and burrowing within a man who makes use of his capacity to receive it, so that the understanding

---

104. *Scripture*, 205.

105. Maximus of Turin, hom.22, cited in *Scripture*, 214.

106. *Scripture*, 213.

107. Ibid., 217.

108. In *Medieval Exegesis*, vol.2, 10.3.

109. As Wood argues, this vision of an organic whole in spiritual exegesis shaped de Lubac's wider theology, as he sought to incorporate disparate elements of theology into each other. Wood, *Spiritual Exegesis*, 1.

110. *Scripture*, 217.

111. Ibid., 220.

112. Wood, *Spiritual Exegesis*, 51. Cf. Barth's and Peterson's non-linear approaches to spiritual reading.

which also believes can grow indefinitely."[113] De Lubac echoes Gregory of Nyssa, who finds knowledge is always moving from beginning to beginning—one is ever a new learner at the edge of inquiry. As John Cassian similarly states, "the beauty of the holier meaning somehow begins to grow with our own growth."[114]

De Lubac's view of Scripture is that of Gregory's—as one makes "progress towards the heights, the sacred words themselves keep pace by disclosing still higher things."[115] Scripture is limitless as the Spirit causes it to be expanded along with the understanding of the one reading it; just as the world is created anew each morning, the Bible is recreated with each reading. Gregory states, the "sacred oracles will grow with you, they will ascend the summits with you. . . . Thus what is said in the Holy Book grows with the mind of those who read it . . . each reader will find in the Holy Book just what he is looking for."[116]

Spiritual Interpretation's Prospects[117]

"A sacred element" was at the heart of the ancients' spiritual exegesis,[118] and so de Lubac finds that certain features of their spiritual interpretation might carry over into the present spiritual reading of Scripture—exegesis today, most importantly, is still to remain christological and attentive to the mystery.[119] Although our attention given to the history of biblical texts might be more of a critical and historical nature, the direction of our exegesis is to move in the same path as that of the ancients. It must recognize, as Moberly states, that "the study of original meaning is both necessary but not necessarily determinative."[120] What is determinative is the greater reality of Jesus. Steinmetz finds medieval exegesis might be a corrective, then, to the narrowing of meaning in modern biblical studies:

113. *Scripture*, 223.

114. John Cassian, *Coll.* 14, c.11, cited in *Scripture*, 223.

115. Gregory, *In Ez.*, 1.2, cited in *Scripture*, 224.

116. Gregory, *In. Ez.*, 1.1, h.7, cited in *Scripture*, 228. Cf. Barth: "The Bible gives to every man and to every era such answers to their questions as they deserve. We shall always find in it as much as we seek and no more." Barth, *Word of God*, 32.

117. 1.6 of *Scripture*.

118. *Scripture*, 66.

119. "No less attentive to the mystery as signified in history, we shall be more attentive perhaps to the historicity of type . . . we shall strive to unite our modern 'historical sense' to that profound 'sense of history' which the ancients were able to draw forth by means of their spiritual exegesis." *Scripture*, 68.

120. Moberly, "Preaching Christ," 239.

> To be sure, medieval exegetes made bad mistakes in the application of their theory, but they also scored noble and brilliant triumphs. Even at their worst they recognized that the intention of the author is only one element—and not always the most important element at that—in the complex phenomenon of the meaning of the text. . . . The medieval theory of levels of meanings in the biblical text, with all its undoubted defects, flourished because it was true, while the modern theory of a single meaning, with all its demonstrable virtues, is false.[121]

While challenges exist in determining the parameters of meanings in Scripture, medieval exegesis offers a way forward to a wider expanse of meaning, and with that, a new flourishing of biblical studies. Although figures like Benjamin Jowett find that "the greatness of the Fathers or Reformers" no longer has "suitableness to our own day . . . their explanations of Scripture are no longer tenable; they belong to a way of thinking and speaking which was once diffused over the world, but has now passed away,"[122] interpreters like de Lubac and Steinmetz argue that the way of thinking in medieval exegesis goes deeper than the mental universe of its own age; it is a truth that still holds today. More than "a way of thinking and speaking which was once diffused over the world," ancient exegesis was a way of understanding the Christian faith that goes beyond its time.

In his concluding remarks to this section of *Scripture*, de Lubac presses home the idea that biblical readers must seek in the Bible a word addressed to them. He finds that "it is Scripture which is questioning us, and which finds for each of us, through all time and all generations, the appropriate question."[123] Citing von Balthasar, de Lubac understands Scripture to be like the Eucharist: it is not simply a remembrance of Christ, but is an ongoing reality of his presence. Reading Scripture is meant to be like the Eucharist, a communion with the living Lord. De Lubac finds hope for this kind of reading of Scripture through the work of other theologians, naming Karl Barth among them,[124] those whose exegesis, he says, is reminiscent of that of the early Fathers. A weakness he sees in some modern theologians' approaches, however, is their reluctance to recognize "a real progress in the order of knowledge from one Economy to the other."[125] The notion of development,

---

121. Steinmetz, "Superiority of Pre-Critical Exegesis," 37.

122. Jowett, "On the Interpretation of Scripture," 66.

123. *Scripture*, 73.

124. Barth seems less aware of de Lubac in his own work, however. Mangina offers a helpful comparison of the two figures in chapter 6 of *Karl Barth: Theologian of Christian Witness*, 164–72.

125. *Scripture*, 77–78.

he maintains, is at the heart of the growth of the church and is what allows spiritual meanings of Scripture to exist.

There is one additional point of de Lubac's conclusion that needs flagging: de Lubac briefly mentions that the "kind of connaturality with Scripture" that marked the Fathers is uncharacteristic of our age.[126] He cites John Henry Newman on this matter:

> This is a practical age: the age of the Fathers was more contemplative; their theology, consequently, had a deeper, more mystical, more subtle character about it, than we with our present habits of thought can readily enter into. We lay greater stress than they on proofs from definite verses of Scripture . . . they rather recognized a certain truth lying hid under the tenor of the sacred text as a whole . . . they are able to move more freely.[127]

Perhaps if there is to be a revival of spiritual exegesis today, what is also needed, then, is to relearn this wholeness of biblical vision, and to strive towards such connaturality with Scripture that the Fathers had.[128] As mentioned in the introduction, the proliferation of biblical scholarship in the academy is, ironically, inversely related to the extent of biblical literacy in the church. More is written on Scripture, but less is Scripture written on the heart. What is necessary for a new spiritual understanding of the Bible is quite simply, more reading of it—back to the sources again.

Reading Towards Christ

Henri de Lubac begins and ends with Christ in his study of spiritual exegesis, as he understands the incarnation of Jesus as that which opens the gateway of spiritual interpretation, bringing it into fresh fields of life, and it is the eschatological vision of Jesus that spiritual interpretation heads towards, its horizon of life eternal. Each sense of Scripture turns in a different manner around Jesus, and in him all the senses are integrated into each other; the revelation of Jesus is the beginning, middle, and end of spiritual exegesis.

What might be done, then, with de Lubac's proposals today? A few brief reflections on the promises and challenges of his approach—first, de

---

126. Ibid., 66.

127. John Henry Newman, cited in *Scripture*, 66.

128. Jenson notes, "The churches most faithful to Scripture are not those that legislate the most honorific propositions about Scripture, or even those that most diligently scrutinize proposed theologoumena for their concordance with it, but those that most often and thoughtfully actually read and hear it." Jenson, "Religious Power of Scripture," 90.

Lubac helpfully sets out a synthesis between theology, exegesis, and spirituality; his "theological vision is one that seeks a reintegration of the reading of scripture, theology and the practice of the Christian life."[129] While theology and biblical studies have been moving closer towards each other in recent times, de Lubac casts this rejoining in light of the history of the church's exegesis, and makes room for spirituality within this alliance, as well. He explains

> In *Histoire et Esprit* . . . I hoped to make a contribution, on the one hand, to the current research into the philosophy or the theology of history and, on the other hand, to the synthesis that is also being sought today within Christianity between exegesis, properly so-called, dogmatic theology and spirituality.[130]

It is de Lubac's joining of spirituality to exegesis and theology that is one of his most compelling contributions; he demonstrates that more than theologically-orientated biblical interpretation, an ecclesial-wide spirituality of openness to and participation with the Spirit of God is needed.

Yet while de Lubac links the project of spiritual interpretation to the life of the church, there are still ways to work out how his understanding of spiritual exegesis might relate to modern biblical scholarship. Work is needed to relate ancient exegesis with what is happening today; as Mark S. Burrows remarks, "the history of biblical interpretation reminds us that the treasures of one generation often become a problematic inheritance for the next."[131] As noted above, de Lubac insists upon using scholarship for spiritual exegesis ("we need . . . the learned in order to help us read Scripture historically").[132] Which aspects of scholarship are required needs fleshing out, however—how far must one plunge into Israel's history? How might modern concerns in understanding the layers of history and multiple contexts within Scripture be related to a Christ-centered understanding of Scripture's whole?

Adele Berlin notes that as so many new approaches and methodologies have sprung up in biblical studies, the change in twenty and twenty-first

---

129. Ayres, "Soul and the Reading of Scripture," 189.

130. Lubac, cited in Hollon, *Everything is Sacred*, 107. Marcellino G. D'Ambrosio points out that de Lubac did not fully chart out the way to that synthesis of these areas; "he did not himself attempt to write a blueprint for their active collaboration in the practical work of exegesis. Leaving that delicate task to others, de Lubac instead limited himself rather modestly to clearing away false oppositions . . . attempting somewhat to clarify the issues involved historically and theologically." Marcellino G. D'Ambrosio, cited in Hollon, *Everything is Sacred*, 107.

131. Burrows, "To Taste with the Heart," 168.

132. *Medieval*, 267.

century biblical scholarship has been "a movement away from the contraction of meaning and toward the expansion of meaning."[133] Yet while biblical texts are recognized as existing in multiple contexts, with more than one meaning, the challenge is whether their many meanings might be a cohesive whole. Childs thus offers one response to this challenge, as with his canonical approach he insists that "the biblical text exerts theological pressure on the reader which demands that the reality which undergirds the two voices [of the Old and New Testaments] not be held apart and left fragmented, but critically reunited."[134] The biblical reader is to understand the parts of the Bible in terms of their own particularities, and then in their wider Christian canonical context and "listen for a new song to break forth from the same ancient, sacred texts."[135] While like the medievals Childs seeks a holistic understanding of the Bible, he does so in a different manner, by listening carefully to each of its parts in their many historical contexts. Childs holds, "Because Scripture performs different functions according to distinct contexts, a multi-level reading is required even to begin to grapple with the full range of Scripture's role as the intentional medium of continuing divine revelation."[136] Childs finds that allegory is intrinsic to the Christian exegetical tradition, but must be reworked today to understand the witness to God in Scripture as an unfolding witness.[137]

Although Childs is making a different move from medieval readers (and the differences are significant), Childs's approach nonetheless offers a modern parallel to the multiple levels of meaning sought in medieval exegesis: for Childs, medieval allegory had its shortcomings but it "correctly sensed the need for interpreting Scripture in ways that did justice to its rich diversity in addressing different contexts, and in serving a variety of functions when instructing the Church."[138] Levenson, from a Jewish perspective, offers a similar argument for recognizing the importance of different contexts of biblical texts:

> Practicing Jews and Christians will differ from uncompromising historicists . . . in affirming the meaningfulness and interpretive relevance of larger contexts that homogenize the literatures of different periods to one degree or another. Just as text has more

133. Berlin, "On Bible Translations," 185.
134. Childs, "Does the Old Testament Witness," 62.
135. Ibid., 62.
136. Ibid., 63.
137. For a study of Childs's growing understanding of allegory, see Driver, *Brevard Childs*, chapter 7, esp. 229–54.
138. Childs, *Biblical Theology*, 122.

than one context, and biblical studies more than one method, so scripture has more than one sense, as the medievals knew and Tyndale, Spinoza, Jowett, and most other moderns have forgotten.[139]

Levenson and Childs hold to the importance of the historical meanings of biblical texts, but will not narrowly restrict the Bible's meaning to one historical sense alone. With his canonical approach, Childs views the history of biblical texts in itself as significant — like de Lubac, he finds there is spiritual importance in history and seeks out its broader meanings, yet he also sees the history of biblical composition as a working of God and worthy of attention. In the following two chapters, we will see through the work of Ellen Davis (a student of Childs) how such an approach might work out in practice.

As de Lubac seeks out the work of God, he sets Jesus at the center of all spiritual reading of Scripture, and so his proposal moreover raises the question of whether a christological crisis is at the root of the decline of spiritual reading in the church and academy today. Francis Watson notes, "'Evangelical' discussions of the trustworthiness of Scripture often seem to bypass the *evangelion*. . . . The result is a doctrine of scriptural 'trustworthiness' or 'authority' in which Jesus himself is relatively marginal."[140] Have Christian biblical interpreters moved too far away from Christ in their interpretations, putting on not just historical lenses but a veil as well? Early spiritual exegetes were so moved by the reality of Jesus that they could not help but see him in every page of Scripture. Commenting upon Augustine's use of the Psalms, and the challenge it poses to interpreters today, Jenson notes,

> [A] very clear control is operative: an interpretation is right if, in a way peculiar to the given text, it draws the reader on in the love of God, patterned and enabled by Christ. This criterion works, of course, only if one believes that God does indeed mold us to life in Christ and thereby move us into God. Which is what Augustine did believe. Query: Where do we now find preachers and teachers who believe this, and so are in position to do what Augustine did? One fears the real problem is a problem of faith.[141]

It may be not just the methods of Christian readers have changed, but the measure of faith brought to their reading, as well. Childs puts it even more starkly, as he suggests that

---

139. Levenson, *Hebrew Bible*, 104.
140. Watson, "Evangelical Response," 288.
141. Jenson, foreword to Byassee, *Praise Seeking Understanding*, xi.

[T]he greatest challenge to the church was not the discovery that a myriad of other secular interpretive options were available for reading the Bible. Rather, it was the growing loss of confidence within the church itself as to whether it actually possessed in the Bible a sacred scripture given as a gracious gift of divine revelation to guide and instruct in the way of salvation.[142]

The exegesis of ancient believers thus challenges the church whether it still believes the Bible is that gracious gift of divine revelation. Moreover, it asks the modern church what it is seeking in its biblical reading and interpretation. It is the question of the resurrected Jesus to Mary, "Whom are you seeking?" Spiritual exegesis seeks a living God in the texts of Scripture, a God revealed in Jesus Christ, who is present in Scripture and the church today. Without returning to particular practices of medieval spiritual exegesis, a resurgence of spiritual exegesis might be viable today, for the result sought in spiritual exegesis is ultimately the knowledge and love of Christ. The end sought in spiritual exegesis is not adding to a body of general knowledge, but adding knowledge to the body of Christ, a knowledge that is ever bound up in love.

---

142. Childs, *Struggle to Understand*, 304.

CHAPTER 6

An Artful Reader: Ellen F. Davis

[T]he teaching life, as I know it, is simply a matter of continually renewing my practices of reading the Bible, and renewing them in public. The only way I know to teach people to read the Bible is to read it myself, afresh, in their presence.

—Ellen F. Davis[1]

Spiritual reading of Scripture is an art, and like any art, the teaching and learning of it is never a straightforward affair. Yet art can (to a certain degree) be taught, and the best way is often by exposure and immersion—inspiration comes through the work of others.[2] In this chapter I look at one artful reader of Scripture, Ellen F. Davis, as an exemplar of the manner of spiritual reading I am exploring in this study. My aim is to see how Davis's artistic handling of the Bible might guide others. Although spiritual reading is not a method and is broader than any one figure or approach, it is through the practices of actual readers of Scripture that this kind of reading is best understood—from its earliest times the art of exegesis has been "partly taught, partly caught."[3] (As Davis herself

---

1. Davis, "Entering the Story," 49.

2. George Steiner argues that the response to art, the "critical act, answerability to poetic and artistic shaping, can be exemplified but not taught. Their transmission from one generation to the next cannot be systematized as can be the handing on of scientific techniques and results." Steiner, *Real Presences*, 37. Steiner is perhaps overstating the case in saying the critical act cannot be taught, but he rightly points out how exemplifying of the critical act is key.

3. Young, *Biblical Exegesis*, 3.

explains art, it is best learned "by sympathy, not in abstraction . . . [by] watching great artists at work."[4]) Davis, a scholar of the Bible and practical theology at Duke Divinity School, is a helpful guide to spiritual readers today, as she is steeped in the academy but has eyes on the church.[5] Davis demonstrates in her work a deep love of God and of the Bible, and with her concerns for the church's life, her reading of Scripture is ever mindful of ordinary believers struggling to know and love God through reading Scripture. Davis takes up similar concerns of Barth and de Lubac (and other theological interpreters), then, but in a strongly praxis-oriented way, and in a way that speaks directly to the western church today. In what follows I will set out and reflect upon some of the broad strokes of Davis's manner of art, before turning in the next chapter to follow her art in practice.

Davis's Manner of Art

Ellen Davis is perhaps one of the most astonished biblical scholars writing today. Astonished in that her writing evidences a deep and abiding awe of Scripture, a sense of wonder that she sets forth as necessary for any kind of engagement with the Bible. In *Wondrous Depth: Preaching the Old Testament*, Davis describes the Old Testament as "a perpetual source of astonishment." She thus encourages preachers to "put [them]selves in the way of that astonishment, and so be overtaken by it."[6] In her own astonished reading of Scripture, Davis practices what she preaches, as her scholarly work is saturated with a sense of being overtaken by the *mira profunditas* of the Bible.[7] Davis's wonder, moreover, is not just childlike—she is a rigorous exegete, often wrestling with the hardest of biblical texts, as well as taking up complex social issues. The knowledge and awe Davis has of Scripture, and her concern for contemporary crises marring the church and the world, work together to produce a reading of the Bible that flows with awareness of God being present and at work in his word and world.

4. Davis, *Wondrous Depth*, xv. Davis's artful reading of Scripture models the suggestion made by Roy A. Harrisville that "It may be that exegesis, interpretation, is not a science, a *Wissenschaft* that allows some space to intuition or divination, but a *Kunst*, an art that uses rules only to fuel or focus its passion." Harrisville, "What I Believe," 24.

5. She explains the focus of her teaching is "how the church may draw upon and be guided by the biblical text in its ministries." Davis, "No Explanations," 102.

6. Davis, *Wondrous Depth*, 2.

7. This phrase Davis takes from Augustine, whom she draws upon in the introduction to *Wondrous Depth*, xi. See also her article "Soil That is Scripture," 37.

Davis's sense of wonder, like any wonder, does not lend itself to neat categorization. Nonetheless, descriptions of her art can be made, especially since Davis is disciplined and reflexive in her practices of biblical reading. Statements of her particular reading manners and spiritual emphases in reading are found peppered throughout her writings, scattered in biblical commentaries, articles, and preaching guides. In Davis's writings unfold decades of concern with what it means to read Scripture well, and she engages the Bible mindful of others, trying to make persuasive not just interpretations of texts but an entire way of reading. Her work challenges both the academy and the church in its claims of what good practices of reading of the Bible look like. Here, rather than a plotted survey of Davis's individual works, I take a thematic approach and draw out some of the key features of biblical reading she emphasizes across her various writings.[8] Mention is needed first of the background of Davis and the context in which she writes—that is, the problems to which she is responding—and following upon that, I will set out traits of reading Davis posits as essential: traits of wonder, imagination, slowness, attentiveness to biblical language, uncertainty, trust, repentance, and spiritual growth.

Davis's Intellectual Background

After studies at the University of California, Berkeley, Hebrew University, Church Divinity School of the Pacific, and Oxford University, Davis undertook her doctoral work in the mid-1980s at Yale University, studying under the prominent figures of Brevard S. Childs and Hans Frei. Davis's work is indebted to theological stances that were being spun out of Yale at the time, particularly, her emphasis on imagination in interpreting Scripture, and her interest in moving past typical liberal/evangelical divides.[9] Childs,

---

8. Although these features of reading could be described as 'virtues of the reader,' a term gaining increasing popularity in circles of theological interpretation (see, e.g., Briggs, *Virtuous Reader*, and Vanhoozer, *Is There Meaning in This Text?*), Davis speaks of these features more in terms of spiritual dispositions, of basic Christian traits or practices.

9. It could be said that Davis was influenced by the "Yale School" of theology, also identified with postliberal theology, but to what extent this Yale school of thought exists/existed is debatable. George Hunsinger argues, "If postliberal theology depends on the existence of something called the "Yale School," then postliberal theology is in trouble. It is in trouble, because the so-called Yale School enjoys little basis in reality, being largely the invention of theological journalism. At best it represents a loose coalition of interests, united more by what it opposes or envisions than by any common theological program." Hunsinger, "Postliberal Theology," 42. While, as Hunsinger states, postliberal theology is far broader than Yale scholars, certain themes nonetheless draw together

more than any other Yale figure, had a strong influence upon Davis.[10] Davis seldom cites Childs directly in her work, but she shares many of Childs's concerns, such as seeking out a theological understanding of the Old Testament that relates to the life of the church, and working across traditional lines of scholarship to offer a comprehensive vision of Scripture. Childs's pressing concern of encounter with God through the Bible marks much of Davis's work, as well. Yet perhaps even more than Childs's particular theological positions, it is his example of life that has inspired Davis, as seen in her reflections made in a Yale Divinity School tribute to Childs's life:

> His scholarship was very fully integrated into his character, it would be very difficult to separate those two. He was a Christian. His work was a form of discipleship . . . I remember Bard saying that in order to teach OT, "you just need to get out of the way," because the text itself is so compelling and interesting. Many academics don't know how to get out of the way—of the text, of their own students—and let something interesting happen around them. Bard did.[11]

Childs's character and entire approach to scholarship seems to have most left its mark on Davis, and in this Childs reflects the manner in which he himself was influenced by his teachers. He describes how as a student who "had fallen under the spell of [Gerhard] von Rad," he slowly came to realize that "what made von Rad's work so illuminating was not his method as such, but the theological profundity of von Rad himself."[12] The theological profundity Childs saw in von Rad characterized his own work, which, as Davis shows, is illuminating still a new generation of biblical interpreters, encouraging them to strive towards greater personal depth in their own work.[13]

---

many Yale professors and doctoral students of the 1980s, even as a neat camp cannot be made of such figures.

10. In several places she gratefully acknowledges Childs's influence, and *Wondrous Depth* is dedicated to him.

11. Yale Divinity School News, "Brevard S. Childs, An Iconic Figure in Biblical Scholarship, Dies at 83," http://www.yale.edu/divinity/news/070625_news_childs.shtml

12. Childs goes on to explain, "The same observation holds true for Wolff and Zimmerli. I am convinced that no amount of methodological refinement will produce a quality of interpretation which that generation achieved whose faith in the God of Israel was hammered out in the challenge to meet the Nazi threat against the life of the church." Childs, cited in Harrisville, "What I Believe," 25.

13. Childs's advice to a student that to become a better exegete he must "become a deeper person" is a remark that has taken on legendary status and been circulated much by his students and readers. See, e.g., Chapman, "Imaginative Readings of Scripture," 420, ft 40. Moberly cites this saying and asks whether "better biblical interpretation may be a fruit of growth as a person." Moberly, "Biblical Criticism," 96.

Davis's published work began with her doctoral dissertation on Ezekiel, *Swallowing the Scroll: Textuality and Dynamics of Discourse in Ezekiel's Prophecy*, a study that is predominantly pursued through historical-critical methods, but takes a theological interest in Ezekiel as a prophet. Davis argues that Ezekiel's prophecies were composed in writing for oral delivery, as from the beginning Ezekiel "conceived his commission to prophesy in a manner congruent with the concept of God's word as text."[14] And so,

> In creating a literary idiom for prophecy, [Ezekiel] took a decisive step toward forging a community which defined itself on the basis of a common text and shared habits of reading . . . he gave those who would attend to him a new disposition for hearing. He began to teach Israel to listen for the authoritative word, not just in single sharp moments of revelation and confrontation, but as it would reecho through the ongoing murmur, not infrequently rising to a clamor, of centuries of interpretation.[15]

Ezekiel's work, as Davis understands it, is the kind of work Davis herself undertakes, as she aims to help the community of faith take on that "new disposition for hearing." Her interest in Ezekiel's prophetic proclamation through the written word was a fitting place to begin her professional scholarship, as her exegetical and historical interests in the Bible almost always grapple with what it means, in this moment of the church's time and place, to hear the murmur of Scripture as the word of God.[16] It is this echo and ongoing murmuring of the Bible that Davis follows, attending both to the historical details of the biblical text and to the reality of God.

Davis's first academic post was at Union Theological Seminary, from 1987 to 1989, and she then returned to Yale to teach Old Testament from 1989 to 1996. She taught at Virginia Theological Seminary from 1996 to 2001, and in 2001 took up a position at Duke Divinity School, where she is currently Amos Regan Kearns Distinguished Professor of Bible and Practical Theology. Davis has been a visiting fellow of Clare Hall, Cambridge, and

---

14. Davis, *Swallowing the Scroll*, 51.

15. Ibid., 139–40.

16. Theodore Hiebert, in his review of *Scripture, Culture, and Agriculture*, describes Davis as "writing much more like a prophet than a historian." Hiebert, "Review: *Scripture, Culture, and Agriculture*," 437. In some ways, Davis's writing does follow in the manner of prophecy which Abraham Joshua Heschel describes: prophecy is "not simply the application of timeless standards to particular human situations, but rather an interpretation of a particular moment in history, a divine understanding of a human situation . . . [A] prophet has responsibility for the moment, an openness to what the moment reveals. He is a person who knows what time it is." Heschel, *Prophets*, xiii–xiv, 106.

she delivered the 2005 to 2006 Hulsean Lectures at Cambridge University (which became the basis of her *Scripture, Culture, and Agriculture*). Along with her research and teaching at Duke, Davis is involved in theological education and community development with the Episcopal Church of Sudan, and she founded and co-directs Duke's Renk Visiting Teachers Program.

Davis's work has been concentrated in Old Testament studies, as seen in her numerous exegetical articles, but her interests in preaching and in reading Scripture theologically have been at front throughout her writings. Davis's second book published was a preaching guide, *Imagination Shaped: Old Testament Preaching in the Anglican Tradition* (1995). Her first full-length biblical commentary was a theological one, *Proverbs, Ecclesiastes, and The Song of Songs: A Theological Commentary* (in the Westminster Bible Companion series, 2000), and her third book, *Getting Involved With God: Rediscovering the Old Testament* (2001), likewise has theological interests at its core. Davis's fourth book was a commentary on Ruth, *Who Are You, My Daughter?: Reading Ruth Through Image and Text* (2003), which pays close attention to the words and imagery of Ruth. In 1998, Davis became a co-leader (with Richard B. Hays) of "The Scripture Project" at the Center of Theological Inquiry in Princeton, New Jersey. Over several seminars in a period of four years, from 1998 to 2002, a group of fifteen scholars and pastors met to discuss how Scripture might be read theologically, and from their conversations and papers was born *The Art of Reading Scripture* (2003), edited by Davis and Hays. In 2005 Davis wrote a second preaching guide, *Wondrous Depth: Preaching the Old Testament*. In 2008, *Scripture, Culture, and Agriculture* took her scholarship in a new direction, as she sought out an agrarian framework for reading the Bible. Agrarian interests have been a constant theme of her recent work (such as with her contribution to *The Green Bible*), and she has translated The Song of Solomon for a new biblical translation, *The Common English Bible* (published October 2011). Her latest book, *Biblical Prophecy: Perspectives for Christian Theology, Discipleship and Ministry* (2014), considers prophets and the prophetic word across the Old and New Testaments.

Davis's Context of Writing

As Davis writes not just in the academy but even more so towards the church, she notices a swarm of spiritual problems that need addressing. Her context is one of modern American mainstream Protestantism, and so while many of her thoughts on Scripture have universal bearing, the particular difficulties with biblical reading she notes are those that characterize a broadly western culture, both within and outside of the church. Davis responds to crises she perceives in the church and in the world; she takes a prophetic voice in speaking into situations of dismay. And like any good prophet, she also discerns hope and possibility in these situations; that hope she finds in the deep reading and living of Scripture.[17]

In *The Art of Reading Scripture*, Davis surmises "the most fundamental need" of the mainstream North American and European church is "to learn again to read and teach the Bible confessionally."[18] This need is put into even starker terms in *Wondrous Depth*, where she proclaims, "the gravest scandal in the North American church in our time" is "the shallow reading of Scripture."[19] What is needed, Davis insists, is for the church to "acknowledge the Bible as the functional center of its life" so that it is "continually reoriented to the demands and promises of Scripture."[20] This need is especially pressing for reading the Old Testament, as there is a "functional loss of the Old Testament in the church."[21] The church as a whole has a crisis of reading the Bible, and that crisis is evinced most obviously in preaching. Davis explains that "the crisis in contemporary preaching" is essentially "an impoverished understanding of the meaning and uses of Scripture."[22]

As Davis speaks mostly to the western mainstream Protestant church, she does not directly address ways of reading that characterize more evangelical, charismatic, or conservative churches that tend to hold Scripture more closely.[23] Yet even in those churches Davis poses that something is off in their relationship with Scripture—they too are charged with "shallow reading," especially when it comes to the Old Testament.[24] In *Getting Involved with God* Davis sets forth as an alternative "a style of spiritually engaged reading that is . . . largely unfamiliar to Christians."[25] And so, while

---

17. As Davis states, "Good biblical exegesis should yield some measure of realistic hope, however chastened, because the Bible itself consistently nourishes such hope." Davis, *Scripture, Culture, and Agriculture*, 5.

18. Davis, "Teaching the Bible," 9.

19. Davis, *Wondrous Depth*, xi.

20. Davis, "Teaching the Bible," 9.

21. Davis, "Losing a Friend," 73.

22. Davis, *Imagination Shaped*, xi.

23. Out of her work in Sudan, Davis notes that her Sudanese theological students read the Bible differently than westerners, for they "live in the Old Testament." Davis, "Land, Life."

24. "[O]ur reading is a simple rehearsal of what (we think) we know rather than an attempt to probe deeper. The assumption of prior knowledge that is fully adequate to new challenges seems to be widely held by 'conservative' and 'liberal' Christians alike." Davis, *Wondrous Depth*, xi.

25. Davis, *Getting Involved With God*, 1.

the problems with biblical reading Davis tackles might be more prevalent in mainstream or liberal congregations, Davis addresses her work to all Christians reading Scripture, as on the whole, the church is in dire need of spiritual reading lessons. While "an earlier generation of biblical scholars" perceived that the church had a need to take the historical character of Scripture more seriously, now "the present struggle" for the church is to learn anew how "to read the Bible as the word of God."[26]

Davis understands that the historical dimensions of the Bible are part of its spiritual meaning as the word of God, but in various and often subsumed ways, and this nuance is an important one. One reviewer of *Wondrous Depth* explains the work as "an invitation to bracket out, to a degree, the historical-critical concerns that seem to render Old Testament texts almost impossibly strange and remote and to engage the Old Testament instead with a habitus of anticipation and imagination."[27] Davis probably would not describe her approach in terms of "bracketing out" historical-critical concerns—as she says in *Wondrous Depth*, "reading the text in light of traditional modes of exegesis as well as modern methods of historical and literary analysis is a great if not indispensible help toward the goal of using the religious imagination more effectively."[28] But the reviewer's comment is not unfair, for what Davis is interested in is a reading that enters fully into the Bible to hear it as the word of God, and to that end, certain historical-critical questions are not as pertinent. (Or they are simply not as interesting—Davis would surely agree with Robert Alter's view that "even where [source] analysis may be convincing, it seems to me a good deal less interesting than the subtle workings of the literary whole represented by the redacted text."[29]) Whether J or E is behind a specific text or when a text may be narrowly dated is not as crucial a concern as what God presently has to

---

26. Davis, "Teaching the Bible," 10. Jason Byassee argues that for all the benefits of critical biblical study, "we as church have failed to digest the methods and results of historical criticism into something that can be fully nourishing to the whole of the church across time and space. And a church that fails to be nourished, like any living organism, runs a perilous risk." Byassee, *Praise Seeking Understanding*, 243.

27. Brown, "Review of *Wondrous Depth*," 545.

28. Davis, *Wondrous Depth*, 69. In *Scripture, Culture, and Agriculture*, Davis likewise explains that "If the question [of an agrarian reading of the Bible] is unusual, the methods used to answer it are not. On the whole, this study will follow procedures that are standard for professional exegesis: paying close attention to rhythm, diction, and the poetics of a text; reading it within the larger literary context and, to whatever extent is possible, in light of the particular historical, social, and even geographical conditions related to its composition and promulgation." Davis, *Scripture, Culture, and Agriculture*, 3.

29. Alter, *Five Books of Moses*, 12.

say to readers through that text. Davis understands critical study's role is to aid the imagination to hear this word of God; the goal of such study is to develop "an educated imagination:"

> The exegetical imagination is enriched by any study, however technical, that draws us into deeper consideration of the words and forms and images of the text, that is, study that forces and enables us to read the text with care, rather than tempting us to talk around or "get behind" it in order to reconstruct social settings or literary layers for which there is no direct evidence.[30]

With all her schooling in historical-critical methods, what Davis does in practice, then, is to hold some critical questions at bay, to see whether they are worth asking of a text, whether they will lead the reader deeper into the subject matter of the text, or mislead the reader into talking around or behind the text. Knowing which historical-critical questions to ask is part of the art of Davis's biblical reading, as some questions are better than others in helping readers to enter imaginatively into the Bible to hear it faithfully as the word of God. Davis explains that in preaching, "the preacher needs to know how to identity a fruitful question. There is, I think, only one criterion: a good question is one that leads you and your hearers more deeply into the story."[31] As Davis's practice shows (see examples in the next chapter), there are no clear-cut rules for what questions will do just that, for each biblical text and each reading setting calls for its own discernment.

A confusion and misdirected concern with historicity is part of the crisis of biblical reading in the church, but among its many factors, Davis identifies this crisis as resulting most fundamentally from the sin of readers: "it is sin, not historical distance," she insists, "which keeps us from hearing the message of Scripture as 'relevant,' that is, life-giving."[32] In her agrarian reading of Scripture, Davis posits sin as the real obstacle to edifying reading: "To put that in theological language, sin—lack of proper knowledge and love of God and neighbor—impedes exegesis."[33] This theological point is one that Davis does not expatiate upon, but she sets it out as a reason for why biblical reading has gone so awry—sin has crept into the church's relationship with Scripture. Although this sin has been described as a loss of biblical authority, Davis notes an even more fundamental problem at root, for what is happening is "a loss of intimacy. For many Christians, profound

---

30. Davis, *Imagination Shaped*, 261.
31. Davis, *Wondrous Depth*, 8.
32. Davis, *Imagination Shaped*, xii.
33. Davis, *Scripture, Culture, and Agriculture*, 27.

friendship with the Old Testament is no longer a live possibility."[34] Scripture is meant to be a friend, the church's guide and companion, but that friendship has withered away of late. The church's disordered biblical reading is due to a disordered love of Scripture, a relationship with the Bible that has slowly been deteriorating over the years in its neglect.[35]

Davis's pointing to the problem of sin in the church's reading of the Bible is a diagnosis also given by others as to what has gone wrong. The effect of sin in reading, however, is not a recent problem, but a hazard throughout the ages. David Lyle Jeffrey traces the struggle to read Scripture spiritually back to the fall of creation, for "in a fallen world no one reader perfectly, or ever, gets it right."[36] Jeffrey explains this condition through biblical language—there is a "split between unrepentant and repentant hearers of the Word, or to put it in still more biblical idiom, between the hard-hearted and broken-hearted reader."[37] What is needed for a right hearing and reading of Scripture is repentance and broken-heartedness, then, for without it the reader cannot read the Bible in keeping with God. Henri de Lubac similarly understands that at the "root of the problem of spiritual understanding" is this need for an act of conversion towards God.[38] John Webster, likewise, wrestles with the question of sin in his theology of reading Scripture, yet his understanding of sin is even more operative than in Davis or Jeffrey or de Lubac, as he explains reading Scripture as "an episode in the history of sin and its overcoming." He posits that "defiance of grace" is the central problem: "Coming to know God, and reading Holy Scripture as a means of coming to know God, can only occur through the overcoming of fallenness." Webster insists that a good reading of Scripture is impossible without this overcoming of sin, as reading requires a "hermeneutical conversion."[39]

---

34. Davis, "Losing a Friend," 73.

35. Chris Webb likewise perceives this lack of love in the church, and explains his book on spiritual reading as an effort to help believers "fall in love with the Bible again." Webb, *Fire of the Word*, preface.

36. Jeffrey, *People of the Book*, 205.

37. Ibid., 362.

38. *Scripture*, 22.

39. Webster, *Holy Scripture*, 87–88, 106. Webster's understanding of the effect of sin and the need for conversion is helpful, for it places the reading of Scripture in light of the human condition, but it is perhaps too strong, as in many ways it does not account for the grace of God that is at work in a reader even before her conversion, or the grace of God that is at work post-conversion as her sin lingers still. Spiritual reading might occur despite the sin brought to it; as Briggs articulates, "Scripture is not a closed book to those not yet virtuous enough to behold in it what is written ... Wise readers get texts wrong.... Neither can insights into texts (or any displays of virtue) come only from those advancing the virtuous life." Briggs, *Virtuous Reader*, 208–9.

Davis notes these perennial problems of sin that effect the ability to hear the word of God, but she explains this sin in terms of a skewed intimacy between the church and its Scripture that clouds readings of biblical texts. Without a sense of closeness to the biblical texts, they have no power in the lives of its readers. She maintains this loss of intimacy and the besetting sins of readers work hand-in-hand, arguing that

> [E]thics informs exegesis, at least as much as the other way around . . . it is not always possible to do good exegesis as a first step. Sometimes important aspects of the text are not visible to an interpreter—or a whole generation of interpreters—until there has been a reordering of our minds and even our lives, until certain gaps have been supplied in the sphere of our "active apprehension."[40]

And so the problem of the church's loss of intimacy with the Bible is complicated by the blindness readers have to "important aspects" of Scripture left unnoticed today because of their own patterns of sin.

These are the pressing problems within the church that stirs up Davis's writing, yet she is also deeply distressed by the enormous ecological crisis around the world (an enormous sin that she sees clouding biblical reading). Western practices of poor land-care and habits of overconsumption (in large part the cause of the global crisis) provoke Davis as spiritual problems, as she suggests that the ecological situation "may be the most far-reaching theological crisis (for it is that) ever to confront the church."[41] Not just in her recent agrarian work, but across her various writings the past twenty years Davis finds Scripture bearing hard upon ecological issues, and she presses the church to recognize the magnitude of this crisis and its deeply spiritual dimensions.

Davis is thus one who enters into a fray of problems that have been centuries in the making—the church's declining love of Scripture, the world's ecological disaster. Both are complex crises, but the immensity of their scale does not ward Davis off. She does not offer complex answers for either crisis, however, but rather solutions that begin in everyday practices.[42]

---

40. Davis, *Scripture, Culture, and Agriculture*, 27.
41. Davis, *Getting Involved with God*, 183.
42. One criticism of her work, however, is that she might do even more to the end of offering practical solutions, especially for ecological issues, for "if we are not all supposed to engage in small-scale farming—as the ancient Israelites did and as Wendell Berry has done (or are we?)—where do we go from here?" Hiebert, "Review," 439.

Davis finds hope originating in the spiritual reading of Scripture, in "practicing hermeneutics as a spiritual discipline" as a way of hearing anew the Bible and drawing close to God.[43] This long-lost love of the church is not yet beyond rekindling.

Wonder

An essential start to the renewal of that love is wonder, a basic striving "to be alert to the presence of God in our midst."[44] As noted above, wonder is a core characteristic of Davis's biblical reading—wonder that is both a sense of curiosity about Scripture and a deepening sense of amazement at it. In her commentary on Ruth, Davis encourages genuine curiosity in reading:

> Why curiosity, a virtue not frequently associated with reading the Bible? Because the biblical writers are at every point urging us to a more probing and wonder-filled way of thinking about things we take for granted when we encounter them in our lives, things we read right past when we find them on the pages of Scripture.[45]

The wonder that is needed for reading Scripture is a way of thinking and seeing the world, a child-like curiosity regained that finds mystery not only in miracles but also in ordinary things. Davis posits that teaching the Bible is not essentially about conveying historical information (though that is indeed part of it), but even more so, it is about imparting "the imaginative skills for wondering fruitfully about the ultimate facts of life ... teaching the Bible confessionally means enabling people to wonder wisely and deeply."[46]

Her connection between wonder and a confessional teaching of the Bible is an important one to note, for Davis's wonder is a particularly directed one, a wonder/curiosity that, as cited above, is "alert to the presence of God in our midst." Such wonder is "wise and deep" and "fruitful" as it considers God through the Bible. (Davis elsewhere describes this wonder as "curiosity in the heart that is disposed to be faithful."[47]) And so, a disposition towards God is basic to one's wonder in reading Scripture—not just any kind of wonder will do, but only the kind of wonder that aims towards God.

---

43. Davis, *Wondrous Depth*, 101.
44. Ibid., xii.
45. Davis and Parker, *Who Are You*, xi.
46. Davis, "Teaching the Bible," 11. Strong resonances of Barth are here—see his emphasis on wonder in *Evangelical Theology*.
47. Davis, *Imagination Shaped*, 253.

This orientation of wonder is an essential mark of spiritual reading that sets its apart from other manners of reading, for biblical readers of all stripes might describe their work as being prompted by wonder. Philologists have a deep curiosity about words and grammatical structures; source critics could spend all day digging with fascination for layers of texts. Biblical scholarship, like any other form of scholarship, is often driven by curiosity and wonder, by scholars' deep and personal interest in their studies. Like other forms of scholarship, biblical scholarship need not be connected to God for it to be caught up in wonder.[48] Yet the kind of wonder Davis is interested in goes beyond intellectuals' random and consuming interests. Davis's wonder presumes a basic interest and openness to God; the reader is pulled to the biblical text to see what might be said truly of God and what God might truly be saying. Wonder stretches beyond the details of the text to the reality of God conveyed through it.

Imagination

As an interest in God prompts spiritual wondering in biblical reading, imagination is the way that wondering is carried out. Davis holds that "fruitful theological wondering resides chiefly in the imagination."[49] In several different writings Davis enthusiastically takes up Garrett Green's proposal that the biblical term "heart" (*lev, kardia*) refers to what we call imagination.[50] Reading with the imagination—with the heart—enables the reader to grapple with the central realities of the Bible. Davis traces the decline of biblical reading to "a neglected and atrophied Christian imagination" and she argues that "the Scriptures are less accessible to the average believer today than before the Reformation . . . because we do not have the imaginative skills to probe the subject matter of the Bible: love and forgiveness, suffering, redemption, the persistence of evil and the birth of boundless hope."[51] (This

---

48. Willimon emphasizes that curiosity must be rightly directed: "Calvin charged that 'the human mind is a perpetual factory for idols.' Idolatry is not necessarily the pastime of the ignorant and the simple. Intellectuals play quite well at this game. Natural inquisitiveness and delight in the novel and the strange, so prevalent in the academy, can be little more than the itch for some new graven image." Willimon, *Peculiar Speech*, 86.

49. Davis, "Teaching the Bible," 11.

50. Ibid., 11; see also *Imagination Shaped*, 249, and "No Explanations," 97. Garrett Green holds that "To call the Bible scripture is to claim that it enables its users rightly to imagine God and the world . . . There are a number of indications that the biblical heart functions very much like the paradigmatic imagination." Green, *Imagining God*, 109.

51. Davis, *Imagination Shaped*, 249.

last claim might need qualifying, for while average believers today may be less able to probe Scripture, they still have been probing love and suffering and evil and hope through other media, such as through film and novels. The disconnect of average believers in reading Scripture is not always due to an inability to imagine about the deepest things of life, but rather, an inability to see how Scripture imagines those matters even more profoundly than they or their present culture do.) As imagination is necessary not only for understanding the Bible but also for understanding its ultimate realities, Davis maintains that imagination is key to encountering God, which is the ultimate aim of reading Scripture.

As noted, Davis draws from Garrett Green with her emphasis on imagination, and she resonates with many other theologians presently exploring the role of the imagination. Stephen B. Chapman suggests that an appeal to the imagination is "[o]ne response to the present state of malaise concerning theological interpretation of the Bible" and this appeal might be "an expression of what theological interpretation currently lacks and a suggestive pointer toward a more promising hermeneutic."[52] Luke Timothy Johnson, likewise, emphasizes the necessity of "Imagining the World Scripture Imagines." He states, "those who practice theology must become less preoccupied with the world that produced Scripture and learn again how to live in the world Scripture produces. This will be a matter of imagination, and perhaps of leaping."[53] Similarly, Richard B. Hays posits a central place for "a way of reading that summons the reader to an epistemological transformation, *a conversion of the imagination.*"[54] Although several recent theologians have made imagination central not just to biblical reading but to the entire theological task,[55] Davis is modest in her use of the imagination; she does not delve into theological explorations of meaning of the imagination, but simply advocates it as one faculty, among many, that a biblical reader must use. Her appeal to the imagination has a rhetorical note, as it evokes a creative manner of reading open to infinite possibilities, even as these possibilities are framed within the tradition of the Christian faith.

---

52. Chapman, "Imaginative Readings," 409.

53. Johnson, "Imagining the World," 3. Walter Bruggemann similarly describes, "Scripture is a relentless *act of imagination* . . . it dares by artistic sensibility and risk-taking rhetoric, to posit, characterize and vouch for a world beyond the 'common-sense.'" Bruggemann, 9, emphasis his.

54. Hays, *Conversion of the Imagination*, x, emphasis his.

55. Trevor A. Hart, for example, is director of the University of St. Andrew's Institute for Theology, Imagination and the Arts; he has done work that brings together theology and the arts through the imagination.

Slowness

So how does one cultivate the wonder and imagination necessary for reading Scripture well? Wonder cannot be coerced, and imagination is not readily taught. Davis finds a starting point, however, as she states, "If there is a secret to getting involved with God through the pages of scripture, then perhaps it is this: *turn the pages slowly.*"[56] Slow reading—this is where spiritual reading begins. "[R]eading the text more slowly is essential for learning to love the Bible."[57] Another way to describe this is patient reading, the characterization Davis uses in her article "The Soil That is Scripture." There she identifies patience in biblical reading as a particular virtue needed in the western church today, as it lives in a culture that "is rife with impatience, and indeed cultivates it."[58] A counter-cultural approach is needed for reading the Bible, Davis insists, a slow movement unlike that used for most other encounters with words in everyday life. Such reading may in turn come to affect how those other encounters are made, as what is learned through the slow reading of Scripture is "a whole new way of thinking and being in the world."[59]

Davis maintains that "speed-reading the Bible cancels most benefits of reading it at all,"[60] for what is lost in a quick turning of pages is attention to words themselves as conveyors of meaning. Western culture has lost its entrancement with words; it is a culture more reckless with words than ever before, and this disposition is reflected in its reading practices. Davis notes, "[w]e are now a society that 'processes' words rather than one that ponders them."[61] Echoes may be heard here of Paul Griffiths (see above, chapter 3), who too is against the quick consumption and processing of words common in western culture. With an overwhelming disregard of words prevalent in the west in both its speed of life and in its technologies, more than ever is a cultivated attention needed to take in the spiritual meaning of the Bible.

It must be noted that even as Davis, Griffiths, and other recent figures (such as Eugene Peterson[62]) rightly point out the challenges of read-

56. Davis, *Getting Involved with God*, 3, emphasis hers.
57. Davis, "Teaching the Bible," 15.
58. Davis, "Soil That is Scripture," 40.
59. Davis, *Getting Involved with God*, 3.
60. Davis, "Soil That Is Scripture," 40.
61. Davis, *Proverbs, Ecclesiastes*, 3.

62. As Peterson states, what is needed in reading the Bible is "ruminative and leisurely reading, a dalliance with words in contrast to wolfing down information." This is "the only kind of reading that is congruent with what is written in our Holy Scriptures, but also with all writing that is intended to change our lives." Peterson, *Eat This Book*, 3. As Peterson suggests, slow reading is needed for other kinds of reading, as well.

ing slowly in a western culture "rife with impatience," this is emphasis on slowness in reading goes back much earlier in the Christian tradition. In 1934, for instance, the English Methodist evangelist W.E. Sangster advised his hearers,

> We shall study [the Bible] every day—and *unhurriedly*. However little time we have at our disposal, let our study of the Book be without haste. There can be little value in a chapter hurriedly scanned and the mind diverted, at once, to something else. Take less. A chapter is often too much . . . Don't make a fetish of finishing a chapter. The deeper you get into it, the less you will need.[63]

While a need for slowness in reading is a refrain among recent writers considering spiritual reading, and a particular trait needed in western culture, the imperative to read "unhurriedly" is basic to the Christian tradition of reading its Scriptures.

Attentiveness to Biblical Language

Such lingering patience in reading, as Davis describes it, is manifested most significantly in attentiveness to words, and so close word-care is another mark of spiritual reading. Davis sets out that "close, imaginative attention to the *words* of Scripture" is "the chief means by which God's nature and will are known."[64] "Listen to the words: this is the first and great command of reading," Davis advises.[65] It is through noticing the actual words of Scripture (not vague abstractions of themes taken from them) that the Bible is encountered well and the possibility is opened up for God to be encountered within it. Acquiring a theological education begins with "learning patience with words, because the biblical writers (and all good theologians who follow them) choose their words with care."[66]

Davis's care for biblical words finds expression in her concerns for poetry and in studying the original biblical languages. The same skills needed for reading poetry are brought to bear for reading biblical texts:

> On the whole, it is better to think of the Bible as poetry rather than as prose, at least as we generally distinguish between those two in our reading practices. You cannot skim poetry for plot,

---

63. Sangster, *God Does Guide Us*, 60, emphasis his.
64. Davis, *Imagination Shaped*, xi, emphasis hers.
65. Davis, *Wondrous Depth*, 9.
66. Davis, "Soil That Is Scripture," 40.

and you cannot read it in distraction ... reading the Bible "as poetry" means slowing down to ponder each phrase, to wonder why this word was chosen and not another, how this line or paragraph or story builds on what precedes and leads into what follows.[67]

A poetic manner of reading the Bible thus means lingering on each of its words, delighting in its resonances and echoes with other words in Scripture. Davis further sets out that viewing Scripture as poetry means recognizing that is has ever-unfolding meanings: "In that sense, all of Scripture is poetry, and surely its inexhaustible potential to say something new and stunningly apt is a large part of what we mean when we call the Bible the word of the living God."[68]

One aspect of Davis's attention to words is that she listens to the ways in which particular verses echo and resonate across the entire canon of Scripture. This move of reading a biblical passage in light of the larger biblical tradition is a basic trait of Jewish and Christian exegesis, and is a move Davis often makes in her exegesis, even though she does not set it out explicitly as one of the key aspects of spiritual reading. Rather, this cross-biblical movement is a basic presumption of her spiritual reading of Scripture and her handling of its words, as the Bible's parts are ever being drawn back into its whole. It is through actual words that canonical-wide connections are often made, and so close attention to biblical words is a means of understanding the entire biblical tradition.

With such attention on the beauty, artistry, and cross-canonical resonance of biblical words, Davis's approach also entails that prominence is given to the original biblical languages. She sets forth learning Scripture's languages as an unparalleled means of learning to love Scripture, for language study "bring[s] you closer to the Word than you ever imagined you could be;"[69] it is "the surest way to gain a sense of the intense excitement of the biblical faith, of how the whole canon endlessly begets interpretations that are new, fresh, and good."[70] In stumbling over Hebrew and Greek, a reader comes to perceive more clearly the Bible's subtlety and artistry, and is pulled into the Bible's ways of thinking. Moreover, study of biblical languages is useful because it cultivates a sense of the strangeness of the Bible.

---

67. Ibid., 41. Davis draws here (as in other places) from Wendell Berry's statement that "a good poem ... cannot be written or read in distraction." Berry, *What Are People For*, 90.

68. Davis, *Scripture, Culture, and Agriculture*, 45.

69. Davis, "Soil That Is Scripture," 41.

70. Davis, "Losing A Friend," 78.

Davis explains that in translations of Scripture she favors "a translational style that retains a 'foreign' inflection, reminding us by its word choices and usages that the English Bible is a translated text."[71] Davis maintains that "it is best to enter this strange new world within the Bible by becoming radically unfamiliar about the language spoken there—at first, uncertain of every letter."[72] By entering into unfamiliar biblical languages, a possibility is carved out for the reader to be more at home in the unfamiliar world Scripture calls its readers to inhabit. A note of Barth is heard here—as he states, "If modern man is earnestly interested in the Bible, he certainly does not wish for its translation into his transitory jargon. Instead, he himself would like to participate in the effort to draw near what stands *there*."[73]

With her mention of "this strange new world" Davis echoes Barth, as do countless other theological readers who likewise find Barth's image an apt depiction of what is happening in the Bible. Barth's understanding of the reality that Scripture conveys directs a certain manner of readerly attention to its words. Peterson, as one inspired by Barth, argues that the heart of spiritual reading is a close attention to biblical words: "the more 'spiritual' we become, the more care we must give to exegesis. The more mature we become in the Christian faith, the more exegetically rigorous we must become. . . . Exegesis is the furthest thing from pedantry; exegesis is an act of love."[74] Although in the academy, biblical exegesis quite often is not "the furthest thing from pedantry," the way in which Barth and Davis and Peterson pay attention to words is indeed not pedantic; it is bound up in their love of and attention to God. Their manner of attention to words is that which Griffiths describes as "to read as a lover . . . [to] savor the words on the page, and to return to them over and over again."[75]

The kind of close reading and attention to biblical words Davis advocates thus has an orientation towards the person of God, and this distinguishes it from other manners of reading that also pay close attention to words. Most notably, spiritual reading differs in this regard from literary approaches to biblical language, and a comparison with Robert Alter, one literary reader of the Bible, will be helpful here.[76] Literary-oriented readers have long lingered over and pondered and found delight in the Bible's

---

71. Davis, "Entering the Story," 53.
72. Davis, "Teaching the Bible," 15.
73. *ET*, 35.
74. Peterson, *Eat This Book*, 53, 55.
75. Griffiths, *Religious Reading*, ix.
76. Here my discussion is limited to the aspect of biblical language within Alter's broader literary approach to the Bible. See chapter 3 for a fuller consideration of the possibility of reading the Bible as a classic work of literature.

words, apart from whether or not they relate those words to the question of God. While some literary critics may limit their interests to the internal dynamics of texts, others are concerned with the broader experiential dimension of reading and trace out how the beauty of the Bible's structures of language and diction creates such an experience. Alter is one of the most careful wordsmiths of the literary studies guild who revels in the Hebrew Bible to that end, painstakingly poring over its words and resonances.[77] He studies biblical words with a primary interest in the experience that happens though reading biblical texts, and shuns any kind of mechanical concept of how words work, as what is most pressing is the experiential power of literature.[78] As Alter explains about literature as a whole, "The formal aspects of the literary text may deserve the nicest attention, but reading is not a matter of nuts and bolts. . . . Most literary works . . . turn on an experiential dimension that is not finally reducible to the formal vehicles through which it is conveyed."[79]

It is this experiential dimension that Alter pays close attention to in his biblical translations and commentaries, as he aims to convey the rich *experience* of reading Hebrew texts. In *The Five Books of Moses: A Translation and Commentary*, Alter sets out his claim that "modern English versions—especially in their treatment of Hebrew narrative prose—have placed readers at a grotesque distance from the distinctive literary experience of reading the Bible in its original language."[80] Alter explains,

> Biblical Hebrew, in sum, has a distinctive music, a lovely precision of lexical choice, a meaningful concreteness, and a suppleness of expressive syntax that by and large have been given short shrift by translators with their eyes on other goals. The present

---

77. See, for example, his *The Art of Biblical Narrative, The Five Books of Moses: A Translation with Commentary, The Literary Guide to the Bible,* and *The Art of Biblical Poetry*.

78. Alter distinguishes his approach from the literary approaches of Formalism, Structuralism, and its descendents, which have in common "a skeptical attitude to the referential qualities of texts and an intense concern for their internal relationships." Alter and Kermode, *Literary Guide to the Bible*, 5.

79. Alter, *Pleasures of Reading*, 11, 206.

80. Alter, *Five Books of Moses*, xvii. Alter explains that there is "something seriously wrong with all the familiar English translations, traditional and recent, of the Hebrew Bible. Broadly speaking, one may say that in the case of the modern versions, the problem is a shaky sense of English, and in the case of the King James Version, a shaky sense of Hebrew. . . . As a consequence, the King James Version . . . remains the closest approach for English readers to the original—despite its frequent and at times embarrassing inaccuracies, despite its archaisms, and despite its insistent substitution of Renaissance English tonalities and rhythms for biblical ones." Ibid., xvi–xvii.

translation, whatever its imperfections, seeks to do fuller justice to all these aspects of biblical style in the hope of making the rich literary experience of the Hebrew more accessible to readers of English.[81]

Alter's interest in biblical words is in their crafted richness and beauty, and his aim as a translator is to convey the experiential, aesthetical dimension of reading Hebrew. He recognizes that many of the Bible's readers come to the Bible with theological interests, but his own interest is not in the way that God is at work through words, but in the way that the words themselves are working. The differences between Davis's and Alter's approaches are made clearer here: whereas Alter pays attention to biblical words essentially because biblical language is *meaningful* in creating an experience of reading, Davis is concerned with biblical language because it is *a means* through which God is known. She maintains that the words of the Bible are how the truth of God is conveyed. It is through the "*words* of Scripture" that "God's nature and will are known."[82]

The contrast between Alter's and Davis's approaches to biblical language is further evinced in the manner in which each understands the value of modern translations of the Bible into English. Alter maintains that the "recent flurry of translation activity, informed by the newly focused awareness of the meanings of biblical Hebrew" has not conveyed the vividness of biblical texts but instead has distanced readers from them.[83] Alter argues that English translations often hinder what the Bible is intending to give; readers are removed from the deep experience of reading the Bible in using translations that are careless of biblical languages and, at worst, "explain away the Bible."[84] As noted above, Davis too gives a high place to attending to the Bible's original languages, but when it comes to biblical translations, she, in contrast to Alter, maintains that

> [W]e are now living in an age of translations. A flurry of translational activity such as we now experience is not a common event in the history of the world; the last great period of Bible translations was the Reformation. So we should recognize this for what it is, a rare gift of the Holy Spirit in our time.[85]

81. Ibid., xlv.

82. Davis, *Imagination Shaped,* xi, emphasis hers.

83. Alter, *Five Books of Moses,* xvii.

84. "The unacknowledged heresy underlying most modern English versions of the Bible is the use of translation as a vehicle for *explaining* the Bible instead of representing it in another language, and in the most egregious instances this amounts to explaining away the Bible." Ibid., xix.

85. Davis, "Entering the Story," 52.

Davis argues that the recent growth of English translations is fueled not just by a growing scholarly competence in biblical languages but moreover by a sense that we must hear anew the Bible "speaking an urgent, unpredictable, and compelling word, the word of the Living God."[86] It is this desire to hear Scripture as the word of God that has prompted and arguably led to many good modern translations.[87] Davis manages both to care for the original biblical languages and to embrace modern translations, and she resolves this possible tension by maintaining that different settings call for different kinds of biblical translations. Davis explains,

> I am not a translational purist; if I were producing a translation for use in public worship, I would for the most part want people to forget that they were hearing a translation. In other words, I would want them to hear themselves being immediately addressed by the Scripture reading ... there is no such thing as an all-purpose translation.[88]

Alter and Davis thus each paint the "flurry" of biblical translations in different ways, one as rampant carelessness, and the other as an outpouring of the Spirit. It seems the truth lies somewhere in-between, for there is merit both in Alter's concerns for what modern translations often do to biblical language, and in Davis's understanding of the spiritual impulse behind recent translational activity. Some modern biblical translations indeed may be careless with biblical words, yet still, there is more to the Bible than its language. Insofar as the Bible is the word of the living God, that word that will never fit neatly into any human language and will ever be speaking anew. But while the impulse may be good to hear that word anew in translating Scripture, even good impulses can be carried out in poor ways. Many modern translations try to fit the Bible into its readers' worlds, rather than take them into the world of the Bible, and the result is a narrow translation focused on the individual.[89] Some translation projects in the west, moreover, are fueled by a consumerist society in which consumer products must ever be repackaged to appeal. In America the Bible-publishing industry (fueled by new translations and editions) is gluttonous; as one journalist notes,

---

86. Ibid., 52.

87. Davis is one of the translators for the recently-published *Common English Bible*, which describes itself as "a bold new translation designed to meet the needs of Christians as they work to build a strong and meaningful relationship with God through Jesus Christ." http://www.commonenglishbible.com/Explore/AbouttheCEB/tabid/196/Default.aspx

88. Davis, *Who Are You*, xii.

89. See comments on the Bible publishing industry in chapter 1.

"Bible publishers manage to sell twenty-five million copies a year of a book that almost everybody already has."[90]

Davis would distinguish between types of English Bible translations—some are indeed better intended and better carried-out than others—yet still, the flurry of translations is hard to evaluate. While the question of western Bible publishing practices moves outside of Alter and Davis's central concerns, the manner in which each approaches the issue of recent biblical translations is telling: Alter focuses on the value of the Bible as an enduring classic in western culture, and with that, the integrity of biblical language, while Davis seeks to discern the work of the Spirit through the Bible's language and witness. In Davis's spiritual reading of Scripture, attention to biblical language is born out of attention to God. She holds to the biblical text, urging study of it in its original languages, but she is open to the many ways in which its words may be heard and translated, as the word of God is heard through it. Such attention to biblical language is made out of a belief, as Barth says, that "Scripture is not mere writing but in its written character is Spirit and life."[91]

Uncertainty and Trust

Perhaps the most valuable aspect of reading in the original biblical languages or hearing different biblical translations is that familiar biblical texts can be heard anew. As Davis explains in her teaching, "Nothing so effectively freshens Scripture for my students as a translation that is at moments radically unfamiliar."[92] Another key part of spiritual reading thus is coming with uncertainty to the Bible. Davis explains, "it is possible to be familiar with the Bible in the wrong way . . . thinking you know what it says without reading it again and looking for what you do not yet know."[93] And so, "wise readers of the Bible are those who are able to free themselves of what they think they already know and listen for the unexpected thing that God now has to say to them."[94] A hunger for the unknown is needed, as a spiritual reader picks up the Bible not knowing what she will hear and take away that day. All texts (both familiar ones and ones less known and ambiguous) are places to encounter the Word of God anew.

---

90. Radosh, "Good Book Business."
91. *CD* I.2, 671.
92. Davis, "Entering the Story," 53.
93. Ibid., 45.
94. Davis, *Wondrous Depth*, 13.

Beneath this comfortableness with unknowing lies a deep trust that Scripture is a good Word from God; trust is the flip side of uncertainty in spiritual reading. Davis grapples with the uncertainties of the Bible out of that trust, as she "confesses that the biblical writings are ultimately the work of the Holy Spirit for the benefit of Israel, the church, and the world," and so there is still "work the Holy Spirit is doing through them even now."[95] Davis's trust entails "a conviction that, no matter how strange or unappealing a given passage may be, there must be something in it for us."[96] Richard Briggs similarly describes trust as that which allows the reader to stay with a text, having "the commitment to stand firm in the midst of the hermeneutical siege ... [in this] coming to a deeper grasp of how God might be at work 'in, with, and under' the text before us."[97] The trust that is brought to Scripture is a trust that God is using all its texts somehow, even in the places that seem odd and uncertain. And so Davis holds that a proper response to reading the Bible, even its ambiguous or troublesome parts, is the liturgical reply, "Thanks be to God."[98]

The trust that is needed to read Scripture well thus requires that something must happen before that reading to set that trust into place. Davis takes the church's trust in Scripture as a starting point for reading the Bible, and she does not spend time considering how that trust is cultivated. Where does it come from—belief in church creeds, immersion in church tradition, in seeing the readings of others? As Davis's concerns are essentially about what to do with that trust, her scarcity of reflection on its origin is not a lack in her work, but merely an area in which she heavily relies upon the church's view towards Scripture, particularly, its formation of the canon. Where more could be said, however, is how this trust in Scripture is sustained and deepened through reading the Bible. (And also how at times it can be unsettled and need rebuilding.) The reader who sets out into the Bible with a willingness to trust its words may find that trust grows stronger with each new reading as the Bible comes to shape his life; he is more willing to be uncertain about what each fresh reading will bring, as he knows its words are deeply good and true. Alternately, however, a reader with a starting trust in the Bible can come to encounter aspects of the Bible that are deeply unsettling, and tear away her trust in its goodness. Work then must be done for that trust to be renewed.

---

95. Davis, "Poetics of Generosity," 630.
96. Davis, *Imagination Shaped*, 245.
97. Briggs, *Virtuous Reader*, 133.
98. Davis, "Soil That is Scripture," 39.

The uncertainty brought to Scripture which Davis advocates starts from the place of trust. It is thus not a doubt or skepticism in the Bible itself, but rather, an uncertainty in ourselves as interpreters, in what we might think the Bible might be saying. It is a stance that sees the Bible as more interesting than ourselves and offering more than we could piece together on our own. Davis looks to Scripture in trust, uncertain of what it means at times, and uncertain of how faithfully she is listening, but always certain that it is a good gift from God. Davis's sense of uncertainty echoes Barth, who maintains that the Word of God must always be encountered anew. More directly, Davis cites Martin Buber's admonition to "Read the Bible as though it were something entirely unfamiliar. . . . Face the book with a new attitude as something new. . . . Do not believe anything a priori."[99]

This approach has merit in opening up the reader to a new experience of hearing God's word, yet where Davis (and Buber and Barth) could say more is on the ways the Bible sounds out the same truths over and over again, and the ways that each fresh biblical reading rests still upon earlier ones. Not every deep reading of Scripture hinges upon being struck by something utterly new; at times the surprising thing in reading may be seeing a familiar text suddenly speak into a new situation. A strong thread of the Christian belief in Scripture is that God not only speaks through the Bible anew, but he also deepens its truths in the hearts of its readers, confirming them again and again in subsequent readings, reminding readers of what they once learned but have again forgotten, placing old truths into new circumstances. Hearing something new in Scripture must be balanced with simply hearing Scripture anew, as what is often needed in the spiritual life is reminding, is pulling-back-to. Moreover, the word that God speaks to a reader today through the Bible often builds upon words he has spoken in days before. Every hearing of Scripture does not have to begin from square one, for the learning that comes from the Bible is a progressive sort, with each new truth of Scripture opening up more.

Although uncertainty and trust in reading Scripture need qualifying, Davis is surely right in emphasizing it as a part of spiritual reading, as it is a posture that essentially seeks to know more. A spiritual reader is humble, one never satisfied with her own biblical interpretations, but ever going on to listen anew, trusting there is more to God and to life than she can ever fully know.

---

99. Quoted by Davis in "Entering the Story," 53, taken from a citation of Martin Buber in Everett Fox, *Five Books of Moses*, ix.

Repentance and Spiritual Growth

Hearing the Bible as a fresh word from God often means that what is heard is a call to repentance. "[W]e are pressed to exercise our imagination," Davis explains, "in order to discover the perspective in which every part of Scripture may be heard as the Word of God, that is, to discover how it calls us to repentance."[100] Davis understands spiritual reading to involve seeking how the Bible calls us "to think and act differently in response to what we hear," to undertake the change of mind that is *metanoia*.[101] Such repentance is wrought out of a reading that is so open to the biblical message that it is willing to hear it against oneself, straining to hear in Scripture not just the realities of God but also the realities of one's own sinful condition.

A spiritual reading of Scripture thus means "having our lives disrupted and profoundly changed by the word God speaks to us through Scripture."[102] What comes about is "a new moral vision" which leads to more ethical living.[103] Repentance and ethical living moreover lead to better Scripture reading, as repenting of sin opens up further aspects of the Bible that were hidden. Repentance is thus an ongoing part of spiritual reading; spiritual reading requires constant turning back to the life of God. In this Davis draws upon Dietrich Bonhoeffer's assessment that "Proper reading of Scripture. . . . grows or diminishes according to my spiritual condition."[104] Reading and repentance flow back and forth in spiritual reading, each leading to a deepening of the other. As Peterson explains, "the living and reading [are] reciprocal . . . the back-and-forthness assimilating the reading to the living, the living to the reading.[105]

In her concern with repentance, Davis suggests that the practice of reading Scripture spiritually is something that grows with the reader, deepening as her Christian life deepens. Davis explains this situation by likening the reading of Scripture to the practice of gardening (with both works requiring humility, love, and patience): "It is not simply that a humble, loving, and patient person is able to make a garden beautiful; reciprocally, the daily work of gardening seems to cultivate those qualities in a person."[106] One who wants to read the Bible spiritually must bring some kind of spiritual

---

100. Davis, *Imagination Shaped*, 264.
101. Davis, "Losing A Friend," 76.
102. Davis, *Wondrous Depth*, 16.
103. Davis, "No Explanations," 97.
104. Bonhoeffer, *Life Together*, 64.
105. Peterson, *Eat This Book*, xii.
106. Davis, "Soil That is Scripture," 37.

disposition to it—a measure of humility, love, and patience—but yet, it is through reading the Bible that these qualities are grown. As Briggs states, "Our ability to understand the Bible as God's book is all a part of our spiritual growth and our relationship with God."[107] James M. Houston similarly explains, "Becoming a Bible reader involves becoming a Christian, in all the depth and fullness of what the apostle speaks of as being 'in Christ.' All the virtues and graces of being a Christian are necessary to grow as a reader of the Word of God."[108]

Here is somewhat of an odd situation, then: on the one hand, reading the Bible well will make the reader more Christ-like; but on the other hand, the more Christ-like the reader is, the better her reading will be. Jeffrey explains that this can seem to come to "a kind of divine catch-22: the reader of Scripture will become, in the largest sense, only as effective an interpreter of its texts as he or she is already a translator of the text in personal life."[109] Spiritual practices on the whole are like this—other ones (such as fasting or prayer) are learned simply by doing them, but the more they are practiced and shape the practitioner, the better they come to be done. The ways in which spiritual practices tend towards spiritual growth are mysterious, however, and one cannot chart out how one's spiritual growth and spiritual reading merge together.[110] Briggs aptly describes this situation:

> The real reader who wishes to read Scripture will not find it easy to correlate their progress along the path of the moral life with their handling of the text; but in various and perhaps unpredictable ways, the one who is engaging with God in the mysteries of holiness, justice, forgiveness, and wisdom will find that their meditations on texts witnessing to these realities are drawn deeper and further than they would previously have had the capacity to see.[111]

It is in coming into the life of God, "engaging with God," that spiritual growth happens and spiritual reading deepens. And this kind of spiritual growth is mysterious because, as Lewis describes, "there is no question of learning a subject but of steeping ourselves in a Personality, acquiring a new

---

107. Briggs, *Light to Live By*, 75.
108. Houston, "Towards a Biblical Spirituality," 10.
109. Jeffrey, *People of the Book*, 178.
110. Serene Jones states, "the process of scriptural formation happen[s] in its own mysterious way.... It happens where life happens, in the chaotic coursings of the everyday, that place where God is alive in the mysterious fullness of each moment's unfolding." Jones, "Inhabiting Scripture, Dreaming Bible," 74.
111. Briggs, *Virtuous Reader*, 210.

outlook and temper, breathing a new atmosphere, suffering Him, in His own way, to rebuild in us the defaced image of Himself."[112] As this image is rebuilt in a biblical reader more and more each day, his reading is also, line by line, made in that image, too.

Concluding Note: The Place of Prayer, and of Jesus?

Davis writes from a church disordered in its reading of the Bible, then, and from a world even more disordered, and she picks up Scripture with wonder, amazed at its words, reading slowly in Hebrew and Greek and paying attention to poetic tones, not quite sure what she will find, but knowing that these words will reorder her life and make it new, as it is doing to all of creation. Davis's wonder, imagination, slowness, attentiveness to biblical language, uncertainty, trust, repentance, and spiritual growth is a whole pattern of movement through Scripture, a way in which to venture deep.

While there is more to Davis's spiritual reading in practice, as will be seen below, here a flag might be raised on two essential aspects of spiritual reading that seem to be missing sustained reflection in her work—the place of prayer and the place of Jesus in the Christian spiritual reading of the Bible. These two aspects of reading are in the background of Davis's approach, but they do not receive as concentrated analysis as the other reading traits mentioned above. Beginning with prayer, Davis doubtlessly posits prayer as a key part of biblical reading; she starts both *Getting Involved With God* and *Wondrous Depth* with the Psalms because of their role as prayers. Psalms "may guide our first steps towards deeper involvement with God, because the Psalms give us a new possibility for prayer . . . they force us to do more than engage in reasonable speculation about God . . . through them we find ourselves talking to the living God."[113] Several of Davis's published sermons are on the Psalms and explore their nature as compelling prayers. However, even with her enthusiasm for the Psalms, and her awareness of the presence of God in reading, Davis seldom discusses how prayer functions in the practice of spiritual reading. How is spiritual reading done ultimately through prayer, through the Spirit's help?

The role of prayer and the need for the Spirit is an aspect of spiritual reading that has been considered more directly by other theological readers. Mariano Magrassi, in his explication of the practice of *lectio divina*, states that in reading Scripture, "Above all else, we will need to pray."[114] Barth saw

112. Lewis, *Reflections on the Psalms*, 95–96.
113. Davis, *Getting Involved With God*, 5, 12.
114. Magrassi, *Praying the Bible*, 60.

prayer as central to biblical reading: "we realise that we cannot read and understand Holy Scripture without prayer, that is, without invoking the grace of God."[115] In his *Evangelical Theology* lectures prayer comes even more to the forefront of biblical reading, as it is done beneath a prayer of "*Veni creator Spiritus!* 'Come, O, come, thou Spirit of life!'"[116] Ever-present prayer is the most essential thing for reading well, for it pulls the reader into remembering the context of Scripture as a work of God, and it hones the reader's dependence upon him. Webster explains that

> Christian reading is thus, very simply, a *prayerful* activity. Prayerfulness is not a spiritual embellishment, or even a preliminary recoil or gathering of resources before proceeding to read in an entirely natural manner ... prayer is the humbling and reorientation of our agency, which now finds its end in hearing God's Word.[117]

Webster holds that spiritual reading involves constantly asking for the Spirit's help in reading aright. Prayer enables the reader to have "teachableness," a spirituality that centers upon being taught.[118]

Unlike Barth or Webster, Davis is not writing a theology of Scripture, so perhaps there is less need for her to outline the role of prayer in her work; prayer is simply presumed all throughout it. Yet still, a sustained reflection on prayer could be helpful, as it would show more clearly the dependence of spiritual reading of Scripture on God's presence and work. Without prayer spiritual reading would be fruitless. Prayer relates the spiritual reading of the Bible to the Spirit who oversees it and ever sustains it.

Prayer, then, in the Christian context, is not just calling on God's help but even more so, it is recognizing the spiritual air one is breathing—the Holy Spirit is at the heart of spiritual reading. Such a Trinitarian awareness leads into the second essential aspect of the spiritual reading of Scripture that Davis could offer more sustained reflection upon—the place of Jesus in such reading. Davis writes as a Christian believer and in her dealings with the Old Testament she is ever aware of its relation to the New Testament and the gospel of Jesus. In her exegesis of Old Testament passages in *Getting Involved With God*, for instance, Davis speaks of Jesus' resurrection, incarnation, death, passion, second coming, power, vulnerability, and obscurity, and the need for Christians to feed on Christ through faith.[119]

---

115. *CD* I.2, 684.
116. *ET*, 58.
117 Webster, *Word and Church*, 83.
118 Webster, *Holy Scripture*, 101,102.
119. Respectively, pages 19, 46, 63, 151, 167, 172, 177, 208.

In many sermons Davis relates Old Testament texts to Jesus—see, e.g., her sermon connecting Moses and Mary in *Getting Involved With God*—and in *Wondrous Depth*, Davis strongly advocates "reading around Christ."[120]

Yet even though she often makes beautiful ties to Christian images and beliefs in her Old Testament exegesis, her work is not that of early and medieval spiritual readers who sought Jesus in all pages of Scripture. Davis understands christological connections in the Old Testament to be a move that Christians may freely make, but do not have to make: "The freedom to preach Old Testament texts christologically is, in my judgment, just that: a freedom that the Christian preacher may exercise at any time and should exercise sometimes, not a requirement for preaching any particular text responsibly."[121] Davis recognizes that different texts call for different moves, and so even while she is in favor of christological exegesis, she insists there is no clear-cut guideline for its use.

A question remains, however, over what place Jesus does hold in Davis's understanding of the Old Testament. To be clear, this critique is not to insist that Davis must relate all her Old Testament exegesis explicitly to Christ, but only that a clearer vision is needed on what she is doing, as an ad-hoc christological reading is in contrast to both early/medieval and modern approaches. As de Lubac has argued (see chapter 5), early spiritual reading of Scripture hinged upon the person of Jesus; it is Jesus who prompted such reading and was seen as its true end. The contrast to modern biblical scholarship is stark: as Webster remarks, Jesus has "virtually disappeared from theological hermeneutics in the modern era."[122] Although Jesus has certainly not "disappeared" in Davis's work, he is a less obvious figure than may be expected for a traditional Christian reading of the Old Testament, and it is unclear how he fits into her broader understanding of Scripture. More clarity is needed on her moves towards Christ, as he is the source of all Christian wonder and trust and repentance and growth, all which Davis pursues in biblical reading. As Barth states, "Christ is that infinitely wondrous event which compels a person, so far as he experiences and comprehends this event, to be necessarily, profoundly, wholly, and irrevocably astonished."[123]

What is needed to round out Davis's account, then, is to cast the practice of spiritual reading of Scripture in light of the prior and ongoing activity of a Triune God. A deepened awareness of prayer might highlight that spiritual reading is about more than the efforts of its readers—it is, as Webster says,

---

120. Davis, *Getting Involved with God*, 45–49, and *Wondrous Depth*, 77.
121. Davis, *Wondrous Depth*, 72.
122. Webster, *Word and Church*, 48.
123. *ET*, 71.

"self-forgetful reference to the prevenient action and presence of God."[124] The work of God is behind all aspects of spiritual reading. That work of God, moreover, is most manifest in the person of Jesus, and an awareness of Jesus will shape spiritual reading in light of the wider Christian life, a life that is centered upon Christ. The nature of reading follows Christian spirituality as a whole in that it hinges upon the work of God as done through Jesus Christ, a work that is accomplished through the gracious action of God. Evelyn Underhill expresses this well (as was mentioned above, chapter 1)— in words that Davis would likely agree with, Underhill points out:

> Our spiritual life is His affair; because, whatever we may think to the contrary, it is really produced by His steady attraction, and our humble and self-forgetful response to it. It consists in being drawn, at His pace and in His way, to the place where He wants us to be.[125]

The same might be said about spiritual reading—"whatever we may think to the contrary, it is really produced by His steady attraction. . . . It consists in being drawn." Spiritual reading, even as its readers take part, is God's affair.

---

124. Webster, *Word and Church*, 43. Webster argues, "what counts as a Christian reading of the Bible will include certain expectations of divine action as axiomatic and operative in acts of interpretation" (73).

125. Underhill, *Spiritual Life*, 35.

CHAPTER 7

Ellen Davis's Art in Practice

WITH ALL HER PROPOSALS on the nature of spiritual reading, Davis's work is ultimately a praxis of Scripture, a reflection of her reading practices on the ground, to which we now turn. Davis's readings of the Bible evince the manner in which her spiritually-engaged approach towards reading is not a methodology or a hermeneutic but rather a spiritual aesthetic, a way of seeing the Bible and responding to its art. Here I consider a few places where Davis has done that, examples of her exegesis in her readings of Psalm 109, Psalm 149, Numbers 11, and the book of Ruth. As the first three examples come from Davis's published sermons and brief theological pieces, in none of them is Davis working out a full exegesis. And so, my aim is to evaluate what Davis does with these biblical passages in light of the limited space she has to comment upon them, and then to supplement her thoughts with reflections of my own. With the last example, her work on Ruth, Davis has written a full-length commentary in conjunction with artist Margaret Adams Parker. My aim with this piece is to trace out how Davis's manner of spiritual reading works on the level of biblical commentary, where her principles have wider space to unfold.

Psalm 109

In *Getting Involved With God*, Davis begins her spiritual reading of the Old Testament with the Psalms—"because they are there," she says. The Psalms are found everywhere, quoted in the New Testament, read in worship services, echoed in poetry and liturgy; they are ubiquitous because they are "the single best guide to the spiritual life currently in print."[1] Davis views

---

1. Davis, *Getting Involved with God*, 7.

the book of Psalms as a good place to begin reading the Old Testament (and the entire Bible) in a spiritually-engaged manner, as the Psalms guide readers towards authentic prayer and openness to God. Such prayer and openness enables spiritual growth, for "profound change happens always in the presence of God."[2] The Psalms "teach us wisdom in prayer" and "help us improve our aim" so that the one praying comes more fully into the presence of God.[3]

Davis offers readings of various psalms in *Getting Involved With God*, covering psalms of lament, cursing psalms, and psalms of praise. Her exegesis of Psalm 109 is particularly striking as an example of spiritually-engaged reading, as she explains through this psalm how the cursing psalms are not only an appropriate form of Christian prayer, but a needed form of prayer. Psalm 109 is a prolonged curse of the psalmist's enemies (the longest of such cursing psalms), with the psalmist calling on God to act on his behalf. It has requests for revenge in one breath, and assurances of God's help in another, and it leaves the modern reader no easy way to grasp its passionate language or tidy up its messy fervor.

Davis cannot cover in a few pages all the psalm's aspects, but she begins her reading of Psalm 109 by pointing out the personal connection to those who are the target of the psalms' curses—this psalm has not only to do with anger, but betrayal, as well. The psalmist, while he is "all prayer" (v. 4), has a prayer for his enemy that is intense, calling for even his enemy's children to wander and beg away from their home. Most churches and lectionaries, taken aback by such lines, do not recite this psalm on Sundays, yet Davis holds that "by clapping our hand over the psalmist's mouth in that way, we lose something the Bible intends us to have . . . an opportunity to bring our own anger into the context of our relationship with God."[4] This psalm, like other cursing psalms, enables its readers and hearers to come before God with full honesty, placing their anger into the context of the biblical faith. What is needed to be healed from that anger is first to offer it to God, to acknowledge bitter feelings "yet not yield to their tyranny."[5]

Psalm 109 helps its readers to "mak[e] that offering of anger" in several ways: first, it gives words for one's anger; second, it assures that "vengeful anger is one mode of access to God;" and third, it sets out that the cry for vengeance is made through an appeal for God to act.[6] The psalm gives voice

2. Ibid., 5.
3. Ibid., 9, 11.
4. Ibid., 24.
5. Ibid., 26.
6. Ibid., 26–27.

to feelings of anger and resentment, helping its readers to articulate their cloudy despair and move past their own sputterings through the sputterings of the psalmist. (Davis recounts how she herself shouted aloud cursing psalms in an empty chapel when as a seminarian she was betrayed by a friend.) Psalm 109 also assures its readers that to be angry at unrighteousness is not to be apart from God (for God "is, like us, outraged by those who violate trust and rupture community").[7] Moreover, the psalm reminds its readers that God is a God of justice who will surely act. An essential point of the psalm is that the psalmist does not take revenge in his own hands but entrusts himself and his enemies to the Lord.

And here is where the rub comes in, Davis points out, for readers of Scripture will know that "God is manifest in judgment of our enemies but also, alas, in mercy towards them."[8] God calls even one's enemies back to himself and may be as merciful to them as he was to the ones they wronged. The moral is: it is an unpredictable thing to ask for others to fall into the hands of the living God. Obliquely Davis drops this Psalm into the wider stream of what Scripture says about God's mercy, as she places its clamoring for justice in light of the mercy we all do not deserve. Yet even in knowing this mercy, a desire for revenge may still burn hot on the Christian's heart, and so Davis emphasizes that one important aspect of Psalm 109 for the Christian life is that a Christian will inevitably encounter attack from others at some point and need words to pray. Even when one is "blessedly free of the feelings" of cursing psalms, they are instructive to read to store up for the time needed.[9]

Davis does not leave Psalm 109 at that, however, for she takes Psalm 109 a riskier step forward, suggesting when we readers are free from our own feelings of resentment, we should turn the psalm "a full 180 degrees, until it is directed at yourself, and ask: Is there anyone in the community of God's people who might want to say this to God about me—or maybe, about us?" And this, Davis finds, is true:

> Here is one of several ways I could answer that question for myself: I am materially privileged beyond most people who are alive at this time, who have previously lived on the earth, or who will live in future generations. By social location, income, and personal habit, I am an active participant in a rapacious industrial economy, regularly consuming far more than I need of the world's goods. I have largely failed to moderate my lifestyle

---

7. Ibid., 26–27.
8. Ibid., 27.
9. Ibid., 28.

in accordance with what I can reasonably expect will be the needs of my great-grandchildren's generation, to say nothing of the present needs of those living in the Two-Thirds World. Yes, there are those who might cry out to God this night or fifty years hence:

> Let [her] memory be cut off from the earth,
> because [she] did not remember to act in covenant faith
> but hounded a person poor and needy,
> crushed in heart, even to death . . .

God give me courage to hear that prayer and act upon what I have heard.[10]

Here in one stroke the psalm is set into Davis's life and wider culture. Davis's reading finds the evil ones of the psalm at work today, only it is we who are they. This last turning Davis takes with Psalm 109 is a move of deep honesty, for she reads the psalm against herself and sees ways in which she is no better than the psalmist's enemies. The context of the psalm becomes the context of her own life, yet in a way that deeply unsettles that life and calls her to change. The psalmist's cry for righteousness and justice is heard against herself. By taking the psalm's anger and prayers for justice personally, Davis hears the psalm as an ever-present demand for the life of God to be lived.

So what are the moves Davis is making throughout her spiritual reading of this psalm; how are her reading principles operating? Her interpretation of Psalm 109 reflects the manner in which her emphases for spiritual reading come to play in various ways in specific texts; each biblical text calls for some principles more than others, and not every principle is always directly employed. Unlike some spiritual and academic guides for reading the Bible, Davis's approach does not entail a step-by-step outline of how to read and exegete a biblical text. Art consists in ever making choices, and the choices she makes at each turn in biblical reading reflect the broader manner in which she views Scripture and its spiritual reading—the Bible is a living entity that ever calls for new angles and responses. She follows both Barth and de Lubac in this; as de Lubac has argued, there is "no method, no scientific procedure which will ever be enough to make us hear 'the music written on the silent pages of the Holy Books.'"[11]

When Davis comes to Psalm 109, an emphasis on uncertainty and trust is one of the strongest reading principles she brings to the forefront—it is evinced from the start in the way in which Davis is willing to stick with

---

10. Ibid., 28–29.

11. *Scripture*, 19. Barth likewise insists, "There is no method by which revelation can be made revelation." *CD I.1*, 183.

Psalm 109, even with the short shrift it gets in lectionaries and in common church practice. Davis trusts there to be worth in the psalm and is willing to keep poring through its words to find a means by which it speaks truly of God and aids the Christian life. She enters into the psalm openheartedly, believing that it is good. One way to resolve the difficulties of this psalm would be simply to attribute its rage to the human nature of biblical authors, and even that would not be without spiritual edification—Clifton Black argues that "as long as we hide from ourselves the pettiness, anguish, injustice, folly, and murderousness of our forefathers in faith, we shall continue to blind ourselves to the same pathologies that God is still laboring to heal within us."[12] Yet this is not how Davis seeks the spiritual benefit of this psalm—she finds that more can be learned here than a poor example of prayer, and holds that this prayer is still, in fact, worth praying. Wonder in her reading is less a sense of amazement than a sense of bewilderment, as she wonders what in this psalm is for the life of faith. Yet that wonder has confidence in finding an answer, and is enabled by her unwavering trust.

With that trust, Davis reads Psalm 109 slowly enough to notice key details, such as that the psalmist is making a prayer and calls on God to act, rather than taking matters into his own hands (v. 1, 21, 26–27). At first glance, her principles of slowness and attentiveness to biblical language do not seem to have an overly strong bearing in her reading of this psalm, however, as in her initial exposition Davis's eye is not caught by its specific words and turns of phrases. Rather than examine the particularities of the psalmist's disdain, Davis wants to understand the impulse behind it and grapple with the sense of the psalm as a whole. She places the psalm in the wider current of the biblical faith, evaluating its cries for justice in light of biblical ideas about God's mercy and justice.

All of the psalm's curses merge together in the first part of Davis's reading of Psalm 109, and attention is not lavished upon particular pleas for vengeance that the psalmist is requesting. A psalm filled with curses might seem to entail that close attention to the words is not as essential, perhaps because in general, words of anger are usually not worth dwelling upon. Yet may it be that in the context of a biblical psalm, such words are worth pondering? The early church took up specific phrasing of this psalm, as Acts 1.20 records that v. 8, "let another take his place," was understood to signify the need for another apostle to take Judas's place. While Davis does not mention this use of Psalm 109 in the Christian tradition, and she does not ponder its specific words in her initial assessment of the psalm, her principles of reading suggest that close attention to even particular curses might have some

---

12. Black, "Journeying through Scripture," 70.

fruitfulness—even without having to go the route of early Christian interpretation. In the case of Psalm 109, attention to the specific wording of the curses may reveal to the reader how deep one's disdain for another can go, such that one wants another's children to "wander about and beg, seeking food far from the ruins they inhabit" (v. 10). With this vivid image the reader may be jarred to recognize feelings that have flooded her own heart; the picture of wandering, hungry children questions the reader whether she might ever be so consumed with hatred and callousness to want that for another.

Throughout her assessment of the psalm a key aspect of Davis's reading is the principle of imagination, which she employs to place Psalm 109 into the context of modern readers' lives, both as a resource for their own prayers, and as a spiritual challenge. Imagination entails understanding the feelings of the psalmist and seeing how those feelings fit into one's present circumstances. One may imagine the psalmist's pleas to be one's own. Imagination is to do more than foster empathy, however, as it can also create a spiritual challenge. Davis presses readers of Psalm 109 to "turn it and turn it" to see how the psalm is calling them to change.[13] And here, in this turning it and turning it, is where Davis's attention to biblical language comes back in, for in the biblical words of "hounding a person poor and needy" Davis senses a connection between the psalmist's enemies and herself—she wonders whether she is one who hounds the poor and needy in the world, whether her lifestyle is causing the oppression of others. With this turning of the psalm, principles of imagination, close attention to language, and repentance come together to pose this searing question.

As Davis understands Psalm 109 to be judging her consumer lifestyle in the western world, she enacts a radical recontextualization of the psalm. Even though "recontextualization" is not a phrase that Davis drops often into her writing, what she does with Scripture (especially in her agrarian readings) might be characterized as such. Her recontextualization, however, is not in terms of what a text "meant" and what it now "means." (Krister Stendahl's famous approach is too rigid for Davis's own paths of movement through biblical texts.) Rather, Davis recognizes the many contexts a biblical text may have when it is placed in light of the entire canon and ongoing Christian tradition. She presses for "a more inclusive view of a text's history, a view that takes into account not only its supposed original meaning but also the abundance of meaning that has been found in the text through the

---

13. Davis, *Getting Involved With God*, 28. Exercising the imagination, as Davis has explained, allows one to find "the perspective in which every part of Scripture may be heard as the Word of God, that is, to discover how it calls us to repentance." Davis, *Imagination Shaped*, 264.

centuries by Jews and Christians."[14] As Jon Levenson similarly argues, "the meaning of a textual unit changes with the other textual units with which it comes into relationship—not just other biblical texts written by authors in other cultural contexts, but also postbiblical documents that the tradition has given us." And so, "a text can say more than any individual author meant; the whole is larger than the sum of the parts."[15]

It is this kind of "abundance of meaning" that is evinced in Davis's reading of Psalm 109, as the psalmist's pleas find a place in the life of western readers. Although the spiritual way that Davis reads the psalm is not anywhere near its original intention, her reading keeps with important aspects of the tenor of it, for it sets the reader in relation to issues of oppression and disregard which are the psalm's central concerns. The psalm's vagueness as to the form of the injustice cried against allows for such a reading. Davis keeps the central issues of the psalm as the focus of her interpretation, only looking for a way in which her life as a reader has a place within those issues. Such a reading of the psalm—putting oneself into it, or rather, being pulled into it—is the goal of spiritual reading, for it allows the Bible to speak jarringly into one's own life. Curses themselves become points of challenge and spiritual growth.

Psalm 149

Davis handles the anger of Psalm 109 in a brilliant way, neither dismissing it nor justifying it, but being judged by it and seeing it as a summons to the things of God. When she considers the cries of Psalm 149, however, she detects a different note, as there she finds more that needs careful handling and unpacking. In her sermon "Self-Inflicted Violence" in *The Art of Reading Scripture,* Davis offers a reading of the praise and violence that mark Psalm 149, and while she presents a challenging sermon, her exegesis of Psalm 149 needs probing. Although Davis is a careful exegete and her scholarly work flows with compelling exegesis, here I mention her sermon on Psalm 149 as one of her less convincing examples, because I find it instructive in revealing the need for spiritual readings of biblical texts to hold closely to those texts.

---

14. Davis, *Wondrous Depth*, 65.

15. Levenson goes on to explain, "When I say this, I am not talking as a mystic or even as a believer. I am talking as a student of literature (I majored in English in college). But I think what I am saying ought to be of great interest to all who see in scripture something more than what was on the mind of the human authors who wrote it, with all their human limitations." Levenson, "Teach the Texts in Contexts."

Davis begins her sermon with a citation of the most dissonant verse in Psalm 149, "Let the high praises of God be in their throat and a two-edged sword in their hand." She notes, "It's bothersome, that cry of violence and praise that erupts in the next-to-last-psalm, disturbing the long crescendo of alleluias with which the Psalter ends."[16] Davis holds all Scripture to be instructive, however, and so even with her discomfort with its violence, she does not want to dismiss the psalm, even this verse. In her sermon Davis brings together these two themes of violence and praise, and along with them, picks up the theme of All Saints' Day, the occasion on which she preached Psalm 149 as its appointed lectionary reading. Her sermon is directed by the wondering what it is in vv. 6–9, with its sword-wielding and vengeance-wreaking, that is befitting of the saints.

Davis finds a way out by turning the sword—to the saints themselves. She envisions the saints as those who are ever setting swords against themselves; the pattern of sainthood is "first withdraw and do battle in your own heart, and then do battle in the world."[17] Saints are those who recognize and fight against their own sin and evil inclinations, giving themselves "completely to that lifelong work of self-inflicted, surgical violence which the tradition calls repentance."[18] Disillusionment with oneself is how saints are made and true praise to God is given. The sword that is picked up is Ephesians' "sword of the Spirit, which is the word of God" (Eph 6:17), that which cuts most deeply, and the saint is one who constantly holds that word before her and prays. The battle is the fight against evil, in which the saints will soldier on to the death, but the victory is already assured. "For over all the fighting and suffering and singing of the saints stands the cross of Christ, the towering sign of that world-shattering conjunction between violence and praise."[19]

Davis's sermon is stirring and draws together well the connection between violence and praise that mark the Christian life, both in the sign of the cross, and in the sword of the Spirit that must be set against evil for the glory of God. Her reading is helpful for painting a picture of a saint as one who battles sin. It is a needed message, and not unorthodox or unencouraging, but yet, this reading of Psalm 149 seems, to use Augustine's analogy, to have left the path for the field. Psalm 149 has an unusual conjunction of praise and violence, but nowhere does it hint of repentance or that the

---

16. Davis, "Self-Inflicted Violence," 294.
17. Ibid., 295.
18. Ibid., 296.
19. Ibid., 298.

violence is a saintly one turned against the self.[20] Davis's interpretation that the sword of the saints is wielded against the self is an exegetical move that actually leads the reader out of the biblical text.

But before exploring how her reading does that, it must be pointed out, however, that Davis has good precedent for her move. She echoes the interpretation Origen makes about swords in his *Homilies on Joshua*:

> Go therefore, even you! Let us prepare ourselves for battles of this kind. Let us thrust Ai through with the edge of the sword, and let us extinguish all the inhabitants of chaos, all opposing powers. Would that I also, just now while I speak the word of God to you, could strike the heart of the transgressor! If I do that, it is certain that with the sword of my mouth I shall slay fornication, slay malice, I shall restrain passion. And if there are any other evil things, I shall exterminate them "with the edge of the sword"; that is, by the word of my mouth, and I shall not leave behind any "who may be saved or who may escape."[21]

Origen explains that when one reads in Holy Scriptures "about the battles of the just ones, about the slaughter and carnage of murderers, and that the saints spare none of their deeply rooted enemies.... You should understand that the wars of the just by the method I set forth above, that these wars are waged by them against sin."[22] Origen's envisioning of the swords turned against sin is exactly the image Davis sets out in Psalm 149; her reading lands solidly in Origen's patch of church tradition.[23]

---

20. As a side note, it may be that the liturgical setting of All Saints' Day is not the best starting point to find a way into Psalm 149, as Davis's emphasis on saints directed her reading. Although Davis wants to keep to church tradition and find what in that tradition has seen a connection between Psalm 149 and All Saints', it may be problematic to make this the *start* of exegesis, as the liturgical connection can overshadow the psalm's internal movement. More could be said on the relationship between biblical interpretation and church lectionaries, but I mention it here only to flag the fact that handling exegesis vis-à-vis the lectionary can produce mixed results, as it seems to have done in Davis's sermon.

21. Origen, *Homily 8*, in *Homilies on Joshua*, 92–93.

22. Ibid., 94.

23. Augustine makes a similar move as Origen, as he turns the sword of Psalm 149 into a metaphor for reproofing others: "Let the 'sword twice sharpened' go forth from you, delay not. Say to your friend . . . 'What kind of man are you, who hast abandoned Him by whom you were made . . . ?' When he begins to blush, when he begins to feel compunction, you have made a wound with your sword, it has reached the heart, he is about to die, that he may live." Augustine, "Exposition on Psalm 149."

By staying with the image of a wielded sword, Davis follows early spiritual interpreters who found great significance in actual biblical words—as R. R. Reno explains about Gregory the Great's exegesis,

> No matter how we might judge the legitimacy of Gregory's exegesis, we must allow that his theological interpretation remains within the verbal atmosphere of the text—something one cannot say about conceptual allegories that dominate modern attempts to provide theological exegesis of the Old Testament. Gregory is not "drawing out" a message in a moment of theological application. His reading involves 'drawing in' the text. In other words, Gregory reads the Scriptures in such a way that the very words of the text are the privileged building blocks for theological insight.[24]

Davis is thus, in the manner of Gregory and Origen, drawing in the building block of the sword in Psalm 149 to find a theological insight for the Christian life. But even as she clings tightly to the psalm's sword, she does not stay with the rest of the wording of the psalm (as patristic interpreters would do, as they would moreover attend to the mystery of Christ). Apart from the sword, Davis does not stay within the "verbal atmosphere of the text."

Davis's reading uses the sword of Psalm 149 to move towards a broader theological message. A reading like Davis's is certainly one way to go with the text—it is a helpful way to make sense of swords wielded against others. But yet Davis's reading raises the question, is this the most fitting way to pursue spiritual interpretation today? As de Lubac has argued, it is the spiritual *impulse* of earlier biblical interpreters, not necessarily their methods, that should be followed.[25] What is needed is to discern what the Spirit is doing in the present age, for "[i]t would be impossible to restore [premodern spiritual exegesis] today in all its fullness . . . in the spiritual order it is an illusion to think that anything can be absolutely acquired, once for all."[26] Although Origen's manner of spiritual exegesis offers a model for Davis's interpretation of Psalm 149, in the long run this type of interpretation is hard to line up with her other reading principles, and it may prove less fruitful than other exegetical approaches. The problem is not just that modern readers have historical and contextual concerns, but even more significantly, that this manner of modern allegorizing interpretation can easily move away from the actual ideas and words of the biblical texts. When she turns

---

24. Reno, "Biblical Theology," 396–97.
25. *Scripture*, 24.
26. Ibid., 64–65.

the sword against the self, Davis makes an interpretive choice that sidelines some of her other central principles of spiritual reading.

The most central principle that is overlooked in this move is attentiveness to biblical language—Davis's interpretation is not one that "draws us into deeper consideration of the words and forms and images" of Psalm 149, or one that "forces and enables us to read the text with care."[27] Although Davis makes a similar move here to that which she made with Psalm 109—turning the psalm against the self, seeing how it calls one to repent—she neglects the central ideas of vv. 6–9 in Psalm 149. Those ideas are that "all [God's] godly ones" are praising God and taking part in the execution of a judgment written against the nations. With Psalm 109, what is at stake is one who has been wronged and cries out for justice. Davis stays with this central idea, dwelling in its images, only turning the perspective of the reader from the one wronged to the one doing the wronging. With Davis's reading of Psalm 149, however, Davis does not ponder the kinds of praises being offered and the ones offering them, and the kind of judgment being urged. Her typical insistence to read the text with care is lost in her sword-spiritualizing move.

Closer attention to things other than swords is needed, then, along with attention to the flow of the psalm. Although Davis picks one verse to dwell upon (verse 6), and need not exegete the entire psalm for the purposes of her sermon, that verse's resonances across the psalm are still necessary to notice. What is most significant is the way that this psalm deals with a collective whole; the people of God are the context for the high praises of God in the people's throats being juxtaposed with two-edged swords in their hands. As vv. 1–6 show, this psalm is a collective praise, with the people together rejoicing in having a Maker and a King, dancing before the Lord with assurance of his pleasure, crowned with salvation and singing still in their laying down. The psalm evokes an entire people caught up in praise, with praise echoing from temple courts to the people's pallets. This collective element of praise gives reason for speculations that Psalm 149 was composed as a festival psalm.[28]

While the switch from praise to swords is abrupt in v. 6, the flow of the psalm is constant, and the turn has the effect of contrasting the people of God with the people not of God. Again a collective whole is envisaged: here the psalmist is not thinking of his own enemies, but the other nations who are not of the people of God, particularly their leaders. They are the ones

---

27. Davis, *Imagination Shaped*, 261.

28. John Eaton envisages this psalm as taking place during "the great pilgrimage festival;" he cites other similar suggestions, such as Mowinckel's proposal that the setting is the autumn festival with cultic dance. Eaton, *Psalms*, 483.

who have done deeds deserving of vengeance and punishments; they have a "judgment written." In contrast to the people of Israel dancing before their King, kings of the other nations will be bound. The godly lie down still singing, while the ignoble nobles are immobilized in fetters. Swords are needed here not for personal vengeance, but for justice in the world in which the nations against God are bound. A firm contrast is made between the ones praising God and the ones being judged.

Even more than swords, then, the psalm picks up larger ideas of Israel executing the Lord's judgment. The phrase "execute vengeance on the nations" (v. 7) recalls Numbers, Ezekiel, and Micah— "go up against Midian to execute the Lord's vengeance on Midian" (Num 31:3); "I will execute judgments upon Moab. Then they will know that I am the Lord" (Ezek 25:11); "I will lay my vengeance upon Edom by the hand of my people Israel" (Ezek 25:14); "I will execute great vengeance on [Philistia] with wrathful rebukes. Then they will know that I am the Lord, when I lay my vengeance upon them" (Ezek 25:17); "And in anger and wrath I will execute vengeance on the nations that did not obey" (Mic 5:15). Julie Woods connects the swords and judgment of Psalm 149 with the oracle of Jeremiah 48, as Jer 48:10 mentions a sword wielded against a foreign nation, and 48:21 and 48:47 speak of judgment upon Moab.[29]

In Psalm 110, the idea of executing judgment makes an even stronger appearance, this time in relation to a messianic figure: "The Lord is at your right hand; he will shatter kings on the day of his wrath. He will execute judgment among the nations, filling them with corpses" (v. 6). Perhaps the "judgment written" in Psalm 149:9 is referring to this—to the Lord's unveiling wrath against the nations, not simply with Israel's present battles with other nations, but even more significantly at the last day.[30] Judgment is linked to both the Messiah and to the glory of God—the end purpose of this execution of judgment, is, as Ezek 25 says, so that the nations "will know that I am the Lord."

This conjunction of the praise of the Lord and the execution of judgment is at the heart of Psalm 149, then; the praise of God is linked to the righting of the entire world. Praise is like "a veritable sword or battle-axe to subdue God's foes."[31] Because the Lord is great and greatly to be praised, so should the entire world be held to account and recognize God's greatness.

29. Woods, *Jeremiah 48*, 198–99.

30. An eschatological meaning is one interpretation of Psalm 149; as Leslie C. Allen argues, "Most probably the psalm is an eschatological hymn that looks forward to a future victory wrought by YHWH on Israel's behalf... this is why the ground for praise in vv. 7–9 looks to the future." Allen, *Psalms 101–150*, 397.

31. Eaton, *Psalms*, 483.

These are moves Davis misses when she jumps straight from the sword to the self; what results is an interpretation focused upon the individual, rather than the corporate people of God and the praises which God is due. The psalm is not about a saint's personal battle against her particular besetting sins (one may look to Psalm 51 for that); it says nothing about the fight against evil in oneself. Rather, it is about the people of God who are in praise of God, and other nations and peoples and rulers are called to account for ways they are far from God. For a Christian reader the psalm urges its readers not to battle within (though this is indeed part of the Christian life), but to be in the people of God and take part in their fight for God's reign. Although the psalm needs the rest of Scripture to flesh out what that battle looks like (in other words, it is not meant to stand alone as a crusader psalm), the psalm in itself presents a coherent message of the people of God—praise God and join his cause.

And so, I see that to a spiritual reader today, what this psalm might suggest is that the godly ones are those who are so caught up in the praise of God that they want the righting of the entire world. They are not content to merely sing alleluia from their beds, but they want to take part in the righteousness of God that calls the world to account. Perhaps even more than Eph 6:17, Heb 4:12–13 is fitting here, as the sword that is picked up by saints today is a sword of the word of God that both pierces their own souls and exposes all creatures to God, to whom they must give account. In reading Psalm 149 in the Christian tradition, the call of the gospel towards peace and grace should, ideally, keep a Christian reader from picking up a sword too easily, as the particular context of this psalm is set into the wider context of the Christian faith.[32] Yet that faith is not without battles of its own, and the movement of Psalm 149 suggests that the godly ones' praise of God remains incomplete if it does not entail in their taking part in the coming of God's ways over all the earth. It is the prayer, "Thy kingdom come, thy will be done." The psalm's communal element moreover reminds its readers that they are always alongside others who are also singing the praises of God, from the festivals of biblical times to the global church today. The psalm's readers are left to look around at where they stand in that throng, and pick up songs of God to sing.

---

32. Woods points out Jesus' rebuke to Peter in Matt 26:52, that those who take up the sword will perish by the sword. She notes, "Here the work of the Lord is not to be executed with the sword and it could be argued that, since Jesus' breaking into the world, the work of the Lord no longer requires the sword. At any rate, it is a generally accepted Christian principle that discipleship entails less wielding the sword and more turning of the other cheek." Woods, *Jeremiah 48*, 215–16.

Numbers 11

With her concerns for the manner in which the Bible guides life today, Davis often hears the Bible speaking into modern problems, particularly the western world's economic (dis)order. Davis finds great reason for Scripture to address everyday activities of buying and selling and consuming, for "our relationship with God is expressed through myriad daily social practices . . . [it is] at every moment inseparable from our relation to the material world."[33] Our dealings with "stuff" are spiritual, and Davis brings out this point in her exegesis of Numbers 11 in *Getting Involved With God*.[34]

In the story of the Israelites grumbling and longing after meat as they march through the wilderness, Davis discerns "a tangled tale of manna and quails, greed and prophecy" in which the central message rests in the two-pronged response of God to pour out meat and pour out prophecy.[35] The congruence between "[u]nbridled greed and free-flowing prophecy" prompts Davis's reflection on Numbers 11, as she sets this story into the context of the greed that marks twenty-first century North American culture, whose "craving *more than enough* is the deadly sin that is wrecking havoc on a global scale."[36] Numbers 11 reminds readers that greed puts them in danger of God's anger, and calls their greed into account. In her exegesis of Numbers 11 Davis probes deeper into the nature of that greed and the spiritual danger it poses. She reads the Israelites' greed to better understand the nature of North American greed, and to find a way out of it.

Davis begins her interpretation of Numbers 11 by moving quickly to Psalm 78, which gives texture to the story by explaining that the Israelites demanded meat "because they had no faith in God, and did not trust his saving power [though] he had opened the doors of heaven" (Ps 78:22, Davis's translation). Davis finds that as the Israelites did not trust God, they could never be satisfied:

> Greed always stems from lack of faith. We crave more than we need because we do not look for God to fill the emptiness we quite accurately perceive in ourselves. In fact, *only* God can fill

---

33. Davis, "Surprised by Wisdom," 276–77.

34. Davis considers the wider wilderness narrative in *Scripture, Culture, and Agriculture*, chapter 4, but there does not specifically deal with Numbers 11. Although her treatment of the Israelites' relationship with God, as symbolized by manna, is more extensive in *Scripture, Culture, and Agriculture*, I find her reading of Numbers 11 in *Getting Involved With God* more pointed and interesting, and more manageable as a brief example of her spiritual exegesis.

35. Davis, *Getting Involved With God*, 202.

36. Ibid., emphasis Davis's.

the emptiness within us. . . . We are trying to fill ourselves with what is not God—the problem is as simple as that.[37]

Davis understands faith as being about trust in God's ability to meet needs and fill emptiness. What greed is about, then, is a lack to perceive one's true needs and bring them before God. As Davis uses Psalm 78's description of the Israelites' lack of faith as a way into the story of Numbers 11, she makes a move outside of Numbers to interpret it, for Numbers does not speak explicitly of lack of faith. More will be noted on this move below, but first, a brief summary of the rest of her interpretation.

Davis makes the connection between the Israelites' lack of faith and their deeper spiritual emptiness to argue that the story of Numbers 11 is essentially about being satisfied with sufficiency. The tragedy of Numbers 11, Davis explains, is that the Israelites failed to see that God had already sent them enough. Manna had been given in abundance, yet the Israelites grew tired of its monotony and demanded more. Their craving was met, but in a way that showed how deadly was their greed, as with the meat still in their teeth a good number of them were struck down. A contrast is made in Numbers between manna and quail, with the one being sufficiency and the other, greed. Manna was "Israel's training in the art of sufficiency" and here they failed to practice that art, to their own undoing.[38] Davis finds a lesson in this for western readers today, as sufficiency is a core art of the spiritual life, and it "becomes an art form only when an aesthetic change takes place within us, so that we come to see the beauty of 'enough' and actually prize it over 'too much.'"[39] Numbers shows graphically just how ugly excessive consumption is, with "the Israelites wading in quail up to their armpits, stuffing themselves until the meat comes out of their nostrils."[40] Davis reads this story as urging its readers to turn away from over-consumption and to be content with having enough and not craving more. Quail piles are never a pretty sight.

How such satisfaction with sufficiency might be attained is found in the rest of the story, Davis maintains, with God's second outpouring in sending the spirit of prophecy. It was so abundant that it fell not just on the gathered assembly of elders, but also in the camp on Eldad and Medad. Davis notes that we are not told the content of their prophesying, but hazards a guess that "the prophets were trying to reorient the people from craving for meat to gratitude for manna. In no uncertain terms they challenged Israel

---

37. Ibid., 204.
38. Ibid., 205.
39. Ibid.
40. Ibid., 206.

to focus on God's faithfulness instead of their own wants."[41] She finds it significant that Eldad and Medad are among those who prophesy, as they reflect how much "God's truth is being uttered in startling and compelling ways."[42] Davis finds this aspect of the story might push the church to recognize ways in which unlikely prophets are speaking God's truth; economists and social activists, for instance, are waking Christians up to see the ways they have ignored God, creation, and the poor. The church would do well to listen to "unordained prophets who speak truth in this matter."[43] Although the church has lagged in responding to the ecological crisis, Davis posits that the church is still the best place to begin to learn a new way, as in its worship (in asking for its daily bread and in receiving the Eucharist) the art of sufficiency is prayed for and practiced.

Davis's reading of Numbers 11 has beauty in its own simplicity and whole-hearted aim. Davis grasps the central concern of the story—the Israelites' greed and God's response in sending down both meat and his Spirit—and she finds it challenging one of the most pressing spiritual problems of her time and place, the material greed of her culture. The nature of greed, as Davis traces in Numbers 11, is being unsatisfied with sufficiency; it is grumbling against one's present situation and failing to thank God for his provisions. Davis sets the story's probing light upon the western world and she finds hope in its prophetic figures, in those who "give a God's eye-view" of situations of dismay.[44] She employs imagination as the overriding principle in her interpretation, as she seeks in this story a parallel "God's eye-view" of the dismay of western consumerism.

While Davis's reading of Numbers 11 is certainly powerful and is a needed message for the church, in a few points her interpretation needs pressing. Most significantly, what is needed in her spiritual interpretation is even closer attention to the text. As with her reading of Psalm 149, here Davis does not employ as carefully her principle of attentiveness to biblical language. Davis is not writing a commentary on Numbers and it would be unfair to demand that she pay attention to every detail, but yet, there are a few features of this story that she does not account for, and which need reckoning with. In jumping quickly to Psalm 78 and in reading for a central message of greed and prophecy, Davis's interpretation overlooks the framing of the story and the place of prophecy within it.

---

41. Ibid.
42. Ibid.
43. Ibid., 208.
44. Ibid., 206.

As Davis begins her interpretation with a move towards Psalm 78, this cross-reference is not a bad move in itself, for it is certainly justifiable to read a biblical passage in light of the entirety of Scripture. Yet, here the effect of moving so quickly to Psalm 78 is that certain details of the story are overlooked as the narrative appears in Numbers. Davis's care for the words and ideas of the biblical text does not come out as strongly in her reading of the Numbers story, as she moves towards a wider theme (that of spiritual emptiness) without dwelling on the passage as it is presents itself in Numbers. Davis finds in Psalm 78 the hook for her interpretation of Numbers 11—the Israelites had a lack of faith. But when she outlines the nature of this lack of faith, Davis moves beyond both Psalm 78 and Numbers to explain that, as she posits that lack of faith is a spiritual emptiness. Such understanding of lack of faith is part of the Christian tradition, but in both Numbers and Psalm 78 the Israelites' lack of faith is much more carnal; it is that they want meat and doubt God will offer it. They are not thankful for what God has provided, nor do they trust God to care about their desires. The deeper problem, as Numbers 11 explains, is that they "have rejected the Lord who is among" them (v. 20). This verse might have been a more fruitful one to dwell upon to explain the nature of the problem in Numbers 11, instead of reaching elsewhere for an idea of spiritual emptiness to place upon it. The effect of bringing the two passages of Psalm 78 and Numbers 11 together is that a spiritual interpretation is made that goes outside of either text. Spiritual emptiness is a good message to preach, but it is not a message that comes clearly out of the story of Numbers 11. Rather, Numbers presents a rejection of the Lord's presence, a failure to see his care.

As Davis heads towards this theme of spiritual emptiness and sufficiency, she neglects to note the story's strong element of the Israelite's rebellion and God's anger. It is mentioned in passing, but an aspect of Numbers 11 that needs better reckoning with is the anger of the Lord that frames this entire chapter. In 11:1–3, the people complain about their misfortunes and when the Lord hears it, he sets a fire to consume some outlying parts (and people?) of the camp. Only when Moses prays does the fire die down. The anger of the Lord appears again in 11:33–34, when a very great plague from the Lord strikes down those who had craved meat. These places are given names of *Taberah* and *Kibroth-hattaavah*; this stretch of the Israelites' journey is marked with memorials of burning and burying.

These two memorials frame the story of the Israelites' demand for meat in a pointed way: *Taberah* makes the rabble's complaints even more brazen, as they cry out for meat on the heels of a previous whining that led to havoc among them. Even as it is a contingent of a rabble that raises this second cry, the people all join in, "everyone at the door of his tent" (11:10), and the carnage as a result of their complaining at *Taberah* seems long forgotten now. *Kibroth-hattaavah* then offers an unsettled end to this story, as a significant aspect of the second outpouring of God's anger is that it happens *after* he sends down a spirit of prophecy and sends out quails. The Lord answers the people with what they want, but yet sends out a plague upon them while the meat is still between their teeth, and those who had the craving are struck down. This second kindling of God's anger is hard to reckon with the rest of the story, as the mercy that God seems to show in sending quails and his Spirit is really a lesson that teaches the Israelites to quit their demanding. As such a great quantity of quail had been sent and collected, the quail they had so eagerly caught and prepared was turned into a reminder of their own greed and self-destruction.

With such a framing of God's anger, a message of greed being answered by prophecy is hard to pull neatly out of the story, as the tale ends not with the people responding to the prophetic word, but with them being struck down by the Lord, and having to eat their just deserts. (This is hardly the message Davis is striving towards in her envisioning the text at work in the church's life today.) Prophecy is less the issue than Israelite rebellion and God's response. Davis posits prophecy as central to the story, but the prophesying of this story, while important, seems to have been of limited extent. The seventy elders prophesy only for a short duration when the Spirit rests on them ("they did not continue doing it," v. 25[45]), and only Eldad and Medad are among the people while the prophecy goes on. Davis imagines the elders prophesying to all the people, suggesting that "they were trying to reorient the people from craving for meat to gratitude for manna."[46] While a creative suggestion, this imaginative move goes beyond the text, as it is unclear what form the prophesying took, and whether it was a direct word to the people.

Moreover, in the flow of the story, the prophetic act *precedes* the sending of the quail, it does not follow it, as Davis's interpretation suggests. Prophecy is not a response to the quail but a prior action. The prophecy marks the elders as now being Spirit-empowered helpers for Moses, and their help is in the form of their ongoing leadership, not ongoing prophesying. Davis's making Eldad and Medad as parallels for unconventional prophets speaking truth to the church today is a move that works to a certain extent, but it overlooks the way that the two figures are part of Israel (thus not outside of the people of God), and they were possibly even among the elders, just

---

45. Textually this verse is difficult, however, a variant reading (as testified in the Vulgate and the Targum Onkelos) is "they prophesied and ceased not."

46. Davis, *Getting Involved With God*, 206.

not gathered with them (v. 26 suggests this, in its wording that Eldad and Medad "were registered"). And so, the prophesy in this story is important more for the way it marks the Spirit of God as coming upon the elders, than it does the elders speaking a prophetic word to the people. Davis is right to highlight the role of prophecy in the story, but needs to be more reflexive on how that prophecy is actually functioning.

A message of greed and sufficiency still comes out of Numbers 11 with these qualifications, but attention to these details of the text deepen a spiritual reading of it even further, as they suggest that greed takes a long time to root out, and that Spirit-empowered leaders are needed to help the people learn to live in God's grace. The Israelites are not left without help, as now the Lord has poured out his Spirit on seventy(-two?) elders, ones who will "bear the burden of the people" with Moses (v. 17). What the people need after their massive quail-collecting and failing are not just sudden bursts of prophecy but leaders committed to them for the long-run, willing to struggle with them as they learn to be the people of God in all things, especially in their very eating. The quail becomes loathsome to the people (v. 20), but only so that their rejection of God, symbolized in it, might become even more loathsome. A prophetic stirring-up of some leaders is only the beginning of the deeper work that must take place among the people. Would that the Lord put his Spirit upon all of them.

Ruth

Davis's reading of Scripture ever seeks out that Spirit in Scripture, striving to understand how it stirs up texts in the lives of its hearers. As the worked examples thus far have come from Davis's briefer pieces (a sermon and essays from *Getting Involved With God*), a look at her commentary work is a helpful addition to these close readings of her art in practice. A commentary has room for attention to detail and wider theological considerations, and through the genre of commentary Davis's concerns emerge in different ways than through her articles and sermons. Davis's commentary on Ruth, *Who Are You, My Daugther?: Reading Ruth Through Image and Text*, presents a compelling illustration of her manner of spiritual reading. Here I will trace out aspects of that reading by first considering the approach to reading Ruth in the commentary as a whole, before delving into specifics on Davis's translation and notes on the first chapter of Ruth.

Reading Ruth Spiritually

Ruth may seem to be an unlikely place to engage in spiritual reading, as the place of God within its story is never overtly stated,[47] but Davis's reading of Ruth carefully traces out the life of God which the narrative portrays. She explains *hesed* as the focus of the meaning of Ruth and the reason for Ruth's appeal: Ruth demonstrates "remarkable transformation: emptiness turning to abundance, desolation and isolation yielding, under the gentle and steady pressure of *hesed*, to new life in family and community."[48] With its embodiment of *hesed*, the book of Ruth is about a small group of people who "speak and act in ways that make God's character more evident, inviting God's blessing, God's action-for-good, into their lives." And so, its story is "one good place to enter into the Bible and attempt to view it in a new way."[49]

Who Are You, My Daughter? is a somewhat unconventional way to enter into the Bible, even by standards of theological commentaries. Co-created with artist Margaret Adams Parker, the commentary seeks to explore the book of Ruth through a fresh translation, notes, and woodcut images that illustrate a running sequence of pivotal scenes. Davis explains that the translation, notes, and images were "from the outset conceived as complementary elements of a single project;" as Parker says, "visual image can be a form of biblical commentary that is both valid and significant."[50] Each piece of translation, note, and image is given due attention through the visual and typographical arrangement of the commentary (which is an oversized book)—translations fill up entire pages, written in large, flowing script; woodcut images are full-paged as well; and much empty space is left between different elements, as in an art gallery, creating space to ponder. The commentary makes a theological statement in its very form: it is not an illustrated commentary of Ruth, but rather, a commentary that illustrates and comments upon Ruth through both word and image. As art was a common mode of biblical interpretation in the medieval church, Davis and Parker's work returns to this tradition, though casting it in a new form in which word and image come even closer together. Davis notes that she and Parker "seesawed back and forth" in their readings of Ruth, "each influencing and reshaping the other's view of it."[51] Like two museum visitors gazing on a masterful painting, Davis and Parker stand before the book of

---

47. Ruth has been interpreted as merely an idyll or romance, without conveying any theological meaning. Hals, *Theology of the Book of Ruth*, 2.
48. Davis, *Who Are You*, xiv.
49. Ibid., xi–xii.
50. Ibid., xv, xxi.
51. Ibid., xv.

Ruth, pondering its strokes and colors, and offering responses through their conversation and artistic responses. Even if the commentary's artwork does not capture the eye of the reader (I must confess I struggled to connect with the woodcut images), the project sets out a way of reading that encourages visualization and varying modes of entering into biblical texts.

With its interest in art as biblical commentary, from the onset *Who Are You, My Daughter?* presents a mode of engagement with Scripture that is characterized by ever-unfolding interpretations and questions, ever-new ways of seeing its stories and the truths of God told through them. Davis and Parker hold to the open-endedness of the biblical message of Ruth, as even though the translation and images "are confined to a single interpretive choice for each moment or phrase, the notes are designed to explain what may not be self-evident and also to raise questions, to disclose ambiguities and roads not taken (this time) by translator and illustrator."[52] One has the sense that Davis and Parker might well go down other roads with Ruth at other times, as the path they take here is construed as one among many. A keen sense of wonder operates throughout the commentary, and that wonder is in keeping with the nature of Ruth, as Ruth tells a story without any summary statements of its meaning; rather, it brims with places in which one might wonder just how God is working.

Who Are You, My Daughter? is an atypical commentary in its form, and Davis's part in the commentary detours from typical commentary practice, as well. Although Davis offers a few introductory thoughts in her preface on the theological meaning of Ruth, her style of commentary is entirely verse-by-verse comment, with no broader introductions or conclusions.[53] Even her introduction to the work is not called an introduction but rather a "Translator's Preface," and absent in it are the traditional commentary notes on a book's origin, date, authorship, purpose, audience, sources, etc. She does engage Ruth's historical context, explore its resonances with the rest of Scripture, mention aspects of Jewish and Christian history of interpretation, and make theological points on Ruth's meaning, but these issues are all peppered throughout her work rather than being sections of their own. Her commentary is caught up with following the turns of the text, and while she presents her own take on how that text turns, the effect of her approach is that she is ever pointing back towards Ruth itself, rather than her own reading of Ruth. As one reviewer notes, Davis and Parker "gently guide the read-

---

52. Ibid., xv.

53. In contrast, her commentary on Proverbs, Ecclesiastes, and Song of Songs offers introductions to each book that are a few pages longer than her translator's preface to Ruth. That commentary does not follow each verse, however, but only select passages—presumably for reasons of space, as it is in the *Westminster Bible Companion* series.

er through the story without displacing it as the main object of attention."[54] In this the commentary succeeds in one of its goals, as stated by Parker in her preface, citing Childs, that a good biblical commentary should "lead the reader back to the biblical text."[55] Although it may have been helpful to have some kind of concluding chapter or overarching discussion of the task of reading Ruth for the Christian spiritual life, Davis's approach is more inductive, teaching verse-by-verse how one might grapple with a biblical text and be led to God through it.

Davis's aim of reading Ruth's words closely with a view towards God puts her commentary in a separate category from critical commentaries of Ruth that also give exquisite attention to Ruth's words. Jack M. Sasson's commentary, *Ruth: A New Translation with a Philological Commentary and a Formalist-Folklorist Interpretation* is even more intricately bound up with the turns of the language of Ruth than Davis's work, as he offers a reading that traces out its literary devices. Like Robert Alter, Sasson is a careful literary reader of Scripture (Sasson is, in fact, a contributor to Alter and Kermode's *The Literary Guide to the Bible*). Sasson's interpretive aim is far from theological, however. As he stated in his preface to the original edition of his commentary,

> I found it distressing that those who label *Ruth* with folkloristic terminology nevertheless proceed to extract from it information of legal and theological import. I tried, therefore, not to abuse the limitations inherent in the folklore genre by strictly delineating the agenda of discussion to topics that could be fruitfully pursued.[56]

Sasson argues that rather than "a hidden God" being operative throughout the events of Ruth, what is really occurring is a typical folklore "sequential function."[57] His study is limited by the genre in which he classifies the book of Ruth, as his starting point of folklore curtails any interest in the spiritual (though this understanding of the folklore genre might itself be questioned). Yet in the second edition of his commentary, Sasson qualified his position:

> I wrote about the marginal value of Ruth for our understanding of Hebrew theological ideology or religious convictions. . . . I should have . . . recognized that these [religious and theological] categories play differently whether Ruth is assessed as an

---

54. Floyd, "Review of *Who Are You My Daughter?*," 143.
55. Childs, "Genre of Biblical Commentary," 192; cited by Parker, *Who Are You*, xxi.
56. Sasson, *Ruth*, xi.
57. Ibid., 221.

independent tale or as part of sacred Scripture. Had I been alert to these distinctions, I would certainly have refrained from blanket censure of efforts to uncover the workings of a providential God.[58]

Sasson, then, leaves room for interest in "the workings of a providential God" by those who read Ruth as part of sacred Scripture, but he sees no role for those workings intrinsically within the story of Ruth itself. Davis, in contrast, reads Ruth out of the assumption that the workings of God are in fact present within Ruth's story and shape its true understanding. Both Sasson and Davis attend closely to Ruth's language, but do this from radically different starting points. Rather than begin with a particular genre classification for Ruth, as Sasson does, Davis begins with the assumption that Ruth has an intrinsic meaning that points towards God, as does all of Scripture.

Such an understanding characterizes other theological commentaries on Ruth, as well, and a comparison with one such commentary, Katharine Doob Sakenfeld's, is a useful contrast. Sakenfeld's commentary on Ruth is written for the *Interpretation* series, a series that aims to produce commentaries that are "the integrated result of historical and theological work with the biblical text." The goal for an *Interpretation* commentary is that it is "both faithful to the text and useful to the church."[59] The style of *Interpretation* commentaries is to leave out printing the biblical text (its "general availability" is taken to deem that unnecessary), and to comment upon passages as a whole, rather than verse by verse.[60] From the start, within the perimeters of its setting in the larger *Interpretation* series, Sakenfeld's commentary will veer in a slightly different direction than Davis's work, as lingering attention upon biblical words is not as prominent a feature. Davis's project is that of a translator and interpreter, who dwells upon Ruth's words and displays them artistically on their own pages, while Sakenfeld has a brief to interpret Ruth primarily in sections of texts and to be mindful of larger questions of meaning in the life of the church.

Even as they start off on slightly different plains, Sakenfeld moves in similar ways as Davis at several points. Her commentary begins with fifteen pages of introductory material, covering the date, purpose, authorship, historical customs, canonical context, and theological themes of Ruth, but she is relatively brief with her discussions of date, purpose, and authorship, as she explains such issues "are informative but not finally decisive for

---

58. Ibid., xv.
59. *Interpretation* "Series Preface," in Sakenfeld, *Ruth*, v–vi.
60. Ibid., v.

assessing the theological significance of the story."[61] Like Davis, Sakenfeld understands theological significance to be found in entering into the many textures and meanings of Ruth; she explains her commentary "seeks to guide readers" through "different ways of experiencing the story by giving explicit attention to alternative interpretations."[62] More so than Davis, Sakenfeld recognizes that interpreters themselves play a strong role in creating those interpretations; she notes, "As we praise Ruth for choosing the unknown, we need to realize that only interpreters, not the text itself, have created the 'known' that Ruth is abandoning."[63] Sakenfeld holds that a reading of Ruth that views it as a happily-ever-after story "is in the end theologically appropriate," but she presses for a more critical reading that notices certain features of the story which might cause difficulties (e.g., its patriarchal framing), and that grapples with those difficulties to arrive at "eventually a more positive assessment."[64]

As a feminist interpreter, Sakenfeld's commentary takes note of feminist strands of interpretation of Ruth (something Davis does not engage directly), but her attention is drawn more towards the text than to its recent interpretive history. She seeks how Ruth might edify the church today, and is more direct and more extensive than Davis in outlining the theological messages of Ruth. Sakenfeld finds the purpose of Ruth to be for instruction of the community's views towards outsiders, and theological themes she mentions in her introduction are "The Peaceable Community," "Examples of Loyal Living," and "The Place of God in the Story."[65] Her aim in her commentary is different from that of Davis, so their two works cannot be mapped onto each other, but on the whole, Sakenfeld's commentary pulls more theological messages out of Ruth to present to the reader, while Davis's commentary gently pushes the reader more towards the text of Ruth so to encounter its theological questions.

Although Sakenfeld's theological reading of Ruth is in many ways close to that of Davis, Davis's commentary clings more tightly to the biblical text as it moves along. Davis offers a reading of Ruth that is truly a *reading*, one that seeks not takeaway messages, but a deeper dwelling in the text. With this aim, Davis's approach is moreover distinct from other theological commentaries on Ruth which delve thoroughly into the historical setting of Ruth—Ronald M. Hals's *The Theology of the Book of Ruth*, e.g., pursues Ruth's theological

---

61. Sakenfeld, *Ruth*, 1.
62. Ibid., vii.
63. Ibid., 34.
64. Ibid., 1.
65. Ibid., 4, 9–16.

meaning by analyzing "the theological intent of the author, bound up as it is with the forms he employs and reflecting as it does the crisis of the age in which that author wrote."[66] While Davis holds to the importance of Ruth's historical setting for understanding certain features of its story, the age of Ruth's composition is not ultimately determinative for Ruth's theological meaning. She understands the theology of Ruth to rest more in its words than in its reconstructed history. Davis, Sakenfeld, and Hals may be working with slightly different understandings of "theology"—for Davis, theology entails the encounter with God that a biblical text presses (the Bible is, after all, about "getting involved with God"), while for Hals and Sakenfeld, theology means more of an understanding of God that a biblical text presents. Even as an encounter with God and an understanding of God are related to each other, they frame theological pursuits in different ways.

In this manner Davis also differs in her approach from sociological and political readings of Ruth. André LaCocque's commentary on Ruth, "a socio-legal commentary," takes as a starting point the legal concerns of Ruth and proposes that Ruth is subversively writing against the strict injunctions of Torah; he argues, "the message of the narrative is not at all as irenic and calm as those who favor a preexilic date. The book of Ruth is antiestablishment. It is doubly subversive: as a 'feminist' book and as hermeneutical key of the Law."[67] LaCocque's argument rests heavily upon a Second Temple dating of Ruth, and although some of his arguments for Ruth's subversiveness are based on the narrative itself (e.g., its role of women and its Moabite ancestress of David), his proposed historical setting of Ruth's composition is essential to his overarching thesis. Just as Sasson makes the genre of Ruth central to its interpretation, Hals and LaCocque make Ruth's dating the pivot for their interpretations. In contrast, Davis does not enter into such historically-driven theological arguments, with the result that her work looks to the received form of the book of Ruth for its theology rather than to its possible historical origins.

---

66. As expressed by John Reumann in his introduction to Hals's *Theology of the Book of Ruth*, vi. Hals's work considers the direct and indirect references to God in the book of Ruth, compares Ruth with other biblical writings, and argues for its dating within the Solomonic era. It offers a theology of the providence of God, but its weakness is that its theological argument rests on a historical reconstruction of Ruth's setting.

67. LaCocque, *Ruth*, 27. LaCocque argues that an early dating of Ruth misses "its principal dimension of subversive narrative." He insists, "if the current story of Ruth is to be understood in the field of tension between Law and commandment, it cannot have been composed during any other era than when such a tension was the expression of an existential problem: the legalistic period of Ezra and Nehemiah." The lesson for the reader of Ruth is "the essence of Torah is love." LaCocque, *Ruth*, 20, 25, 30.

Davis still keeps closely enough to Ruth's historical setting, however, to not land on another end of the theological interpretive spectrum—medieval readers who understood Ruth as "one long allegory," with Ruth representing the church; Boaz, Christ; and Naomi, the synagogue.[68] Lesley Smith explains that in the Ordinary Gloss (*Glossa Ordinaria*), Ruth is

> a series of changing allegories, containing a fluidity of imagery that marks much medieval exegesis. . . . Modern readers may find the shifting sands confusing and treacherous—we are never quite sure we are putting our feet on firm ground; but for medieval exegetes this variety only signaled more possible uses for the material, and they were happier to leap between stepping stones, supplying the rest of the path in their own heads.[69]

Davis's approach is not that of the "fluidity of imagery," nor the extensive allegorizing that marked earlier spiritual exegesis. Yet in many ways, however, she has kept with the tenor of medieval interpretation, as she is happy to hold to multiple meanings and to understand many "possible uses for the material" of Scripture. As she embraces the multiplicity of meanings in the Bible, Davis is one who "reaps the benefits of deconstructive and other such approaches, but without their off-putting narratological schemata and jargon."[70] In her reading of Ruth, Davis combines the instinct of the medieval with the awareness of the historian and the concerns of the theologian; she picks up varying interpretive methods as the words of Ruth unfold.

Ruth, Chapter 1

My following comments will focus on Davis's translation and commentary on the first chapter of Ruth in *Who Are You, My Daughter?* As a representative sample of her interpretive work of Ruth as a whole, Davis's notes on the first chapter evince her spiritual reading principles at work—there she pays close attention to biblical language, reveling in nuances of Hebrew words, and she notes the ambiguities of certain passages, positing that the openness of the story enables genuine engagement with it. Attentiveness to language and wonder are the spiritual reading principles most concretely at work, along with an awareness of the wider biblical tradition in which Ruth is operating.

---

68. Although Naomi shifts in meaning—sometimes she is also the early church. Smith, *Medieval Exegesis In Translation*, ix.

69. Ibid., xv.

70. Floyd, "Review of *Who Are You My Daughter?*," 144.

Her comments on chapter 1 first come out in her preface to *Who Are You, My Daughter?*, in which Davis's attentiveness to language is at the forefront. She begins the preface by setting out her goals as a translator, explaining that her translation is meant to sound like one, as this rendering of Ruth is meant for "people who are willing to take the time to dwell on a text ... to ponder the implications of curious word choices, the follow a trail marked by the repetition of key words."[71] As has been noted above, Davis posits there is "no such thing as an all-purpose translation" and she offers this translation as intended primarily for study, not for public reading.[72] Davis explains that this approach gives her the freedom to make peculiar word choices, two of which emerge in the first chapter. The "outstanding example" of this is how she translates *kallah*, "daughter-in-law." Davis explains this word has a particular resonance in Hebrew, as it also is the ordinary word for "bride." While in English, "daughter-in-law" can be "a perfunctory statement of relationship," "bride" connotes "joy, hope, expectation, perhaps trepidation."[73] And so, to keep that resonance, the sense of *kallah* also meaning "bride" in Hebrew, she creates a neologism to render *kallah* as "bride-daughter." In holding to the Hebrew sense of bride, particular textures of Ruth come clear: "In the context of this story, the (otherwise ordinary) word [*kallah*] acquires poignancy: these 'brides' are in fact widows."[74] Davis's translation is a means of capturing a narrative poignancy of Ruth.

A second example of Davis's careful word choice, which she explains in the preface, is her choice to render *davaq* consistently throughout Ruth as "stick with" (1:14, 2:8, 2:21, 2:23)—Ruth "stuck with" Naomi, and then Boaz and Naomi advised Ruth to "stick with" the female field workers. Other translations offer different words in those places—e.g., the ESV renders 1:14 as "clung" and 2:8, 2:21, and 2:23 as "keep close," while the KJV renders *davaq* as "clave" in 1:14, "abide here fast" in 2:8, and "keep fast" in 2:21 and 2:23. Davis notes that such a move misses a particular point being made with *davaq*: "The verbal repetition draws a line concerning Ruth's initial protective action toward Naomi on the road back to Bethlehem with the reciprocal concern of these elders for her, a young stranger in the land who is perhaps more vulnerable than she perceives herself to be."[75] The repeated

---

71. Davis, *Who Are You*, xii.
72. Ibid., xii.
73. Ibid., xii.
74. Ibid., 13.
75. Davis, *Who Are You*, xiii. In contrast, Sasson posits, "In 1.14, its use is at once simple and moving" but when "Boaz employs the verb to advise Ruth to remain with his workers, one has the feeling that the narrator has unfolded a playfulness a bit too daringly." Sasson, *Ruth*, 28.

use of *davaq* indeed leads to this interpretation, but a slight modification of Davis's point must be made, in that Boaz employs the word *davaq*, but not Naomi. In 2:21 it is Ruth who is speaking, reporting Boaz's words back to Naomi, and in 2:23 it is Ruth once again practicing *davaq*. Naomi's advice to Ruth in 2:22, in contrast, is to "go out" with the young women—she uses the verb *yasa'*, not *davaq*. A minor point, this detail does not overturn the broad point that Davis is making—that Ruth demonstrates *davaq* to Naomi and another manner of *davaq* comes to protect Ruth. But as Davis is making this point through noticing the actual biblical words of Ruth, what needs qualifying is her attention to those words. The "reciprocal care of these elders" for Ruth is seen primarily in a verbal connection between Ruth's actions and Boaz's words.

When Davis begins her commentary on chapter 1, she keeps to this manner of close attention to biblical words as she plunges straight into exploring Ruth's words, verse by verse. She starts her comments with an explanation of "the judges judging," noting the pre-monarchy backdrop to the story of Ruth. Davis does not linger long upon historical details, however; as Ruth's history is not the goal, but Ruth's story, Davis limits her historical discussion to the most pertinent information that helps that story along. Even as she feels free to speculate that the author of Ruth was probably writing in the time of the monarchy, she does not enter into academic debates of the origin and purposes of Ruth. Yet historical information can still provide great insight into biblical texts, and when it is helpful, Davis eagerly picks it up. With verse 1 she looks to historical setting to explain the name of Bethlehem and its role as breadbasket for Jerusalem, and notes the ironic reversal of expectations, that pagan Moab was more fertile than Israel.

Davis posits that this is "the first of many reversals of expectation and situation in this story, in which the 'ordinary' upheavals that affect and periodically devastate every human life are seen to be occasions for the operation of God's grace and also of human kindness."[76] Here, in just one line, Davis has moved from the historical to the theological, without any pause. This is her style throughout her commentary on Ruth, and although it could be judged as too seamless by more historically-focused commentators, it is an approach of integrating history with spiritual reality. Just as the "ordinary" upheavals of Ruth are places where God's grace is operating, so too the "ordinary" aspects of biblical texts are places where that grace is still working. In discerning its historical background the spiritual realities of a biblical text come even more in view, and noting the historical particularities brings out unchanging aspects of God's character and work.

76. Davis, *Who Are You*, 5.

In her comments on 1:2, Davis explores the descriptive aspect of characters' names in the book of Ruth, that is, how their names tell something about their roles in the story. Elimelekh, "My-God-is-king,"

> is important in this story chiefly for his absence. Yet in his very absence, his name stands as a reminder that there is another source of protection for his family—less obvious, but ultimately reliable—namely, the God who is sovereign over all the circumstances of human lives.[77]

Davis here moves quickly again from specific words to interpretive theological meaning—although the book of Ruth says nothing about the significance of Elimelekh's name, Davis attends to the possibilities, whether or not the author of Ruth intended them. Elimelekh's name may not remind Naomi or the narrator of God's protection, but it reminds Davis of such, and she points to this as one way to understand his name's significance.[78] The meaning of his name within the story is sought by the contour of the story, as other names also seem to indicate their bearers' natures. Mahlon ("Sickness") and Kilyon ("End-of-the-line") "bespeak the destiny of those who will bear them," while Orpah ("Back-of-the-neck") "will eventually turn her back on Naomi."[79] When it comes to Ruth, however, Davis posits that her name is curiously not "transparent to meaning"—Davis wonders,

> [P]erhaps the very fact that Ruth's name cannot be fully "decoded" is itself one clue to the complexity of her character. . . . Ruth is the most fully developed character in the book; all the action revolves around her surprising initiatives. She cannot be reduced to a capsule description.[80]

With her musings on Ruth's name, Davis is using linguistic details to make an interpretive choice, as other translators have offered interpretations of Ruth's name—the *Glossa Ordinaria*, e.g., drawing from Jerome's explanations of Jewish names, explains Ruth's name as "seeing," "hurrying," or "ceasing."[81] Davis, however, clings more closely to modern philology to find

---

77. Ibid., 5.

78. Another way, which LaCocque mentions, is to read Elimelek's name as signifying his piety, a piety that makes his "defection" to Moab all the more shocking. LaCocque, *Ruth*, 39.

79. Davis, *Who Are You*, 6, 10.

80. Ibid., 10.

81. "The Ordinary Gloss," trans. Smith, *Medieval Exegesis In Translation*, 11. From the side of modern interpreters, LaCocque understands Ruth's name to mean "to water," and suggests that she provides her Israelite hosts with the help that her Moabite ancestors had refused the Israelites. LaCocque, *Ruth*, 3.

Ruth's name opaque, and significance residing in that opaqueness. Davis's move to understand the meaning of names is like patristic and medieval traditions in that it is born out of a view towards the Bible that sees each detail as potentially significant. Yet where early interpreters took the significance of biblical names as simply an interpretive given, Davis arrives at this view from the particulars of Ruth—to Davis the meaning behind names is a significance that the Hebrew vocabulary of Ruth itself suggests, rather than being a general interpretive principle. And within these verbal wordplays in Hebrew, different conclusions may be reached according to how the translator chooses the render the names.

When 1:2 speaks of Moab, Davis explains how Moab, from the Israelite perspective, "was definitely on the wrong side of the tracks."[82] Here again a larger biblical and historical context is needed, especially when 1:4 speaks of Moabite wives. In translating 1:4, Davis keeps the Hebrew word order in the sentence, "And they took for themselves wives, Moabites." She notes that in the Hebrew text this "first sentence hints at a small drama . . . we have to wait until the end of the sentence to know the kind of wives the young men actually took."[83] Even as Hebrew word order has some flexibility, Davis finds that order as intentional in this instance, as it gives emphasis to the fact of the sons' wives being Moabites.[84] Davis explains the staunch Israelite prohibition against marriage to foreigners, especially Moabites (Deut 23:3–4), and notes how Ruth is repeatedly called "Ruth the Moabite" (1:22, 2:2, 2:21, 4:5, 4:10). Having the history of Israel in mind as well as attention to the style of the Hebrew prose, Davis finds one line speaking legions. And here again Davis moves freely from the historical and textual to the theological, as she points out that Ruth

> will reverse some of the expectations that attach to her nationality, or at least some of them . . . through her sexual actions, not only is a family preserved, but the nation Israel is built up and

---

82. As Davis mentions, Jewish midrash criticizes Elimelekh's decision to leave. Davis, *Who Are You*, 6.

83. Ibid., 9.

84. Elsewhere, in her article "Entering the Story," Davis cites this example as one instance in which teaching biblical Hebrew, and reading the text slowly with her students, "slowed [her] down enough to ponder the implications of every sentence, with its possible nuances, ambiguities, and hidden meanings. Here is one intriguing possibility . . . we know that they 'took . . . wives, *nashîm*' just an instant *before* we hear the identifying adjective: '*Moaviyyot*, Moabites' . . . In that moment's delay, the drama of the tale begins to unfold." Davis, "Entering," 54, emphasis Davis's.

(through the person of her great-grandson David) moved into deeper relationship with God.[85]

"[D]eeper relationship with God" is language that goes past the scope of the book of Ruth; such terminology is foreign to the author of Ruth, and Ruth grapples more with human relationships than relationships with God. Yet Davis reads Ruth fluidly, casting it in light of the ongoing canonical story, and putting that story into modern spiritual language. Even as she looks closely at contexts and biblical words, those are considered in light of the ongoing Christian tradition and understanding of God.

As she works her way through the book of Ruth, Davis notices its points of ambiguity that allow for more than one avenue of interpretation. 1:4 offers the first instance of this, in which it is unclear what "ten years" refers to—whether it is to the time that begins when Elimelekh's family first come to Moab, or to the period after the two sons took wives. Davis views this statement as a place in which "the narrator invites inquiry by means of a gap or ambiguity."[86] Davis wonders into that gap, posing that if the ten years begin after the marriage of Ruth, she would have been barren for a long time, having born the shame of childlessness before the disaster of being widowed. (Davis points out that the medieval rabbis thought it was this situation, which creates greater significance in Yahweh's giving Ruth a son.) Moreover, ten years after her marriage would signify Ruth's attachment to Naomi, having lived together as a family for a decade. However, if Naomi's boys were young when they went to Moab and they have been there a total of ten years, the implication would be that Ruth is a young widow, one who still had a whole life that she could start over again. Davis reads the narrative as leaving this question open:

> Neither of these alternative interpretations is more inherently correct than the other. And while they are mutually exclusive as "historical" possibilities, maybe the storyteller deliberately leaves both open to our imaginations. For each of them leads us to see through the lens of the biblical text a somewhat different aspect of the human situation. Our reading is richer precisely because we can identify the sufferings and the achievements of these two women in more than one way.[87]

Davis's reading strategy is to see the positive side of ambiguity, as it invites readers to wonder about the women of the book of Ruth and to identify

---

85. Davis, *Who Are You*, 9–10.
86. Ibid., 10.
87. Ibid., 11.

with them in different ways. Another strategy that could be taken here, however, which Davis does not mention, is to view the ambiguity as signifying that Ruth's age is simply not an essential aspect of the story. Whether she is young and brimming with endless possibility, or nearing middle-aged and barren, the story that unfolds in her life is one of immense surprise and hope. Ruth is one who is seized by more than seemed imaginable, and such an overtaking of new life is powerful, whatever her age. Although Davis holds that narrative ambiguity invites wonder, at times such ambiguity may rather simply direct one's attention towards more important things. As Sakenfeld notes on the text's silence as to why Elimelekh and his sons died, "the narrator's lack of attention to any reason suggests that the answer to the question is not the central meaning of the story."[88] What is needed in biblical spiritual reading, then, is discernment on *when* to wonder—are all ambiguities in biblical texts calling for creative wondering? Davis speaks much of "fruitful" questions and wondering, and would seem to posit that most, if not all, trails of biblical wondering are useful.[89] But if a "fruitful question" is "one that leads you and your hearers more deeply into the story,"[90] the issue is how to know when a wondering will bear fruit.

It seems in this case that wondering about Ruth's age will not yield many fruits that lead deeper into the story, as there is no way of knowing what her age might be, and her age is not central to the story. While there may be benefit from such wondering in the reader's ability to identity with Ruth, as Davis points out, such wondering is not as useful in opening up avenues of the story. Ambiguities in biblical texts are of different orders; some are textual and some are situational, and where Davis could be more careful is to distinguish between different kinds of ambiguities and wonderings. A wondering that leads to greater identification with a biblical character is not the same as one that opens up depths of the text. As Michael H. Floyd points out in his review of *Who Are You, My Daughter?*, "Davis treats various kinds of ambiguity that are philologically quite different on more or less the same plane . . . readers might relate to different kinds of ambiguities differently if they were somehow enabled to."[91]

Davis finds layers of meaning not just in ambiguity, however, but even more so in seemingly straightforward pieces of the narrative. One word can sound off endless echoes, as happens in 1:6 where *shûv* first appears, with

---

88. Sakenfeld, *Ruth*, 21.

89. Biblical reading, she explains, requires "the imaginative skills for wondering fruitfully about the ultimate facts of life . . . fruitful theological wondering resides chiefly in the imagination." Davis, "Teaching the Bible," 11.

90. Davis, *Wondrous Depth*, 8.

91. Floyd, "Review of *Who Are You My Daughter?*," 144.

"and she turned back." Davis finds the verb *shûv* as "represent[ing] the central movement of the first part of the book;" it is used twelve times in first chapter alone (vv. 6, 7, 8, 10, 11, 12, 15, 16, 21, 22).[92] For this reason, Davis titles her comments on chapter one, "Turning Back." Repetition of *shûv*, Davis explains, highlights the word's thematic significance, which elsewhere in the Old Testament represents "a powerful spiritual reorientation, a turning to God and away from sin or false worship." She notes, "It is striking in this connection that Ruth is twice described as 'the one who turned back with Naomi from the field of Moab' (1:22; 2:6). Although Ruth is not literally returning to Israel and its God, she and Naomi are equal partners in a radical reorientation."[93] A close attention to words has thus sent a simple verb resonating with spiritual meaning—the turning back of Ruth and Naomi is cast on the plain of Old Testament repentance and reorientation. While Davis is reading Ruth verse-by-verse, she is bearing in mind the outcome of the story and the story's place in the broader canon of Scripture, and her comments move freely between the particularities of verses and the wider resonances they evoke.[94]

Strangely, Davis does not comment on the rest of 1:6, which contains the first mention of the presence and activity of YHWH: Naomi "had heard in the field of Moab that YHWH had visited his people, to give them bread" (Davis's translation). In her notes on this verse, Davis explains the divine name of YHWH, but she does not offer any comments on the significance of YHWH's act. It is a peculiar omission, as this verse offers potential for reflection on both God and biblical language. Kirsten Nielsen notes that "visited," *pqd*, also means "looked after," and she connects this word to its use in Gen. 21:1 and 1 Sam. 2:21, where God enables Sarah and Hannah to conceive.[95] Yet even as Davis is following what the story of Ruth says about God, she does not seize this overt mention of YHWH as a place to reflect theologically, to wonder what the narrator is telling. At the end of Ruth, in Davis's comments on 4:13, "and YHWH gave her pregnancy," Davis notes that this verse and 1:6 are the only two places where the narrator of Ruth states that God is acting directly. It is still not a major point of reflection, however, in contrast to other commentators who understand 1:6 and 4:13 to be framing the entire narrative of Ruth. Sakenfeld comments, "within the broad parameters of the gifts of daily bread and of human life itself, the

92. Davis, *Who Are You*, 13.
93. Ibid., 13.
94. In contrast, Sasson is again unconvinced by the narrator's use of language when it comes to the "*leitmotif* quality" of *shûv* in the first chapter, and maintains that the narrator "unfolded his playfulness a bit too loosely in this context." Sasson, *Ruth*, 37.
95. Nielsen, *Ruth*, 46.

book of Ruth presents God's working as hidden and mysterious, like yeast at work in a loaf of bread, until all is transformed."[96] As Davis reads Ruth spiritually, Ruth's most spiritually-sounding places are not necessarily the places in which she finds the most theological fruit. (Yet I would posit, with the commentators above, that there is much theological fruit to be found in those places, and it is peculiar that Davis does not seize that.)

Davis moves to 1:8 to suggest the significance of "house of her mother," noting that women's power "would prove to be world shaping, even though in a traditional society such as Israel, the exercise of women's power was less publically visible than that of men."[97] She does not offer prolonged feminist musings, however, but gives attention to this dimension of the verse as one aspect of its interpretation. Overall Davis evinces a concern for gender issues in Ruth, but not a preoccupation with it. In contrast to the commentary of Danna Nolan Fewell and David Gunn, *Compromising Redemption*, Davis does not exploit the feminist potential of Ruth. In this Davis's work is similar to that of Sakenfeld, who, although having deeper feminist concerns than Davis, finds Fewell and Gunn's work "strained as it reads nearly every speech in the entire story as disguising the speakers' true motives."[98] Sakenfeld, like Davis, "imagine[s] a greater degree of ambiguity of motivation in all the characters of this story than has usually been done,"[99] but feminist concerns do not become overriding in the commentaries of either interpreter. More so than gender relations, Davis seeks out the larger patterns of relations between the characters of Ruth, and their relations to God.

In 1:8–11, Davis comments upon biblical understandings of *hesed*, rest, and weeping, and finds significance in Naomi's calling Orpah and Ruth "my daughters," rather than "bride-daughters," as a closeness between them is implied. In 1:11 Davis briefly explains the practice of levirate marriage, but does not enter into a lengthy discussion of what is understood by that in the Old Testament (as many other commentators have done). With 1:13, Davis ponders the cause of Naomi's bitterness, suggesting that the text can mean that Naomi's deepest pain is seeing that of her daughters-in-law's affliction, or that Naomi sees her daughters-in-law as the cause of her bitterness, or that Naomi sees herself as more afflicted than the young women.

---

96. Sakenfeld, *Ruth*, 15. Nielson is more direct in her commentary: "[W]ith these two verses the author also characterizes the chief feature in the book's image of God: Yahweh provides bread and babies. In this way the theology corresponds precisely to the plot, where famine and childlessness are overcome." Nielsen, *Ruth*, 30.

97. Davis, *Who Are You*, 17.

98. Sakenfeld, *Ruth*, 26.

99. Ibid., 26.

Davis sets out and leaves these interpretive options open, as she does at many other points in her commentary.

In 1:14 Davis offers further reflections upon the significance of *davaq*, as Ruth "stuck by" Naomi. Davis posits that *davaq* "calls to mind" Gen 2:24, "what is perhaps the foremost biblical statement about the voluntary attachment of one person to another." Ruth is thus creating "a foundation of love on which a new family structure may be built." *Davaq* also hints adhering to God: "Perhaps the narrator means for us to hear the Torah injunction echoing behind the forceful declaration of loyalty to Naomi *and her God* that Ruth will soon make."[100] Yet that declaration must be read carefully, Davis goes on to argue, as although 1:16 is a beautiful statement (frequently read at weddings), "we should be cautious of sentimentalizing it." Davis understands that "the moment is not tender" as "the wills of these two determined women stand in acute tension at this point."[101] In her commentary Davis translates 1:16 as

And Ruth said,
> "Don't press me to leave you,
> to turn back from (following) after you.
> For where you go, I will go.
> And where you stay-the-night, I will stay.
> Your people (is) my people,
> and your God, my God."[102]

Davis explains that she departs from the more familiar translation, "Your people will be my people" because the Hebrew does not include a future-tense verb, or a verb at all. Although the future tense is implied by the surrounding clauses (going away, staying the night), Davis suggests that Ruth is saying that she and Naomi already share two things—a people and a God. Her translation, she explains, "implies that what they already share is the basis for sharing all the contingencies in the near and far future."[103] At the center of Davis's spiritual reading of this passage is a willingness to allows its Hebrew words and grammatical structures to reshape its traditional interpretation, and open up other ways of understanding its meaning.

Although Ruth's declaration has been read as a conversion statement, Davis finds the narrative leaves open Ruth's views towards the God of Israel, whether its God is one among many whom she may now worship. Davis

---

100. Davis, *Who Are You*, 23.
101. Ibid., 27.
102. Ibid., 26.
103. Ibid., 27.

explains that the question is ultimately whether Ruth is declaring devotion primarily to Naomi or to Naomi's God. She thinks it is more likely the former, as the reference to "your God, my God" is not prominent in Ruth's speech. Moreover, Davis states another reason "to think that Ruth is moved primarily by attachment to Naomi is simply that that is how many people come to God. . . . Many, and perhaps most, people come to God because they know and love someone who knows and loves God."[104] Again, Davis posits that this question should be left open:

> But we cannot finally choose between the two interpretations, nor should we. They point to different ways that love of God and love of another human being may be bound together in our experience. Each kind of devotion may have temporal primacy and lead eventually to a deepening of the other.[105]

Davis allows the openness of Ruth's declaration to lead her into contemplating how it is that "people come to God" and love of God and others is known. The text thus leads Davis into pondering the spiritual realities of which it speaks, and Davis's reading strives not towards a definitive hermeneutical answer of what comes into question, but a deeper engagement with that question. It is an inviting way to read, as rather than wrestling out an interpretation to be argued for definitively, a larger issue of faith is engaged. Yet Davis might allow more room for one to "choose between the two interpretations," as she herself often makes interpretative decisions that shape her reading of biblical texts. As the earlier examples of her exegesis have shown, a choice of interpretative possibilities can be a fruitful way to engage issues of a biblical passage, as one's interpretive choice will highlight aspects of that passage. What might be done with that choice, however, is to hold it open-handedly, to leave it open for further revision and rethinking, as the Bible is ever returned to with eyes of faith.

At the end of chapter 1, Davis comments on Naomi's use of *Shaddai* in 1:20, noting Shaddai's resonances with Israel's ancestral stories and positing that it is a name better left untranslated. She also links Naomi's use of Shaddai to the book of Job, as Job frequently uses this word when he too makes "a poetic cry of rage and pain."[106] Davis's third comment on Shaddai requires even more poetics. She posits that the name of Shaddai derives from an ancient Semitic word meaning "mountain," a word that in Hebrew

---

104. Ibid., 28.
105. Ibid.
106. Ibid., 35.

also means "my breasts." Although she notes that these meanings are *shaddai* are homonyms, Davis is intrigued by this connection and suggests

> The coincidence of meanings for Shaddai may be significant in the context of our story. For Naomi presents herself as a woman whose body has been emptied of all possibility of nurturance. Could this bitter naming of God as Shaddai be a reminder of her own breasts, which once nurtured sons who are no more? At the end of the book, she will in fact hold another son to her body, and that expresses Naomi's own restoration to full life.[107]

Davis reads like a church father or midrashic rabbi here, as the resonances of words and meanings are captivating her imagination. She lands further back in interpretive tradition, while at the same time offering insights one might find in feminist hermeneutics. However, this interpretation of *Shaddai* seems a step too imaginative, as it rests upon a translation of an ancient Semitic root for a name for God, a name that Davis herself does not want to translate. In her willingness to offer several meanings of *Shaddai* Davis presents an interpretation that seems too bound in creative speculation. Although Naomi becomes the nurse for Obed, it is a weak textual link between her breasts and her understanding of God.

More interesting with this verse is the observation Sakenfeld makes, that as Naomi "speaks of her return as God's action, action in which she sees nothing but sorrow, Naomi unknowingly anticipates the ways in which God will continue to work behind the scenes for the redemption of her tragedy."[108] Sakenfeld's comment holds to the words of the text, tracing the irony that Naomi speaks of God as "bringing her back empty," right as her return is a way that God is at work in beginning to fill her anew. Whereas Davis's comments on Naomi's outburst lead to increasing speculation, Sakenfeld's prompt an increased observation of the details and movement of the text.

Davis concludes her notes on chapter 1 with a comment on "at the beginning of the barley harvest," noting the historical timing of the grain harvest season and the possibilities that season offers for migrant workers. Even as she notes how this comment summarizes and concludes chapter 1, she peculiarly does not posit that the mention of harvest offers a glimmer of narrative hope and possibility. (Sakenfeld notes, "God's gift of food, the theme of full or empty, and the context for the following chapter are all lifted up implicitly in the notice."[109]) Davis does not want to run too far ahead with the story of Ruth, and in places like this (and 1:6) she sometimes errs on the

---

107. Ibid., 35.
108. Sakenfeld, *Ruth*, 36.
109. Ibid., 36.

side of reticence. Her reading of Ruth is like that of a storyteller who moves through the story slowly and dramatically and allows its elements to unfold in due time. What emerges in Davis's commentary is not an easily-extracted overarching interpretation of Ruth, but rather a series of reflections on Ruth that are truly that, reflections pointing back to the beauty of the original.

Pages Still Turning

Any good piece of art leaves its beholders or hearers with much to walk away with, and Davis's artistic handling of Scripture does not fail in that. Her manner of spiritual reading sets out a way of seeing the Bible and entering into its life, and it presses the reader to consider her own ways of biblical reading. Even when a reader like myself finds places to disagree with particulars of her biblical interpretations, Davis's own approach often sets the terms of that debate, as her close attention to God's work in Scripture calls the reader to probe what form that work might take in a given biblical passage. Davis is ever sending the reader back to the biblical text. As these examples of her biblical interpretations have shown, Davis's manner of spiritual reading requires great care and skill, for it is not easy to correlate a deep concern for biblical texts with a deep concern for the life of the Bible's readers and the world today. An eagerness to bring biblical texts to bear upon modern situations can end up skewing those texts, or at least, missing central parts of them. But at the same time, the Bible is ever-unfolding new meanings and any given interpretation can only pick up part of its many meanings. Davis's strength is in recognizing this reality and seeking out what meanings of Scripture are most pressing upon readers today. As the Bible speaks anew, spiritual reading must be done anew, for there is ever more to be heard.

More than just more to think about and strive to hear, Davis's spiritually-engaged reading also has the effect of encouraging the biblical reader to long for more in reading Scripture. Davis has understood her life's work to be about teaching others to read the Bible, and she accomplishes that through her own readings that convey a contagious wonder and longing towards the Word of God found in Scripture. Such longing to hear more and know more, Davis explains, is at the heart of the spiritual life and of biblical reading:

> Not satisfaction but the expansion and purification of holy desire is the surest sign of God's presence with us. So the art of the spiritual life is the art of learning to live with longing, with the

eager expectation that God's presence will be felt yet again in our hearts, in our midst, and always in new ways.[110]

Those new ways may indeed be in pages of Scripture, turned over once again.

---

110. Davis, *Proverbs, Ecclesiastes*, 302.

CHAPTER 8

Conclusion

IN *EVANGELICAL THEOLOGY* BARTH describes theology as a "*living* procession" after the living God; theology's work is to describe holistically "the dynamic interrelationships which make this procession comparable to a bird in flight, in contrast to a caged bird."[1] Eugene Peterson perhaps has this vision in mind when he begins his own work of spiritual theology; there he explains, "Writing about the Christian life (formulated here as 'spiritual theology') is like trying to paint a picture of a bird in flight. The very nature of a subject in which everything is always in motion and the context is constantly changing—rhythm of wings, sun-tinted feathers, drift of clouds (and much more)—precludes precision."[2] As the spiritual reading of Scripture is at the heart of the kind of spiritual theology that Barth and Peterson pursue (and that I have followed them in), it indeed is like a bird in flight—its contexts and contours are always changing, as it is following the One who hovered over the waters of creation, and descended like a dove upon Jesus at Jordan's banks. With this Spirit at work in a spiritual reader, the stillness and quietness and sheer everydayness that can be found in, e.g., my great-grandmother's Bible reading, disguise the fact that around her are lively spiritual realities constantly turning, like the wheels of the Ethiopian's chariot, for the Spirit is always moving.

Although birds in flight are ever moving, paintings of such birds still exist, and so also the spiritual reading of Scripture is thought and written about. The Spirit's work in the Bible is ultimately beyond all our charting, but it continues to call for a human response, a response of seeking to understand Scripture and to grapple with the practice of reading it, in order to enter into its life more fully. What has been offered in this study is one such

1. *ET*, 10, emphasis Barth's.
2. Peterson, *Christ Plays*, xi.

response, as I have sought to understand what is happening when Scripture is read spiritually, that is, when it is read to encounter God. C. S. Lewis said, "We must never assume that we know exactly what is happening when anyone reads." He adds a footnote to this, however: "I do not say we can never find out."[3] It may be beyond us to find out all that is happening when believers read the Bible, yet still we look to see how much we can learn, how much further back and further in we can go.

I set out below a brief summary of where we have ventured in this study, with notes on areas requiring further surveying and charting out. Following upon this, I offer a summary sketch of what I find to be the spiritual reading of Scripture in a western Christian context today—this sketch is my own snapshot of what might be portrayed (albeit only in part) of the spiritual reader and the ever-moving work of the Spirit in the reading of the Bible.

First, where we have been: I began in the introduction by explaining the context in which this work has been done; that context is important to make clear, for "spiritual reading" is an amorphous term (flighty indeed!) and needs grounding in a particular time and place. The western context of my work is important to bear in mind, for the spiritual reading of the Bible will keep on changing according to time and place. The technological culture of the west has changed, and will undoubtedly continue to change, the practices of spiritual reading. I am admittedly a Luddite myself, and so although I did not explore the connections between new technologies and spiritualities of reading, this is an important area in which my research could be taken.[4] It may be that just as the codex offered the early church new ways to express its understanding of the place of Scripture in the Christian life, new technologies may offer fresh ways of understanding how God speaks anew through the Bible to the church today. Likewise, more research needs to be done into other cultural practices of biblical reading, as cultures outside of the west have much to offer to the global church for its understanding of how to listen to and live with a living Word in its midst.[5]

As I set my work within the western context of the individual reading of the Bible, I noted the theology in which I was operating: I pursued this

---

3. Lewis, *Experiment in Criticism*, 48.

4. Alan Jacobs enthusiastically pursues such issues; see comments above, chapters 1 and 3, and his article "Christianity and the Future of the Book." See also Hipps, *Flickering Pixels*.

5. Philip Jenkins offers a compelling exploration of this in *New Faces of Christianity*..

study out of a Wesleyan-Orthodox understanding of the Bible and sanctification. I find this most helpful for understanding the practice of spiritual reading, for there the work of God and the work of humans come together. Even as God is always prior and primary, his Spirit invites humans into participation with him. In the practice of spiritual reading we see perhaps the clearest illustration of the participatory nature of sanctification—the Bible was created through God and humanity's coming together, and its spiritual reading involves the same.

As the Bible itself reflects a close and intertwined relationship between God and its human authors and readers, more could be said on the presence of God in biblical reading. Another direction my research could be taken is to consider inspiration anew, that is, how the Spirit of God both has formed the Bible and uses it to form the church today. Although hermeneutics may offer some help in this direction,[6] more theological work needs to be done.[7] Inspiration offers a category that holds together the previous and ongoing work of God in the Bible, that is, God's speaking-once and speaking-still in Scripture. As Robert Jenson points out in his article "A Second Thought About Inspiration," "there is someone in the picture beside the author, first readers, and us:"

> It was . . . a function of the old doctrine of inspiration [footnote: "even if unbeknownst to the propounders of the doctrine"] to trump the created author and first readers with a prior agent, the Spirit, and prior readers, the whole diachronic people of God, preserved as one people through time by that same Spirit.[8]

And so, Jenson finds that Bible produced by all of its "tradents and editors and canonizers, can be the textuality of the one Word—who is Jesus—because the Spirit made and makes all of these one community with that Word."[9] A fresh understanding of inspiration—of the Spirit of God who works throughout all of the Bible's history—might give new life to the church's reading of its Bible. The practice of spiritual reading makes clear

---

6. Francis Watson, e.g., finds hermeneutics offers a way "to hold together the past and present moments of divine speech . . . a theological conceptuality that does justice to this unity has proved hard to find. The problem is best addressed by drawing on the resources of nontheological hermeneutics." Watson, "Hermeneutics and the Doctrine of Scripture," 131.

7. Joel Green notes that in modern theological studies, "we have no common language for conversing about inspiration." Green, "Scripture and Theology," 11.

8. Jenson, "Second Thought," 396.

9. Ibid., 398.

the vital importance of this work of the Spirit, and calls for the manner of the Spirit's work to be pursued anew in each generation.

Just how to pursue that Spirit is the pressing question. Benjamin Jowett, who could be seen as the figure *par excellence* against the kind of spiritual reading I have been exploring, nonetheless was one who, like today's theological interpreters, was truly seeking God in Scripture. He explains, e.g., that in overseas missions work,

> [I]t is not the *Book of Scripture* we should seek to give [other peoples], to be reverenced like the *Vedas* or the *Koran*, but the truth of the Book, the mind of Christ and his Apostles, in which all lesser details and differences should be lost and absorbed. We want to awaken in them the sense that God is their Father, and they His children—that is of more importance than any theory about the inspiration of Scripture.[10]

Jowett's desire to "awaken in them the sense that God is their Father, and they His children" beautifully reflects Jowett's awareness of the end goal of Scripture. Yet where his approach differs from that of spiritual reading is the way that goal is pursued, how God is understood as being involved in that pursuit. Spiritual reading is an approach that insists that we are not on our own for the task of reading the Bible. Perhaps a theology of the inspiration of the Bible might better help readers to arrive at the end of being awakened to God through Scripture, for inspiration seeks to make clear how the Spirit of God is the one doing the awakening, turning hearts towards God through the reading of the Bible.

It is the church that has classically articulated such claims of the work of the Spirit of God in Christian Scripture, and it is through the witness of the church that most Christians come to receive and understand and live its Scriptures. In chapter 2 I thus explored the role of the church in spiritual reading. There I argued that the church is necessary for the spiritual reading of Scripture, as it has both formed the canon and set out ways of reading it well. William Abraham argues that the process of canonization is "the adoption of a complex means of grace;"[11] as the examples of recent biblical readers have shown, the church is needed to receive well the complex offering of grace in the Bible. The nature of the Bible is such that it is meant to be received within the community of faith. My comparison of the church

---

10. Jowett, "On the Interpretation of Scripture," 72, emphasis his.
11. Abraham, *Canon and Criterion*, 28.

with approaches of biblical scholarship and of reading the Bible as a classic was intended to demonstrate how necessary the church is as a framework of spiritual understanding of the Bible.

Much more could be said, of course, on how this framework is not as neat as my study may have made it seem. In many times and places the church's angles of reading have been skewed; examples abound of bad ecclesial readings of Scripture. Being in the church is no guarantee of good spiritual reading, as the church is not yet perfected in wisdom and holiness. Moreover, the church as a whole is divided in its readings of Scripture, and it does not speak with one voice. Different branches of the church read and interpret the Bible in different ways, and the church does not always challenge one's practices of biblical reading. And with such a wide array of churches, it is always possible to leave one branch of the church for another in order to find a church whose readings of the Bible more closely mirror one's own.

Perhaps what is needed to make clear, then, is the nature of the church as the body of Christian believers across history and space; it is this overarching flow of the church that gives guidance to spiritual reading. Local examples of bad readings are, on the whole, corrected by the broader church's understanding and witness. A good reading of Scripture is not one that is sanctioned by one particular local church or denomination, but one that may stand in the larger light of the universal church's creeds and testimonies and teachings. Even as there are still many issues that may not be agreed upon in this wider tradition, there is a common rule of faith that gives a baseline for practicing spiritual reading. The difference between spiritual reading and biblical interpretation is important to point out here—spiritual reading is about a *practice* of entering into and grappling with Scripture, while biblical interpretation is more directed towards the end results and consequences of that grappling (although those end results are, of course, closely tied up to the practices of reading employed). As a manner of spiritual reading is more commonly shared across the church than a mode of biblical interpretation, the church gives a basis for spiritual reading, despite its shortcomings.

What complicates this vision of spiritual reading as taking place within the church is that the Bible and the church are never apart from the horizons of their cultures, and that the church is continually growing in its own understanding of its Scripture. And so thorny issues (such as women's roles in church leadership) are ones that call for much probing into how the Bible is speaking out of and into its culture, as well as probing into how the church is growing in its understanding of the nature of gospel and the communal Christian life. Genuine growth in biblical understanding does take place within the church, as the Spirit of God continues to lead the church in its understanding of the Bible and shape the church into the image of Christ. (As de Lubac has insisted, there is movement in the history of the church; its own grasp of its faith is growing as the Spirit is growing the church.) And so even though the church is not a perfect exemplar of spiritual reading, it is still the place from which spiritual reading may begin. It must be remembered that the church, even more than being the body of Christian believers, is the body of Christ, the very place where the Spirit of Jesus dwells. Christ is betrothed to the church and is in it and is washing it by the water of the word (Eph 5:26). Because Jesus is in the church, so too should the spiritual reading of Scripture be.

In chapter 3 I considered how reading itself is an act with spiritual dimensions, and I surveyed some of the spiritual impulses behind the modern study of western literature. As the language used to talk about reading classical works of literature is similar in many ways to the language used to talk about reading Scripture, I sought to explore the spiritual dimensions to the reading of great literature. What emerged was the confusion often present in modern accounts of the reading of great literature, as various voices contest what its reading is actually for. I looked at Jacobs and Lewis to understand how Christians might approach reading literature in general, and turned to Griffiths to trace out whether a general manner of reading religious works might exist. I find that it does not, as the particular beliefs of the Christian faith fundamentally shape the Christian reading of Scripture; they are the realities in which the spiritual reading of the Bible occurs, and they give structure to particular practices of reading.

In chapters 2 and 3 I spoke of the possibility of reading the Bible as a work of literature, and it is important to make clear that I am not arguing against reading the Bible in a literary manner, a manner that uses the insights of modern literary criticism. My goal is not to set spiritual reading over and against literary reading, but rather to point out how spiritual reading requires something more than a literary approach. Yet as I mentioned in the introduction, close literary readings greatly enrich the spiritual reading of Scripture, and the modern tools of literary criticism have helped the Bible to become more alive to its readers today. The nature of the Bible is such that it is literary, a written text meant to be read. While the Bible need not always be approached as a written document (Graham and Griffiths pointed out that many other modes of engaging sacred writings exist), and the Bible has given life to the church in more ways than in its actual reading (such as through preaching, visual art, and music), the situation of twenty-first century western Christian readers is now that the Bible is primarily a literary document to them. For literate western readers, then, literary readings will be part of what it means to encounter Scripture well. In this time and place, the reading of the Bible is caught up in the broader patterns of reading in our culture. And so literary approaches to reading Scripture are helpful tools, as they bring out the rich textures of the Bible for readers steeped in a culture of written words. One of the most useful tools of a literary approach is its insistence on close attention to words and language; as Griffiths and Davis (among others) have noted, modern western consumer culture is often careless with words. A literary reading urges a biblical reader to pay close attention to the words of the Bible, as its actual language is the means through which its concerns are heard, and God may be known.

I mentioned in the introduction that it seems a great risk God has taken in putting his words into ever-turning pages of human words. There is truly a *theological* dimension to the written nature of the Bible; the medium is part of the message.[12] Something about God is revealed in the very *script*-ness of Scripture. The nature of the Bible as a written means of revelation calls for greater consideration, and one direction my research could be taken is to probe more fully what this written choice of revelation says theologically about God and the ways in which God may be encountered. Why, among many possibilities, would God choose the seemingly fragile means of written revelation?

Barth has already tackled that question to some degree, and in chapter 4, I studied Barth's theology of biblical reading, as he makes the reality of God clear and argues forcefully for the work of God in the Christian reading of the Bible. From *Church Dogmatics* to *Evangelical Theology* we see a movement of Barth seeking out more fully the role of the human reader of Scripture, and the spirituality of reading that is required to encounter God. Barth could say more about the potential for genuine growth in that spirituality, yet his concern for the primacy of God in biblical reading is a much-needed corrective to the often overly self-confident readings of Scripture in the church and academy. What Barth sets out is a reminder of the reality of the situation in which a reader picks up the Bible—the only reason that reading can take place is because God has already done, and is doing, something. Barth's insistence on the work of God, paired with the participation and response of the human reader, captures well the dynamic relationship between God and biblical readers. Moreover, his insistence on love in *Evangelical Theology* makes clear that this relationship is one primarily grounded in love. The act of reading Scripture should ultimately be an act of love, both

---

12. A point raised to me by Stephen Chapman.

the love of God that is shown to humankind, and the love of humans who respond to God. Love is thus a mark of biblical reading that needs greater theological reflection. More so than wisdom or understanding, the love of God is the aim in spiritual reading, and from that love, all else is added.

Barth addresses the complex intermingling of God and humanity in the practice of biblical reading, and the struggle to understand this cooperation of God and humanity is beneath many tensions between critical biblical scholarship and biblical readings undertaken in faith. As mentioned in the introduction, the movement of theological interpretation is one attempt to work out how modern biblical studies and Christian belief might relate to each other. What this study of spiritual reading has shown is that what is needed in spiritual biblical reading today is not less criticism but rather more faith—by "faith" I mean not a cognitive ability, but a greater trust in the active work of God in Scripture, a willingness to pursue that work of God through all manner of enquiry. Spiritual reading is to be faithful reading in that it strives to trust that the Spirit of God is present and working in the Bible today, in all manner of ways.

An illustration of a parallel phenomenon might help to make this clear: in commenting on different understandings of healing held by churches in the global North and South, Philip Jenkins notes that North Christians all too often neglect the reality of healing:

> The backwoods preacher putting his hand on a sick person and commanding, "Heal!"—in a suitably caricatured Southern accent—is a comic stereotype. But we should not exaggerate the supposed dichotomy between religion and "real" healing. The worst offense committed by global North Christians is not that they use conventional medicine, but that so few recognize its spiritual dimensions. If one proclaims Christ as the divine Wisdom, views the Spirit as the presence of God in the world, then we should acknowledge the divinely inspired inquisitiveness and creativity that gave rise to anesthesia and antisepsis. . . . The scientific imagination is—or should be—a religious impulse.[13]

It seems the same might be said about spiritual and "scientific" understandings of Scripture—the "worse offense" committed by many western readers of the Bible today is not that they use criticism, but that they neglect its spiritual dimensions. The critical study of the Bible, with its "inspired

---

13. Jenkins, *New Faces of Christianity*, 190.

inquisitiveness and creativity" that gave rise to approaches such as textual criticism and redaction criticism and literary criticism "is—or should be—a religious impulse." And so to reconcile modern biblical studies with theology and spirituality requires more than a movement of methodology—it requires a spiritual movement of faith, one that believes in the real presence of God and seeks to discern just how the Spirit is "the presence of God in the world." To say that spiritual reading is to be marked by faith is to say that it is a reading that deeply trusts in the work of the Spirit of God, a work that is ever beyond our neat categorizing.

Henri de Lubac sets out powerfully this belief that the Spirit of God is indeed present in the world and in the church, and in chapter 5 I followed de Lubac's history of medieval exegesis to explore the manner in which the church has approached its Scripture in light of Christ. De Lubac finds Jesus as the clear goal of the early and medieval church's movements of spiritual reading, and he argues that Jesus must still be the guiding light of spiritual exegesis today. More than just the *telos* of spiritual reading, Jesus is present in all parts of biblical reading, from its beginning to its end. I noted in my conclusion to chapter 5 that this presence of Jesus in Scripture is often overlooked in both ecclesial and academic reading of the Bible today; Jesus is not usually seen as primary to the task of biblical reading. Is it that there is a christological crisis in the church's biblical reading, then? How might the church seek more ardently its Lord Jesus in all manner of its biblical reading? As the church believes that it is through Jesus that the God the Father is known, so too it must discern more clearly how it is through Jesus that all Scripture is understood. There is a need for Jesus to come alongside biblical readers on the rough roads of their wonderings, to open their hearts to understand the Scriptures (Luke 24:32). De Lubac has illustrated beautifully how the early and medieval church sought this Jesus throughout all its reading of Scripture; the challenge is to imagine how that might take place today, in the light of modern critical approaches and methods.

In chapters 6 and 7, I looked at Ellen Davis as one presently immersed in the task of advancing the spiritual reading of the Bible in the church. As she writes towards the church by using the best tools of the academy, Davis offers a compelling integration of biblical scholarship, theology, and spirituality. She is practical, as well (more so than many other theologians and biblical scholars with similar concerns), and chapter 6 considered the particular practices and postures that she identifies as essential marks of spiritual reading. In chapter 7 I examined Davis's exegesis of four Old Testament texts in order to see how her approach works out in practice. Although I differ with her interpretations in various places, Davis helpfully models the kind of work that must be done for the task of relearning the spiritual reading of the Bible in the present day. Davis does leave open, however, the question of the role of Christ in Old Testament reading. She is happy to allow for an ad-hoc approach, explaining that a christological move must not always be made. As noted above, however, this claim needs pressing. How is it that God may be encountered in the Old Testament apart from an understanding of Christ? Is Jesus necessary for all biblical reading? Can the Old Testament be read on its own, as leading up to the gospel, but essentially not changed by "the Fact of Christ" of which de Lubac spoke? These questions, again, need further pursuing.

Just where to pursue those questions is itself a question. I have written this work from a location of both church and academy, as the conjunction of the two is needed for such a study. Although the study of spirituality has not held much ground in the secular university, it is rightly coming into consideration as an area deserving of academic interest. In his 2008 presidential address to the Society of Biblical Literature, Jonathan Z. Smith remarked, "I would insist with equal vigor that phenomena such as devotional practices of Bible study have a proper place within the histories of biblical interpretation as well as in ethnographies of practices within Jewish and Christian religious communities—topics of appropriate study for both the SBL and the AAR."[14] While Smith insisted that more attention must be paid to the ethnography of reading, and I agree, my project has been less an ethnography of the Christian reading of the Bible, and more a theological exploration of how that reading might be understood. What is needed to grasp the practice of Christian spiritual reading, I argue, is a theological understanding of the faith of the biblical reader. Again, by "faith" I mean the understanding of God and essentially the trust of God that is operative in a reader's life; it is the belief that shapes the act of reading. It is less a cognitive belief and intellectual assent than a trust that the Spirit of God is near and is working. As I have started from a place of a Christian belief and paid attention to that belief in the spiritual reader, this work has studied the extent to which a Christian belief informs the practice of the spiritual reading of the Bible. The issues I flagged for further consideration are questions that need

---

14. Smith, "Religion and Bible," 5.

pursuing in a context that recognizes religious belief as truly a significant factor for grasping the phenomenon of biblical reading.

Spiritual reading is a practice, and like many other practices, a step-by-step approach or summary of main points can be less helpful than actually seeing it take place. And so, rather than a bullet-point summary of spiritual reading at the end of this study, I offer a sketch of a spiritual reader of the Christian Bible today, noting the spiritual realities and the spiritual practices that are shaping her reading. I began this work with a brief series of images of three spiritual readers of Scripture in the past, and so I end by sketching out an image of what a spiritual reader might look like today:

She sits in a crowded coffee shop, with a steaming latte and open Bible laying flat on the table before her. Around her are all sorts of readers—professionals who come in for a coffee and quick read of the newspaper before heading to the office; free-lance writers who do their work from that coffee shop, their ubiquitous laptops ever before them; and students with stacks of notes and classic works of literature strewn out across their tables. She is one amongst many readers, yet her reading is of a different sort. It may not look that way to anyone surveying the scene, but there is something happening in her reading that is different from all the information- and pleasure- and self-improvement- types of reading around her.

Her reading is rather a kind of *meeting, an encounter*. Even as it involves aspects of information and pleasure and self-improvement, it is about something much more, the *meeting-with-God* that is the heart of spiritual reading. This is essentially the difference between her reading and all the other sorts—she came into that coffee shop not to be left alone to read, but to read with God, to be encountered by God. What that encounter may look like is hard to say—the God of the Bible shows up in various ways, from fire to quiet whisper to flaming tongues. Most likely this morning it will be in the form of a word or phrase of Scripture that strikes her heart, that speaks into some situation of her life, or that tells her something about the person of God. The basic nature of spiritual reading is that in it the reader begins with a desire that God may be known in the act of reading. With this, moreover, comes the recognition that God is present before she is; the presence and activity of the Spirit of God is prior to all efforts of biblical reading.

Her reading is then a *prayerful* reading, one that seeks God. She might begin by praying before she starts reading, asking the Spirit of God to open her heart and mind to hear what she needs to hear. Or she might dive straight into her reading, and pray as she goes, holding her questions and thoughts before God in a constant stream of conversation. In her praying she comes to trust God with her doubts and wonderings, and her prayer is a means by which the end goal of spiritual reading (to be with God) is part of the entire process. Prayer is also a reminder of the role of the Holy Spirit, as *the Spirit is needed* to come into the act of her biblical reading to bring it to life and to bearing fruit.

She did not grow up reading the Bible—only in her adulthood did she come to the Christian faith through the witness of a friend. The Bible she reads is a gift from that friend, a tangible reminder that for the spiritual reader *the Bible is a gift mediated through the church*. The church is the means by which God has worked in order to form the Christian Bible, and it continues to be the body that passes the Bible along and bears witness to it as speaking the truth about life and God. As she reads the Bible on her own, she is part of the community of faith, and she has a place to take all her questions and interpretations. She sets herself in the wider wisdom of the church. Even as her local church and its leaders cannot provide her with all she needs to know in order to read Scripture well (and could even lead her astray), she draws upon the resources of the wider universal church, and looks towards other church figures, past and present, for help in receiving the Bible.

Our reader's practice of spiritual reading is moreover *a learned reading*. She has learned from both the church and the wider culture how to read well, and she meditates on Scripture by way of various practices of learning. She reads with close attention to language, as she learned in school that any great work of literature must be read with great care given to its words. When she comes up with questions about the contexts and interpretations of various biblical passages, she reaches for biblical references and commentaries and dictionaries (yet usually she does this later, after her reading, as her task now is to immerse herself in the actual words of Scripture). She does not know Hebrew or Greek, but she often looks up the original meanings of particular words. In her efforts to wrestle with the words and meanings of biblical texts, there is a clear reflection of the *divine-human relationship at work in the Bible*. She responds to the offering of grace in Scripture by working out her salvation as God works in her.

Her reading is *slow*, lingering. Although when she first began reading the Bible she read quickly, trying to cover as much ground as possible, the more she has read the Bible, the slower she has become. Sometimes she will sit in the coffeeshop for an hour and only read a few verses, as its words plunge her into great mysteries of the faith. Sometimes she will read more quickly, such as when she reads of Israel's battles or of oracles against the nations, but even then a slowness comes in at the end of her reading, as she wonders what could possibly be the use of those passages. She reads in light of the gospel, linking all of Scripture towards Christ. Her reading is a reading in *trust*, in the belief that God may speak through any part of Scripture. Even as she encounters difficulties and does not always feel that God is near and speaking, she persists in the *hope* that the seed of the word is working within her.

As the aim of her reading is to encounter God, the product of her reading is her *growth towards Jesus Christ*. The more she reads Scripture the more she grows as a follower of Jesus, and knows Christ in her reading. Her sanctification is worked out in many ways, but one of the most daily and tangible ways is through her biblical reading. She comes to read the Bible better as her practice of spiritual reading deepens through the years, as her growth in her faith leads her towards a greater awareness of God and being formed into the image of Christ.

Such is one spiritual reader today, one image of the Spirit of God working in a reader who earnestly seeks out that Spirit in Scripture. Perhaps more than anything else, what must be recalled is that in the presence of this reader, and of all other Christian readers, and in the presence of the church is the living Jesus, he who might guide all practices of biblical reading. With Jesus in their midst, spiritual readers find the way, the truth, and the life of their reading. Mariano Magrassi explains, "The Fathers, recognizing the Spirit as the author of Scripture, ask its readers to be men and women of the Spirit and friends of Christ, even before they are perfect exegetes."[15] It is this being "men and women of the Spirit and friends of Christ" that truly marks the spiritual readers of the Christian Bible, those who seek in Scripture their Lord and their God.

---

15. Magrassi, *Praying the Bible*, viii–ix.

Bibliography

Abraham, William J. *Canon and Criterion in Christian Theology: From the Fathers to Feminism*. New York: Oxford University Press, 1998.
———. *The Divine Inspiration of Holy Scripture*. Oxford: Oxford University Press, 1981.
Adam, A. K. M., et al. *Reading Scripture With the Church: Toward a Hermeneutic for Theological Interpretation*. Grand Rapids: Baker, 2006.
Adler, Mortimer J., and Charles Van Doren. *How to Read a Book: The Classic Guide to Intelligent Reading*. New York: Simon and Schuster, 1972.
Allen, Leslie C. *Psalms 101–150*. Nashville: Thomas Nelson, 2002.
Alter, Robert. *The Five Books of Moses: A Translation and Commentary*. New York: W. W. Norton, 2004.
———. *The Pleasures of Reading in an Ideological Age*. New York: W. W. Norton, 1996.
Alter, Robert, and Frank Kermode, eds. *The Literary Guide to the Bible*. London: Fontana, 1989.
Auden, W. H. *Secondary Worlds*. London: Faber and Faber, 1968.
Augustine, Saint. "Exposition on Psalm 149." *Nicene and Post-Nicene Fathers*, Series 1, Vol. 8. Translated by J. E. Tweed. Edited by Philip Schaff. Buffalo: Christian Literature, 1888. Online: http://www.newadvent.org/fathers/1801149.htm
———. *On Christian Teaching*. Translated by R. P. H. Green. Oxford: Oxford University Press, 1997.
Ayres, Lewis. "The Soul and the Reading of Scripture: A Note on Henri de Lubac." *Scottish Journal of Theology* 61.2 (2008) 173–90.
Barth, Karl. *Church Dogmatics. Vol I.1: The Doctrine of the Word of God, Prolegomena to Church Dogmatics*. Edited by G.W. Bromiley and T.F. Torrance. Translated by G. W. Bromiley. Edinburgh: T. & T. Clark, 1975.
———. *Church Dogmatics. Vol I.2: The Doctrine of the Word of God*. Edited by G. W. Bromiley and T. F. Torrance. Translated by G. T. Thomson and Harold Knight. London: T. & T. Clark, 2004.
———. *The Epistle to the Romans*. Translated from the sixth edition by Edwyn C. Hoskyns. London: Oxford University Press, 1968.
——— *Evangelical Theology: An Introduction*. Translated by Grover Foley. New York: Holt, Rinehart and Winston, 1963.
———. *The Word of God and the Word of Man*. Translated by Douglas Horton. Gloucester: Peter Smith, 1978.

Benedict XVI. "Address of His Holiness Benedict XVI to the Participants in the International Conference Organized to Commemorate the 40th Anniversary of the Dogmatic Constitution Divine Revelation 'Dei Verbum.'" 16 September 2005. Online: http://www.vatican.va/holy_father/benedict_xvi/speeches/2005/september/documents/hf_ben-xvi_spe_20050916_40-dei-verbum_en.html

Berger, Peter L., and Thomas Luckmann. *The Social Construction of Reality: A Treatise in the Sociology of Knowledge*. New York: Doubleday, 1967.

Berlin, Adele. "On Bible Translations and Commentaries." In *Bible Translation on the Threshold of the Twenty-First Century: Authority, Reception, Culture, and Religion*, JSOT Supplement Series 353, edited by Athalya Brenner and Jan Willem van Henten, 175–91. London: Sheffield Academic, 2002.

Berry, Wendell. *What Are People For?* New York: North Point, 1990.

Biggar, Nigel. *Hastening That Waits: Karl Barth's Ethics*. Oxford: Clarendon, 1993.

Billings, J. Todd. "How to Read the Bible: New Strategies for Interpreting Scripture Turn Out To Be Not So New—And Deepen Our Faith." *Christianity Today*, October 2011. http://www.christianitytoday.com/ct/2011/october/how-to-read-bible.html

———. *The Word of God for the People of God: An Entryway Into the Theological Interpretation of Scripture*. Grand Rapids: Eerdmans, 2010.

Black, Clifton C. "Journeying through Scripture with the Lectionary's Map." *Interpretation* 56.1 (2002) 59–72.

Bloom, Harold. *How to Read and Why*. London: Fourth Estate, 2000.

Bonhoeffer, Dietrich. *Life Together*. Minneapolis: Fortress, 1996.

Booth, Wayne. *Company We Keep: An Ethics of Fiction*. Berkeley: University of California Press, 1988.

Bouteneff, Peter C. "All Creation in United Thanksgiving: Gregory of Nyssa and the Wesleys on Salvation." In *Orthodox and Wesleyan Spirituality*, edited by S. T. Kimbrough, Jr., 189–210. Crestwood, NY: St. Vladimir's Seminary, 2002.

Bouyer, Louis. *Parola, Chiesa e Sacramenti nel Protestantesimo e nel Cattolicesimo*. Brescia: Morcelliana, 1962.

Briggs, Richard. "Christian Theological Interpretation Built on the Foundation of the Apostles and the Prophets: The Contribution of R. W. L. Moberly's Prophecy and Discernment." *JTI* 4.2 (2010) 309–18.

———. *Light to Live By: How to Interpret the Bible*. Bletchley: Scripture Union, 2005.

———. *The Virtuous Reader: Old Testament Narrative and Interpretive Virtue*. Grand Rapids: Baker, 2010.

Breck, John. *Scripture in Tradition: The Bible and Its Interpretation in the Orthodox Church*. Crestwood, NY: St Vladimir's Seminary, 2001.

Brown, Sally A. "Review of *Wondrous Depth*, by Ellen F. Davis." *Theology Today* 63.4 (2007) 542–46.

Brueggemann, Walter. *An Introduction to the Old Testament: The Canon and Christian Imagination*. Louisville, KY: Westminster John Knox, 2003.

Burnett, Richard E. *Karl Barth's Theological Exegesis: The Hermeneutical Principles of the Römerbrief Period*. Grand Rapids: Eerdmans, 2004.

Burrows, Mark S. "To Taste with the Heart: Allegory, Poetics, and the Deep Reading of Scripture." *Interpretation* 56.2 (2002) 168–80.

Busch, Eberhard. *Karl Barth: His Life from Letters and Autobiographical Texts*. Translated by John Bowden. Philadelphia: Fortress, 1976.

Byassee, Jason. *Praise Seeking Understanding: Reading the Psalms with Augustine*. Grand Rapids: Eerdmans, 2007.

Cavanaugh, William T. *Being Consumed: Economics and Christian Desire*. Grand Rapids: Eerdmans, 2008.

Certeau, Michel de. *The Practice of the Everyday Life*. Translated by Steven Randall. Berkeley: University of California Press, 1988.

Chapman, Stephen B. "Imaginative Readings of Scripture and Theological Interpretation." In *Out of Egypt: Biblical Theology and Biblical Interpretation*, edited by Craig Bartholomew, et al., 409–47. Grand Rapids: Zondervan, 2004.

Childs, Brevard S. *Biblical Theology of the Old and New Testaments: Theological Reflections on the Christian Bible*. London: SCM, 1992.

———. "Does the Old Testament Witness to Jesus Christ?" In *Evangelium, Schriftauslegung, Kirche: Festschrift für Peter Stuhlmacher zum 65*, edited by Jostein Adna, et al., 57–64. Göttingen: Vandenhoeck & Ruprecht, 1997.

———. "The Genre of the Biblical Commentary as Problem and Challenge." In *Tehillah le-Moshe: Biblical and Judaic Studies in Honor of Moshe Greenberg*, edited by Mordechai Cogan, et al., 185–92. Winona Lake, IN: Eisenbrauns, 1997.

———. *Old Testament Theology in a Canonical Context*. London: SCM: 1985.

———. *The Struggle to Understand Isaiah as Christian Scripture*. Grand Rapids: Eerdmans, 2004.

Chyrsostom, John. *Homilies on Genesis*, 35.3. In *Acts, Ancient Christian Commentary on Scripture New Testament*, Vol. 5, edited by Francis Martin, et al. Downers Grove, IL: InterVarsity, 2006.

———. *Homily 1 on Matthew*. Translated by George Prevost, revised and edited for New Advent by Kevin Knight, http://www.newadvent.org/fathers/200101.htm.

Clooney, Francis X. "Review of *Religious Reading: The Place of Reading in the Practice of Religion*, by Paul J. Griffiths." *The Journal of Religion* 82.2 (2002) 298–300.

Cunningham, Mary Kathleen. *What is Theological Exegesis? Interpretation and Use of Scripture in Barth's Doctrine of Election*. Valley Forge, PA: Trinity, 1995.

Cyprian. Epistle to Donatus. In *Ante-Nicene Christian Library: Translations of the Writings of the Fathers Down to AD 325*, Vol. 8. Edited by Alexander Roberts and James Donaldson. Translated by Robert Ernest Wallis. Edinburgh: T. & T. Clark, 1868.

D'Ambrosio, Marcellino G. "Henri de Lubac and the Recovery of the Traditional Hermeneutic." PhD diss., Catholic University of America, 1991

Daley, Brian E. "Is Patristic Exegesis Still Usable?" In *The Art of Reading Scripture*, edited by Ellen F. Davis and Richard B. Hays, 69–88. Grand Rapids: Eerdmans, 2003.

Darnton, Robert. "Reading: Harvard Views of Reading, Readership, and Reading History." Harvard University Library Open Collections Program. Online: http://ocp.hul.harvard.edu/reading/

Davis, Ellen F. "Entering the Story: Teaching the Bible in the Church." In *Sharper Than a Two-Edged Sword: Preaching, Teaching, and Living the Bible*, edited by Michael Root and James J. Buckley, 44–62. Grand Rapids: Eerdmans, 2008.

———. *Getting Involved With God: Rediscovering the Old Testament*. Boston: Cowley, 2001.

———. *Imagination Shaped: Old Testament Preaching in the Anglican Tradition*. Valley Forge, PA: Trinity International, 1995.

———. "Land, Life and the Poetry of Creatures." Interview with Krista Tippet on *Speaking of Faith*, Minnesota Public Radio, aired June 10–16, 2010. Online: http://being.publicradio.org/programs/2010/land-life-poetry/

———. "Losing a Friend: The Loss of the Old Testament to the Church." *Pro Ecclesia* IX:1 (2000) 73–85.

———. "No Explanations in the Church: Two Sermons on the Prophets." In *Touching the Altar: The Old Testament for Christian Worship*, edited by Carol M. Bechtel, 95–121. Grand Rapids: Eerdmans, 2008.

———. "The Poetics of Generosity." In *The Word Leaps the Gap: Essays on Scripture and Theology in Honor of Richard B. Hays*, edited by J. Ross Wagner, C. Kavin Rowe, and A. Katherine Grieb, 626–45. Grand Rapids: Eerdmans, 2008.

———. *Proverbs, Ecclesiastes, and the Song of Songs*. Louisville, KY: Westminster John Knox, 2000.

———. *Scripture, Culture, and Agriculture: An Agrarian Reading of the Bible*. Cambridge: Cambridge University Press, 2009.

———. "Self-Inflicted Violence." In *The Art of Reading Scripture*, edited by Ellen F. Davis and Richard B. Hays, 294–99. Grand Rapids: Eerdmans, 2003.

———. "The Soil That is Scripture." In *Engaging Biblical Authority: Perspectives on the Bible as Scripture*, edited by William P. Brown, 36–44. Louisville, KY: Westminster John Knox, 2007.

———. "Surprised by Wisdom: Preaching Proverbs." *Interpretation* 63.3 (2009) 264–77.

———. *Swallowing the Scroll: Textuality and the Dynamics of Discourse in Ezekiel's Prophecy*. Sheffield: The Almond, 1989.

———. "Teaching the Bible Confessionally in the Church." In *The Art of Reading Scripture*, edited by Ellen F. Davis and Richard B. Hays, 9–26. Grand Rapids: Eerdmans, 2003.

———. *Wondrous Depth: Preaching the Old Testament*. Louisville, KY: Westminster John Knox, 2005.

Davis Ellen F., and Margaret Adams Parker, *Who Are You, My Daughter? Reading Ruth Through Image and Text*. Louisville, KY: Westminster John Knox, 2003.

Davis, Ellen F., and Richard B. Hays, eds. *The Art of Reading Scripture*. Grand Rapids: Eerdmans, 2003.

Davis, Philip, ed. *Real Voices: On Reading*. Basingstoke: Macmillan, 1997.

———. *The Experience of Reading*. London: Routledge, 1992.

Dawkins, Richard. "Richard Dawkins Lends His Support to the King James Bible Trust." Online: http://www.kingjamesbibletrust.org/news/2010/02/19/richard-dawkins-lends-his-support-to-the-king-james-bible-trust.

Donoghue, Davis. *The Practice of Reading*. New Haven, CT: Yale University Press, 1998.

Driver, Daniel R. *Brevard Childs, Biblical Theologian: For the Church's One Bible*. Tübingen: Mohr Siebeck, 2010.

Dumont, Charles. *Praying the Word of God: The Use of Lectio Divina*. Oxford: SLG, 1999.

Eagleton, Terry. *Literary Theory: An Introduction*. Minneapolis: University of Minnesota Press, 1998.

Eaton, John. *The Psalms: A Historical and Spiritual Commentary with an Introduction and New Translation*. London: T. & T. Clark, 2003.

Eliot, T. S. *The Sacred Wood: Essays on Poetry and Criticism*. London: Faber and Faber, 1997.

Esler, Philip F. *New Testament Theology: Communion and Community*. London: Augsburg Fortress, 2005.

Fee, Gordon D., and Douglas Stuart. *How to Read the Bible for All Its Worth: A Guide to Understanding the Bible*. Grand Rapids: Zondervan, 1993.

Floyd, Michael H. "Review of *Who Are You My Daughter?* by Ellen F. Davis." *ATR* 86.1 (2004) 143–44.

Ford, Nigel. *The Lantern and the Looking-glass: Literature and Christian Belief*. London: SPCK, 1997.

Foster, Richard. *Life With God: Reading the Bible for Spiritual Transformation*. New York: HarperCollins, 2008.
Fowl, Stephen E. *Engaging Scripture: A Model for Theological Interpretation*. Malden: Blackford, 1998.
———. *Theological Interpretation of Scripture*. Eugene, OR: Cascade, 2009.
———, ed. *The Theological Interpretation of Scripture: Classic and Contemporary Readings*. Cambridge: Blackwell, 1997.
Gamble, Henry Y. *Books and Readers in the Early Church: A History of Early Christian Texts*. New Haven, CT: Yale University Press, 1995.
Gaventa, Beverly Roberts. "To Glorify God and Enjoy God Forever: A Place for Joy in Reformed Readings of Scripture." In *Reformed Theology: Identity and Ecumenicity II: Biblical Interpretation in the Reformed Tradition*, edited by Wallace M. Alston and Michael Welker, 107–15. Grand Rapids: Eerdmans, 2007.
Godsey, John D. "Barth as a Teacher." In *For the Sake of the World: Karl Barth and the Future of Ecclesial Theology*, edited by George Husinger, 202–14. Grand Rapids: Eerdmans, 2004.
Graham, William A. *Beyond the Written Word: Oral Aspects in the History of Religion*. Cambridge: Cambridge University Press, 1987.
Green, Garrett. *Imagining God: Theology and the Religious Imagination*. Eerdmans: Grand Rapids, 1989.
Green, Joel B. "The (Re-)Turn to Theology." *JTI* 1.1 (2007) 1–3.
———. "Scripture and Theology: Failed Experiments, Fresh Perspectives." *Interpretation* 56.1 (2002) 5–20.
Griffiths, Paul. "Reading as a Spiritual Discipline." In *The Scope of Our Art: The Vocation of the Theological Teacher*, edited by L.Gregory Jones and Stephanie Paulsell, 32–47. Grand Rapids: Eerdmans, 2002.
———. *Religious Reading: The Place of Reading in the Practice of Religion*. New York: Oxford University Press, 1999.
Guigo II. *The Ladder of Monks*. Translated by Edmund Colledge and James Walsh. Kalamazoo, MI: Cistercian, 1979.
Haddon, Mark. "The Right Words in the Right Order." In *Stop What You're Doing and Read This!*, 75–96. London: Vintage, 2011.
Hadot, Pierre. *Philosophy as a Way of Life: Spiritual Exercises from Socrates to Foucault*. Edited by Arnold I. Davidson and translated by Michael Chase. Oxford: Blackwell, 1995.
Hals, Ronald M. *The Theology of the Book of Ruth*. Philadelphia: Fortress, 1969.
Harrisville, Roy A. "What I Believe My Old Schoolmate is Up To." In *Theological Exegesis: Essays in Honor of Brevard S. Childs*, edited by Christopher Seitz and Katherine Greene-McCreight, 7–25. Grand Rapids: Eerdmans, 1999.
Hauerwas, Stanley. *Character and the Christian Life: A Study in Theological Ethics*. San Antonio, TX: Trinity University Press, 1974.
Hays, Richard H. *The Conversion of the Imagination: Paul as Interpreter of Israel's Scripture*. Grand Rapids: Eerdmans, 2005.
———. "Reading the Bible with Eyes of Faith: The Practice of Theological Exegesis." *JTI* 1.1 (2007) 5–21.
Hiebert, Theodore. Review of *Scripture, Culture, and Agriculture*, by Ellen F. Davis. *Biblical Interpretation* 18 (2010) 437–39.
Hipps, Shane. *Flickering Pixels: How Technology Shapes Your Faith*. Grand Rapids: Zondervan, 2009.
Heschel, Abraham Joshua. *The Prophets*, Vol. 1. New York: Harper Colonphon, 1962.

Hollon, Brian C. *Everything is Sacred: Spiritual Exegesis in the Political Theology of Henri de Lubac*. Cambridge: James Clarke, 2010.

Houston, James M. "Towards a Biblical Spirituality." In *The Act of Bible Reading*, edited by Elmer Dyck, 148–73. Carlisle: Paternoster, 1996.

Hunsinger, George. *How to Read Karl Barth: The Shape of His Theology*. New York: Oxford University Press, 1990.

———. "Postliberal Theology." In *The Cambridge Companion to Postmodern Theology*, edited by Kevin J. Vanhoozer, 42–57. Cambridge: Cambridge University Press, 2003.

Hurtado, Larry W. *The Earliest Christian Artifacts: Manuscripts and Christian Origins*. Grand Rapids: Eerdmans, 2006.

Illich, Ivan. *In the Vineyard of the Text: A Commentary to Hugh's Didascalicon*. Chicago: The University of Chicago Press, 1993.

Jacobs, A. J. *The Year of Living Biblically: One Man's Humble Quest to Follow the Bible as Literally as Possible*. New York: Simon & Schuster, 2007.

Jacobs, Alan. "Christianity and the Future of the Book." *The New Atlantis* (2011) 19–36.

———. *The Pleasures of Reading in an Age of Distraction*. Oxford: Oxford University Press, 2011.

———. "*The Pleasures of Reading in an Age of Distraction*: A Discussion with Alan Jacobs." *The New Atlantis*, The Hudson Institute, 3 June 2011. Online: http://www.thenewatlantis.com/publications/the-pleasures-of-reading-in-an-age-of-distraction

———. *A Theology of Reading: The Hermeneutics of Love*. Cambridge: Westview, 2001.

Jamison, Abbot Christopher. *Finding Sanctuary: Monastic Steps for Everyday Life*. London: Phoenix, 2010.

Jeanrond, Werner. *Text and Interpretation As Categories of Theological Thinking*. Dublin: Gill and Macmillan, 1988.

Jeffrey, David Lyle. *Houses of the Interpreter: Reading Scripture, Reading Culture*. Waco, TX: Baylor University Press, 2003.

———. *People of the Book: Christian Identity and Literary Culture*. Grand Rapids: Eerdmans, 1996.

Jenkins, Philip. *The New Faces of Christianity: Believing the Bible in the Global South*. Oxford: Oxford University Press, 2006.

Jenson, Robert W. "The Religious Power of Scripture." *Scottish Journal of Theology* 52.1 (1999) 89–105.

———. "A Second Thought About Inspiration." *Pro Ecclesia* 8.4 (2004) 393–98.

———."The Strange New World Within the Bible." In *Sharper Than a Two-Edged Sword: Preaching, Teaching, and Living the Bible*, edited by Michael Root and James J. Buckley, 22–31. Grand Rapids: Eerdmans, 2008.

Jerome. Letter 22.17,37. Translated by W. H. Fremantle. Revised and edited for New Advent by Kevin Knight. Online: http://www.newadvent.org/fathers/3001022.htm.

Johnson, Gregory O. "From Morning Watch to Quiet Time: The Historical and Theological Development of Private Prayer in Anglo-American Protestant Instruction, 1870–1950." PhD dissertation, Saint Louis University, 2007.

Johnson, Luke Timothy. "Imagining the World Scripture Imagines." In *Theology and Scriptural Imagination*, edited by L. Gregory Jones and James J. Buckley, 3–18. Oxford: Blackwell, 1998.

Jones, Serene. "Inhabiting Scripture, Dreaming Bible." In *Engaging Biblical Authority, Perspectives on the Bible as Scripture*, edited by William P. Brown, 73–80. Louisville, KY: Westminster John Knox, 2007.
Jowett, Benjamin. "On the Interpretation of Scripture." In *Interpretation of Scripture and Other Essays*, 1–76; reprint from *Essays and Reviews*, 1860. London: George Routledge & Sons, 1932.
Keuss, Jeff. "George Steiner and the Minotaur at the Heart of Love: Review of *Real Presences*, by George Steiner." *Literature & Theology* 18.3 (2004) 351–57.
Kelsey, David. *The Uses of Scripture in Recent Theology*. London: SCM, 1975.
Kort, Wesley. *"Take, Read": Scripture, Textuality, and Cultural Practice*. University Park, PA: Pennsylvania State University Press, 1996.
Koskie, Steven J. "Seeking Comment: The Commentary and the Bible As Christian Scripture." *JTI* I.2 (2007) 237–49.
"Krish Kandiah and the Weightwatchers Approach to Reading God's Word," *Christianity Today*, 18 January 2011. Online: http://www.christiantoday.com/article/krish. kandiah.and.the.weightwatchers.approach.to.reading.gods.word/27377.htm
LaCocque, André. *Ruth: A Continental Commentary*. Translated by K. C. Hanson. Minneapolis: Fortress, 2004.
Legaspi, Michael C. *The Death of Scripture and the Rise of Biblical Studies*. Oxford: Oxford University Press, 2010.
L'Engle, Madeleine. *Walking on Water*. New York: North Point, 1980.
Levenson, Jon D. *The Hebrew Bible, the Old Testament, and Historical Criticism*. Louisville, KY: Westminster John Knox, 1993.
———. "Teach the Text in Contexts." *Harvard Divinity Bulletin* 35.4 (2007). Online: http://www.hds.harvard.edu/news-events/harvard-divinity-bulletin/articles/teach-the-text-in-contexts
Lewis, Alan E. "Review of *Evangelical Theology: An Introduction*, by Karl Barth." *Religious Studies* 18.2 (1982) 255–57.
Lewis, C. S. *An Experiment in Criticism*. Cambridge: Cambridge University Press, 1961.
———. *Reflections on the Psalms*. Glasgow: Collins, 1981.
———. "The Weight of Glory." In *The Weight of Glory: And Other Addresses*, edited by Walter Hooper. New York: HarperCollins, 2001.
Logan, Stephen. "Amazed and Confused in the Quest for Clarity." *Times Higher Education Supplement*, 14 November 2003. Online: http://www.timeshighereducation.co.uk/story.asp?sectioncode=21&storycode=181184
———. "Literary Theorist." In *The Cambridge Companion to C.S. Lewis*, edited by Robert MacSwain and Michael Ward, 29–42. Cambridge: Cambridge University Press, 2010.
Lubac, Henri de. *At the Service of the Church: Henri de Lubac Reflects on the Circumstances That Occasioned His Writings*. San Francisco: Communio, 1993.
———. *Medieval Exegesis. Vol. 1: The Four Senses of Scripture*. Translated by Mark Sebanc. Grand Rapids: Eerdmans, 1998.
———. *Medieval Exegesis. Vol. 2: The Four Senses of Scripture*. Translated by E.M. Macierowski. Grand Rapids: Eerdmans, 2000.
———. *Scripture in the Tradition*. Translated by Luke O'Neill. New York: Herder & Herder, 2000.
Madueme, Hans. "Theological Interpretation after Barth." *JTI* 3.I (2009) 143–56.
Magrassi, Mariano. *Praying the Bible: An Introduction to Lectio Divina*. Collegeville, MN: Liturgical, 1998.

Mangina, Joseph L. *Karl Barth on the Christian Life: The Practical Knowledge of God.* New York: Peter Lang, 2001.

———. *Karl Barth: Theologian of Christian Witness.* Burlington, VA: Ashgate, 2004.

Maurice, F. D. "On the Friendship of Books." In *The Friendship of Books and Other Lectures*, edited by Thomas Hughes, 1–32. London: Macmillian, 1904.

McCormack, Bruce L. "The Significance of Karl Barth's Theological Exegesis of Philippians." In Karl Barth, *The Epistle to the Philippians* (40th anniversary edition), translated by James W. Leitch, v–xxv. Louisville, KY: Westminster John Knox, 2002.

McKenzie, Tim. "'I Shall Win at the Odds'—George Steiner's Wager on the Meaning of Meaning: A Review of *Real Presences*, by George Steiner." *Literature & Theology* 18.3 (2004) 357–62.

McLuhan, Marshall. *The Gutenberg Galaxy: The Making of Typographic Man.* London: Routledge & Kegan Paul, 1962.

Milbank, John. *The Suspended Middle: Henri de Lubac and the Debate Concerning the Supernatural.* London: SCM, 2005.

Moberly, R. W. L. "Biblical Criticism and Religious Belief." *JTI* 2.1 (2008) 71–100.

———. *The Bible, Theology, and Faith: A Study of Abraham and Jesus.* Cambridge: Cambridge University Press, 2000.

———. "Christ in All the Scriptures? The Challenge of Reading the Old Testament as Christian Scripture." *JTI* 1.1 (2007) 79–100.

———. "'Interpret the Bible Like Any Other Book'? Requiem for an Axiom." *JTI* 4.1 (2010) 91–110.

———. "Preaching Christ from the Old Testament." In *'He Began With Moses . . .': Preaching the Old Testament Today*, edited by Grenville J. R. Kent, et al., 233–50. Nottingham: Intervarsity, 2010.

———. "Theological Interpretation, Presuppositions, and the Role of the Church: Bultmann and Augustine Revisited." *JTI* 6.1 (2012) 1–22.

———. "What Is Theological Interpretation of Scripture?" *JTI* 3.2 (2009) 161–78.

Morrison, Blake. "Twelve Thoughts About Reading." In *Stop What You're Doing and Read This!*, 13–35. London: Vintage, 2011.

Nielsen, Kirsten. *Ruth: A Commentary.* London: SCM, 1997.

Noonoo, Jemimah. "Reading the Bible: Taking on Biblical Illiteracy," *The Houston Chronicle*, 5 June 2009. http://wwww.chonr.com/CDA/archives/archive.mpl?id=2009_4750019

Nunberg, Geoffrey, ed. *The Future of the Book.* Berkeley: University of California Press, 1996.

Nussbaum, Martha C. *Love's Knowledge: Essays on Philosophy and Literature.* Oxford: Oxford University Press, 1990.

O'Connor, Flannery. *Mystery and Manners: Occasional Prose.* Selected and edited by Sally and Robert Fitzgerald. London: Faber and Faber, 1972.

Olson, Glending. *Literature As Recreation in the Late Middle Ages.* Ithaca, NY: Cornell University Press, 1982.

Origen. *Homilies on Joshua.* Edited by Cynthia Whire and translated by Barbara J. Bruce. Washington, DC: Catholic University of America Press, 2002.

Parks, Tim. "Mindful Reading." In *Stop What You're Doing and Read This!*, 55–73. London: Vintage, 2011.

Peterson, Eugene. *Christ Plays in Ten Thousand Places: A Conversation in Spiritual Theology.* Grand Rapids: Eerdmans, 2005.

———. *Eat This Book: A Conversation in the Art of Spiritual Reading*. Grand Rapids: Eerdmans, 2006.

———. "Foreword: *Caveat Lector*." In *The Act of Bible Reading*, edited by Elmer Dyck, 7–9. Carlisle: Paternoster, 1996.

Plotz, David. "Biblically Speaking: David Plotz Discusses *Good Book*, His Chronicle of Reading Every Single Word of the Bible." *Slate*, March 4, 2009. http://www.slate.com/id/2212970/pagenum/all/#p2.

———. "Blogging the Bible: A Harvard-educated Reformed Jew Grapples with the Old Testament." *Christianity Today*, April 2009, 64.

Quiller-Couch, Sir Arthur. *On the Art of Reading*. Cambridge: Cambridge University Press, 1928.

Radosh, Daniel. "The Good Book Business: Why Publishers Love the Bible." *The New Yorker*, 16 December 2006. http://www.newyorker.com/archive/2006/12/18/061218fa_fact1

Reno, R. R. "Biblical Theology and Theological Exegesis." In *Out of Egypt: Biblical Theology and Biblical Interpretation*, edited by Craig Bartholomew, 385–408. Grand Rapids: Zondervan, 2004.

———. "'You Who Once Were Far Off Have Been Brought Near': Reflections in the Aid of Theological Exegesis." *EA* 16 (2000) 169–82.

Sakenfeld, Katharine Doob. *Ruth*. Louisville, KY: John Knox Press, 1999.

Sangster, W. E. *God Does Guide Us*. London: Hodder & Stoughton, 1963.

Sarisky, Darren. "What is Theological Interpretation? The example of Robert W. Jenson." *IJST* 12.2 (2010) 201–16.

Sasson, Jack M. *Ruth: A New Translation with a Philological Commentary and a Formalist-Folklorist Interpretation*. Sheffield: Sheffield Academic, 1995.

Schneiders, Sandra M. "Biblical Spirituality." *Interpretation* 56.2 (2002) 133–42.

———. "The Gospels and the Reader." In *The Cambridge Companion to the Gospels*, edited Stephen C. Barton, 97–118. Cambridge: Cambridge University Press, 2006.

———. *The Revelatory Text: Interpreting the New Testament as Sacred Scripture*. New York: HarperCollins, 1991.

Smith, Jonathan Z. "Religion and Bible." *JBL* 128.1 (2009) 5–27.

Smith, Lesley. *Medieval Exegesis In Translation: Commentaries on the Book of Ruth, Translated with an Introduction and Notes*. Kalamazoo, MI: Medieval Institute, 1996.

Steiner, George. "'Critic'/'Reader.'" In *Real Voices on Reading*, edited by Philip Davis, 3–37. Basingstoke: Macmillan, 1997.

———. *Language and Silence: Essays 1958–1966*. London: Faber, 1967.

———. *No Passion Spent: Essays 1978–1996*. London: Faber & Faber, 1996.

———. *Real Presences: Is There Anything in What We Say?* London: Faber and Faber, 1989.

Steinmetz, David C. "Calvin and the Irrepressible Spirit." *EA* 12 (1996) 94–107.

———. "The Superiority of Pre-Critical Exegesis." In *The Theological Interpretation of Scripture*, edited by Stephen E. Fowl, 26–38. Cambridge: Blackwell, 1997.

Stendahl, Krister. "The Bible as a Classic and the Bible as Holy Scripture." In *Presidential Voices: The Society of Biblical Literature in the Twentieth Century*, edited by Harold W. Attridge and James C. VanderKam, 209–15. Atlanta: Society of Biblical Literature, 2006.

Studzinski, Raymond. *Reading to Live: The Evolving Practice of* Lectio Divina. Collegeville, MN: Cistercian, 2009.

Treier, Daniel J. *Introducing Theological Interpretation of Scripture: Recovering a Christian Practice.* Nottingham: Apollos, 2008.

———. "What Is Theological Interpretation? An ecclesiological reduction." *IJST* 12.2 (2010) 144–61.

Underhill, Evelyn. *The Spiritual Life.* Harrisburg, PA: Morehouse, 1955.

Vanhoozer, Kevin J. "Spirit of Understanding: Special Revelation and General Hermeneutics." In *Disciplining Hermeneutics: Interpretation in Christian Perspective,* edited by Roger Lundin, 131–66. Grand Rapids: Eerdmans, 1997.

Vanhoozer, Kevin, Daniel J. Treier, and N.T. Wright, eds. *Theological Interpretation of the New Testament: A Book-by-Book Survey.* Grand Rapids: Baker Academic, 2008.

Watson, Francis. "Barth's Philippians as Theological Exegesis." In Karl Barth, *The Epistle to the Philippians* (40th anniversary edition), translated by James W. Leitch, xxvi–li. Louisville, KY: Westminster John Knox, 2002.

———. "The Bible." In *The Cambridge Companion to Barth,* edited by John Webster, 57–71. Cambridge: Cambridge University Press, 2000.

———. "Does Historical Criticism Exist?" Unpublished paper presented to the Society of Biblical Literature Annual Meeting, New Orleans, November 2009.

———. "An Evangelical Response." In *The Trustworthiness of God: Perspectives on the Nature of Scripture,* edited by Paul Helm and Carl Trueman, 285–89. Grand Rapids: Eerdmans, 2002.

———. "Hermeneutics and the Doctrine of Scripture: Why They Need Each Other." *IJST* 12.2 (2010) 118–43.

———. *Text, Church, and World: Biblical Interpretation in Theological Perspective.* Grand Rapids: Eerdmans, 1994.

———. *Text and Truth: Redefining Biblical Theology.* Grand Rapids: Eerdmans, 1997.

Webb, Chris. *The Fire of the Word: Meeting God on Holy Ground.* Downers Grove, IL: InterVarsity, 2011.

Webster, John. *Barth's Moral Theology: Human Action in Barth's Thought.* Edinburgh: T. & T. Clark, 1998.

———. *Holy Scripture: A Dogmatic Sketch.* Cambridge: Cambridge University Press, 2003.

———. "Reading Scripture Eschatologically (I)." In *Reading Texts, Seeking Wisdom: Scripture and Theology,* edited by David Ford and Graham Stanton, 245–56. London: SCM, 2003.

———. *Word and Church: Essays in Christian Dogmatics.* Edinburgh: T. & T. Clark, 2001.

Wettenhall, Edward. *Enter Thy Closet, or a Method and Order for Private Devotion.* London: John Martyn, 1666.

Wilken, Robert Louis. "Foreword." In *Medieval Exegesis, Vol. 1: The Four Senses of Scripture,* by Henri de Lubac, ix–xii. Grand Rapids: Eerdmans, 1998.

Williams, Rowan. "Historical Criticism and Sacred Text." In *Reading Texts, Seeking Wisdom: Scripture and Theology,* edited by David Ford and Graham Stanton, 217–28. London: SCM, 2003.

Willimon, William H. *Conversations with Barth on Preaching.* Nashville: Abingdon, 2006.

———. *Peculiar Speech: Preaching to the Baptized.* Grand Rapids: Eerdmans, 1992.

Wood, Susan K. *Spiritual Exegesis and the Church in the Theology of Henri de Lubac.* Grand Rapids: Eerdmans, 1998.

Woods, Julie Irene. *Jeremiah 48 as Christian Scripture*. Eugene, OR: Pickwick, 2011.
Work, Telford. "Meager Harvest." *Christianity Today* 53.2 (2009) 28–31.
Wright, Stephen I. "An Experiment in Biblical Criticism: Aesthetic Encounter in Reading and Preaching Scripture." In *Renewing Biblical Interpretation*, Scripture and Hermeneutics Series I, edited by Craig Bartholomew, et al., 240–67. Grand Rapids: Zondervan, 2000.
Young, Frances M. *Biblical Exegesis and the Formation of Christian Culture*. Peabody, MA: Hendrickson, 1997.
Zylstra, Henry. *Testament of Vision*. Grand Rapids: Eerdmans, 1961.

www.ingramcontent.com/pod-product-compliance
Lightning Source LLC
Chambersburg PA
CBHW032057230426
43662CB00035B/585